Foreword by
ELIZABETH BEISEL
Three-Time USA Olympian, World Champion, & Author

MANIFESTING YOUR DREAMS

INSPIRING WORDS OF ENCOURAGEMENT, STRENGTH, & PERSEVERANCE

STORIES COLLECTED BY MARLA McKENNA

Manifesting Your Dreams
Inspiring Words of Encouragement, Strength, and Perseverance

Contributing Editor: Marla McKenna

Foreword: Elizabeth Beisel

Associate Editors: Lyda Rose Haerle, Griffin Mill

Contributing Authors: Kristi Allen, Vidal Cisneros Jr., Brenda E. Cortez, Donna Drake, Manette Kohler, Jennifer Longhofer, Mary Markham, Paula H. Mayer, Kylie McGowan, Marla McKenna, Sharon Maniaci, Natalie M. Miller, Markos Papadatos, Nastassia Putz, Lucas J. Robak, Connie F. Sexauer, Marie Sumnicht, Penny Tate, Cheryl Thoma, Debbie Truncale

Cover Design: Marla McKenna

Interior & Cover Layout: Michael Nicloy

All images have been provided by the individual contributors.

ISBN: 978-1945907494

Published by Nico 11 Publishing & Design; Mukwonago, WI

Quantity order requests may be emailed to the Publisher: mike@nico11publishing.com

Manifesting Your Dreams
Inspiring Words of Encouragement, Strength, and Perserverance

ISBN: 978-1945907494

NICO 11 PUBLISHING & DESIGN
MUKWONAGO, WISCONSIN
www.nico11publishing.com

Be well read.

Printed in the United States of America

MANIFESTING YOUR DREAMS

Table of Contents

Introduction

I asked God to bring me 20 authors for *Manifesting Your Dreams*, and that's the exact number I manifested. Others showed interest and inquired, but the authors featured in this book are the ones who made the cut. I believe their chapters were meant to be shared in this collection of unique and inspiring stories.

All of the coauthors manifested their dreams by using the law of attraction, actual manifesting tools like vision boards, or they worked extremely hard to accomplish their goals and dreams by believing they could—by changing their thoughts and focusing on the positive. Others found their life's purpose on the other side of trauma or tragedy and fought their way through to find healing, peace, and to reach a new dream.

The common thread woven throughout these chapters is they *did not give up.* They found courage and persevered through whatever challenges they faced.

It reminds me of a poem I read in college which I have engrained in my memory:

My life is but a weaving between my God and me.
I do not choose the colors, He worketh steadily.
Ofttimes He weaveth sorrow, and I in foolish pride,
forget He sees the upper and I the underside.
Not till the loom is silent and shuttles cease to fly
will God unroll the canvas and explain the reasons why.
The dark threads are as needful in the skillful weaver's hand
as the threads of gold and silver in His pattern He has planned.

- Author unknown

Sometimes in life, when we get caught in the web of dark threads, and dark times, we search for any golden strand of hope to grab onto, to save us from the struggles, the fears, and those negative thoughts that are constantly replaying in our mind. However, we don't have to permanently live in those dark, negative times—we have the power to save ourselves, to live a beautiful life with gratitude, and to find purpose; it all starts with our thoughts.

Your thoughts are very powerful and can manifest into something bigger, that being something negative or positive depending on the direction of your strongest thoughts. You have the power to manifest your dreams.

Here are some powerful words to consider:

"Watch your thoughts, they become your words; watch your words, they become your actions; watch your actions, they become your habits; watch your habits, they become your character; watch your character, it becomes your destiny."
– Lao Tzu

"Your thoughts are a creative power to use to materialize your dream."
– Rhonda Byrne, author of The Secret

The Law of Attraction is best described by this statement from Albert Einstein: "Everything is energy and that's all there is to it. Match the frequency of the energy you want, and you cannot help but get that reality. It can be no other way. This is not philosophy. This is physics."

"Be careful how you think; your life is shaped by your thoughts."
– Proverbs 4:23 (GNB)

It is with much gratitude that I take a moment to thank God for bringing all of these wonderful authors together and allowing me to collect and share their stories and find an even stronger purpose in my life.

It is also with deep gratitude that I thank my mom and dad for believing in me, supporting my dreams, and loving me always.

A very special thank you to Elizabeth Beisel for her amazing and beautifully written foreword. Her story couldn't be more perfect for this book, and it is truly an honor to have her share it with us. Who knows better than an Olympian about manifesting a dream!

This book has taken my dream to the next level, and I thank each author for sharing their heart, their story, and their soul. We are like family now, and I couldn't be more grateful for this blessing. *We did it!*

I now invite you to read *Manifesting Your Dreams*; some stories will make you laugh, and some will make you cry, but I hope all will inspire you and even challenge you to shift your thinking and energy frequency to a positive setting. Go after your dreams, don't wait, and don't ever give up. Make it happen. Live your life's purpose. You too can manifest your dreams!

– Marla McKenna

Foreword

By Elizabeth Beisel

Dreams, no matter how big or small, fuel us. They keep us up late at night, push us through our darkest moments of doubt, and remind us why we dedicate ourselves to a journey that might lead to failure. The pursuit of a dream is not for the faint of heart. It takes time, sacrifice, resilience, and perseverance. But let me tell you, when a dream comes true, it is the deepest form of happiness we can experience as humans. I have only experienced this feeling once in my life, and it happened the moment my biggest dream came true.

My first memory of the Olympics was nothing out of the ordinary. In fact, it was probably a carbon copy of what most people experience. It was seven-year-old me, sitting on the couch with my parents, watching swimming during the 2000 Sydney Olympic Games on NBC. Me being a swimmer and knowing that swimming is never broadcasted on television, it was going to take a natural disaster to peel my eyes away from the television.

While watching the best swimmers in the world compete at the pinnacle of their sport, something special happened; it was the first time I truly grasped what the Olympic Games represented, and I knew I had to be there one day. Not to spectate, but to compete. When the allotted hour of swimming was over on NBC, I sprinted to the dial-up computer and opened the search engine and typed in "odds of becoming a U.S. Olympic Swimmer." Before my parents could get to the computer to see what I was up to, the search results popped up and revealed the number ".0065%." I turned around to see my parents looking over my shoulder with their jaws to the floor and watched the color drain from their skin. The look of wanting to protect me from such wild aspirations was plastered across both of their faces. Without missing a beat, I stood up and displayed a huge smile on my face and said "Mom…Dad…there's actually a *chance!*"

Here is the reality. *Everyone* has a chance. Dreams do not discriminate against their pursuers.

But the biggest and wildest dreams come with the greatest risk for failure and disappointment. So, when the search results popped up with that .0065%, all I saw was a chance. But in all fairness, not a great one.

Growing up in Rhode Island, the odds were already stacked against me. In a region dominated by hockey and lacrosse, swimming is nothing more than a skill you have to ensure your safety at the beaches during the summer. The last Olympic swimmer from the state of Rhode Island was a woman named Clara who competed in the 1948 London Olympic Games. There were two swim teams in the entire state, and neither of them had ever produced an athlete that was even close to competing at an Olympic caliber. I was also the smallest. In swimming, the difference between winning and losing is sometimes hundredths of a second, and typically the fastest swimmers are the tallest swimmers. My coach relentlessly tried to convince my parents to sign me up for gymnastics or diving, reasoning "She's just too small. She might be fine now, but there's no way she will ever be able to keep up with kids her age once she's a teenager. You're setting her up for failure." As I progressed in the sport, we had coaches reach out from California, Texas, and Florida, telling my family and I that if I ever wanted to swim in the Olympics I would have to move to one of those states and swim for a more prestigious program like theirs. Needless to say, the Beisels stayed in Rhode Island, and I continued to pursue my dream of being an Olympic swimmer.

A few months after watching the Sydney Olympic games on television, an Olympic swimmer named Amanda Beard who had competed in those very Olympic games, was hosting a clinic for young swimmers in Boston. It was the talk of the town, and I begged my parents to take me to meet her. My parents agreed and made the trek to Boston on a cold November morning. I sat in the back seat with my swimsuit, cap, and goggles on the entire ride. I was ecstatic. The clinic was held at Harvard University, and I remember thinking it was the most beautiful pool in the entire world. Amanda walked out in her Olympic sweats and had all of us sit down on the bleachers while she stood in front of us and spoke. I was enamored by her. She was brilliant, beautiful, and an Olympic hero. At the end of her motivational speech she looked at the 60 of us and paused. She emphatically and carefully said one sentence, making eye contact with each and every one of us. "At least one of you in this room will be an Olympian one day." I remember hearing that and getting full body chills, knowing it was going to be me. Knowing I was going to be a part of that .0065%. Knowing that one day, I was going to be hosting a clinic like Amanda and inspiring the next generation of Olympic hopefuls. That night when I got home, I wrote one line in my journal that I still have to this day. It simply read "I will be an Olympian one day."

Eight years later in 2008, my dream came true. I became an Olympian, and one of my teammates representing the United States of America that year was Amanda Beard.

Between the time of my clinic with Amanda and my qualifying for the Olympic team, I dedicated my life to the pursuit of my dream. I treated every single day as an opportunity to get better and made the most out of everything. Every single action had a purpose. I said no to things that everyone else was saying yes to. My dream poured over into every crevice of my life, and as crazy as my dream was, I wholeheartedly believed I could do it. I write this now having competed in three Olympic Games and winning two Olympic medals in the process.

For a dream to come true it does not require talent, a certain IQ, specific physical attributes, or any other false prerequisites society might force upon you. A dream come true requires hard work, uncompromising belief in yourself, and a fiery passion towards your pursuit. My dream took eight years to accomplish, and time was always the true test. I never put an expiration date on my dream because I knew I would never stop trying. I believe every single thing we put out into the Universe comes back to us at some point. The authors in this book have defied the odds, put themselves out there, and have manifested their biggest dreams. I commend them for finding their life's purpose and making the world a better place while doing so. The Universe heard all of them, and it responded. Now it's your turn, as the reader, to become inspired and fearless in the pursuit of your own dream. Here's to becoming a part of your own unique .0065%.

Photo credit: Kateland Cornine

Elizabeth Beisel is one of the most well-respected Olympic athletes of the past decade and is widely regarded as the consummate "team leader" among all Olympians. As a 3-time Team USA Olympian (2008, 2012, 2016), 2-time Olympic medalist and the team captain of the 2016 US Olympic Team, Beisel has had one of the most accomplished and remarkable athletic careers in history.

As impressive as Beisels' athletic accomplishments are, it is her reputation as a team leader, mentor, and motivator that has led to such a loyal following among fans and strong relationships with sponsors. Beisel is an ambassador for the Olympics, Women in Sports and often speaks to corporations about how to be a team leader. Her perspective spans across three Olympic Games, is easily one of the most unique and sought after views on leadership in the world.

Beisel began swimming at age 5, following her mother, who swam at the University of Rhode Island. She grew up in Rhode Island and graduated from North Kingstown High School in 2010. She trained with Blue fish Swim Club under coach Chuck Batchelor.

In 2008 she solidified her place on the international swimming stage by qualifying for the U.S. Olympic Team. At 15, she was the youngest member of the squad. Beisel cites this moment as her favorite moment in the sport, "I have won plenty of medals and broken plenty of records, but the happiness I experienced when I made my first team in 2008 is second to none. As a little girl, all I ever wanted to do was compete on the Olympics. When that dream finally turned into reality, it was one of the best days of my life."

Beisel currently lives in Saunderstown, RI where she keeps an active role in advancing women's sports, and is a sought after national speaker. She is involved with organizations focused on sustainability, including Dow Chemical, an Olympic Sponsor, and Save the Bay. In Spring 2019, she was the Keynote Speaker on behalf of Dow Chemical Company at the American Institute of Architects Conference in Las Vegas, Nevada, where she related the importance of sustainability with the Olympic Games. Further, as a Rhode Island native growing up with a close connection to the ocean, Elizabeth has become an advocate for Save the Bay. This nonprofit organization is dedicated to improving and protecting Narragansett Bay, located on the northern side of Rhode Island Sound. She is very passionate about ocean sustainability and preserving the world's oceans, and is excited to partner with organizations and events that share similar values. Beisel's other interests include sur fing, hanging at the beach, and traveling to cool new places around the globe!

Elizabeth's highly anticipated first book, *Silver Lining*, written with Beth Fehr, will be released February 2020.

MARLA McKENNA

"What lies behind us and what lies before us are tiny matters compared to what lies within us."

- Ralph Waldo Emerson

Detour to Destiny

All I needed was a 4.0 to slightly nudge my overall grade point average up just a bit to get accepted into the journalism school at the University of Wisconsin-Madison. I was a pretty good student but I hadn't excelled enough to receive a 4.0 before. But I wanted this and I didn't give myself any other options. I believed I could do it.

I began manifesting long before I even knew what "manifesting" was. Graduating from U.W. was all I focused on. BELIEVING was the key. I proudly displayed a poster of Bascom Hall, the infamous building located on campus at the top of Bascom Hill, in my U.W. Stout dorm room. This poster was the first site I saw when I greeted the morning, and it was the last image etched in my mind before I went to sleep. I remember staring at it as I studied for my exams and wrote my essays. Those study days and nights were long, and the sacrifices were many. The poster featured my favorite quote by Ralph Waldo Emerson, *"What lies behind us and what lies before us are tiny matters compared to what lies within us."* I knew I held the power within me to manifest this dream.

When the semester ended at Stout, and grades were about to be revealed, I anxiously waited with anticipation. If I did achieve a 4.0, I would need all of my professors to write my official grade on a separate note card and sign it, and then I'd have to submit each signed card showing my "A" to the admissions office at U.W. There was no time to wait for my transcripts. Becoming a Wisconsin Badger and graduating from U.W. was something I had always wanted. I just knew that's where I wanted to attend and graduate from college. I had envisioned it in my mind for almost 10 years.

I began my college career at the University of Wisconsin-Marathon Center in my hometown of Wausau, WI with the transfer to Madison in mind, but I unexpectedly changed my major and attended U.W. Stout—taking a *detour to my destiny*. Ultimately in the end, fate, the Universe, and I believe God intervened, and I changed my major back to my true love of writing, marketing, and advertising.

The semester ended.

I did it!

I achieved a 4.0, plus I received the Chancellor's Award.

And so my future in writing began, and so did the journey to my destiny.

The Real Bascom Hall - What a Site to See!

I remember the first day I walked up that hill to Bascom Hall. I transferred midyear, so the air was brisk on that January morning, but it didn't matter to me. Even if the winter sky was dreary and overcast, it was all sunshine and warm feelings for to me. When I reached the top after a long trek up that hill, I looked back to see what I had accomplished—that beautiful campus and my uphill journey to get there. I made it. Bascom Hall was no longer a poster in my life, it was real—a presence in my life and a real knowing that I could do anything I set my mind to.

My first news writing and reporting class had me off and running right out of the gate. We were assigned to choose a topic to write about, something we loved. My love was entertainment. Bryan Adams was always a favorite of mine; while growing up, his poster hung on my bedroom door. Of course, I always wanted to meet him one day. He was performing that week at the Dane County Exposition Center/Coliseum in Madison. I already had my ticket and was going to the concert. While in class, my professor aloofly suggested I contact the venue and ask them if I could interview Bryan Adams for my assignment. I must have looked at him like he had two heads, *sure I'll just call Bryan Adams and ask him for an interview…* but he wasn't joking. He was very serious. *Taking a chance, because what did I have to lose, I did just that.* I contacted the venue and asked for an interview with Bryan Adams. I actually ended up interviewing Bryan Adams' tour manager, along with the events coordinator and marketing manager of the Dane County Coliseum, and I landed a paid marketing internship right then and there that day. *And guess what?* I met Bryan Adams. It happened backstage before the concert. What a day! What a dream come true, and all I did was ask.

I learned a lot about marketing and promotion, and I experienced so much happiness during that internship. I loved it. Backstage with Bon Jovi was fun, and watching the production and filming of their music video while in the audience was a blast!

Plus, I had the opportunity to chauffeur the lead singer of 38 Special, Don Barnes, from his hotel to the venue. I was pretty excited because I was a fan of their music. The other band members had gone on before him in a van, but I was the one asked to wait. Thinking back, it makes me laugh because it was a sticky, humid Wisconsin summer day for their "June Jam" concert appearance, and my college car had no air conditioning. Plus, I know as we drove to the venue, I'd say I was probably a bit chatty with him…what can I say, I was nervous, haha! He was gracious and carried on the conversation. I watched the concert from backstage, and I enjoyed every minute of it. The car ride there must not have been too bad for the rock star because he rode back with me after the concert and so did fellow band member Donnie Van Zant. It was definitely a cool experience for this college girl.

When I think about it, these were just fun bonuses for me in manifesting one of my dreams.

Little did I know more of these exciting manifestations would come true—two posters (my visualizations) manifested. *What other posters/visions would I manifest?*

Oh, the Places You'll Go!

Graduation day was finally here! My manifested dream transformed into a reality; filled with emotion, I proudly walked across that stage and graduated from the University of Wisconsin. The future was bright and wide open for me to pursue. "I was off to great places, I was off on my way!" – quoting Dr. Seuss and my favorite book, *Oh the Places You'll Go.*

Fast forward several years…I worked for a few corporate companies as account executive, marketing specialist, and coordinator. The jobs well-suited me at the time, and I gained valuable experience in graphic design, writing, and marketing. The corporate world allowed more stability for me to attain the joy of becoming a mom, and my beautiful daughters, Julia and Ashley, were born. I found a job where I was able to work from home during their entire childhood. That was a dream come true opportunity for me, what a blessing. I was able to take on a career full-time and be a full-time mom, juggling two very important positions in my life. The girls and I did everything together. They grew up knowing that Mom worked from home and was always there; we adjusted our schedules accordingly. It was perfect.

Then the year 2011 made its grand entrance into my life. It came in like a lion. I had worked in the marketing department at the same company for almost nine years when they decided to transfer my position to their New York City corporate office. So just like that, I was out of a job, and my life drastically took another detour. I was devastated. *Big changes were coming!* I just didn't know it at the time.

While facing this crossroads, I didn't know what destination I would reach from this unexpected detour. Looking back though, God knew exactly what He was doing, as this was the year my first children's book was released. These events forced me to focus on my new path.

Manifesting My Dreams…
Mom's Big Catch - 2011

My true passion is revealed. I had always wanted to write a children's book when my girls were born but I didn't know how to accomplish that. *How do you publish a book?* That seemed so far out of reach—a feat only celebrities achieved. I needed an original idea, something that hadn't been written before. *But what?* Then it happened. You could say the idea was literally dropped in my lap while enjoying a family day, actually my birthday, at Miller Park cheering on the Milwaukee Brewers. And so, I ran with it. *What a gift!* However, it would be another two years before I would actually write the book, even though the story continued to brew in my mind. My daughters would be the "stars" in the book, as well as my sweet dog, Sadie—*that* I knew for sure. *My girls continue to be the inspiration behind my books.*

Finally, one night I couldn't sleep and just got up and wrote the book. It was as if God spoke to me and said, "It's time." I don't quite know how to explain it, but it was like the words just flowed right through me, and the book magically wrote itself. It was then that another uphill journey began. It was a two-year collision course of disappointments and rejection after submitting my work to countless publishers, but I didn't give up. When I finally received a contract to publish my first book, it was as if I felt God's hand of favor showering me with His blessings. That book would be called *Mom's Big Catch*, and it would be a home run! Little did I know then how it would change my career and my life.

Rick Springfield

During my teenage years, no one owned more real estate on my walls than Rick Springfield. His posters and featured magazine covers lined them like wallpaper, and his many hits blasted from my enormous, black speakers. Just like every other teenage girl, I waited for my favorite rock star's songs to be played over the airwaves, as I took in my daily dose of Dr. Noah Drake on General Hospital. Then we all stood in long lines at the movie theater anticipating the release of his first major motion picture, *Hard to Hold*. Rock star, television star, movie star...*what teenage girl didn't want to meet Rick Springfield?* I told myself I'd meet him one day. At the time that was just a young girl's fantasy; however, I also saw it in my mind and hung onto that vision. The manifestation was already set in motion.

Many years passed, and the day finally came when I actually saw Rick Springfield in concert, but it wasn't until I was 28 years old...a far cry from that teenage girl. Our seats seemed like they were way out in left field, but that really didn't matter to me. I was finally at his concert.

About six more years went by, now I was a wife and full-time mom with two beautiful daughters, a new home, and a full-time job. Life was busy. Driving home after a day at the office, which was rare since I worked from home, I just happened to have the "right station" tuned in on my car radio.

Coincidence? I don't believe in coincidences.

The Universe? I'd say absolutely.

They were giving away Rick Springfield tickets for a concert in Milwaukee that night. I just needed to be caller number 10. So, I pulled over and frantically dialed the radio station's number. The phone began to ring. I waited patiently thinking...*who really ever wins concert tickets on the radio, right? I mean who actually gets through?*

Me! I got through. The announcer answered my call, "You are caller number 10, and you're going to see Rick Springfield tonight at Potawatomi!"

My life took a wonderful detour that night and this ongoing journey has opened my world to beautiful, new, and lasting friendships—friends I am so grateful for.

Those new friends invited me back to the concert the next night, and to my surprise there was a meet and greet after the show. *What? Meet Rick Springfield? Yes, I would definitely make that happen.*

The lengthy line wound through the theater and gave me time to think about what I'd say to Rick. As the fans in front of me disappeared, one by one, I tried to hide a few long-awaited tears filling my eyes. Finally face-to-face with Rick Springfield, I just said, "I've waited so long to meet you." Then he kindly replied with a warm smile, "Aw, sweetheart," and gave me a hug. *And that was the first time I met Rick Springfield.* Everything couldn't have fallen into place more perfectly. Little did I know then how the stars were aligning from my first manifestation.

Fast forward a few more years to 2010, Rick's memoir, *Late, Late at Night,* was released—a brilliant must-read, by the way. It was then that I spoke to Rick at his book signing. This was just months before the release of my first book, *Mom's Big Catch*. I mentioned my book and asked him if he would match my donations (from partial proceeds of my book) to the Linda Blair WorldHeart Foundation. *What did I have to lose by asking him?* He said, "Absolutely," without hesitation. I gave him a letter with all of the information and asked if we could talk more when I saw him on the fan trip in November, a cruise to the Bahamas.

What struck me at that meeting was Rick's genuine excitement for me that I had written a book. I was so excited for him and his new book, yet when I told him about mine, he seemed just as excited for me.

When I saw Rick on the cruise, he confirmed his "yes" to matching my donations. Plus, I had the wonderful opportunity to speak with Rick's wife, Barbara, about my book too; she is a lovely and beautiful soul, and she was very supportive. I was immediately connected to Rick's management right then and there. And that's how it all began. *I just asked him.*

*"When Marla approached me about matching a donation for the Linda Blair WorldHeart Foundation, I thought about how much this would mean for the awesome dogs Linda rescues and takes care! It's a great opportunity to help a fantastic organization, and **Mom's Big Catch** is a very fun story for kids. I am happy to support this project."*
- Rick Springfield

The Linda Blair WorldHeart Foundation
lindablairworldheart.org

From that moment on, I worked with Rick's wonderful management team, communicating and sharing *Mom's Big Catch*, step-by-step, as the book came alive through its illustrations. My illustrator and I created the "Give a Dog a Home" logo—an illustration of my sweet Sadie girl. I contacted Linda Blair, introduced myself, and told her of my intentions to donate partial proceeds from my books to her foundation. I wanted to help the dogs she rescues and takes care of. She was sincerely grateful and so very kind. It has been a blessing getting to know her, and I truly believe Linda is an angel on Earth. I am so grateful for her.

Dogs have always held a special place in my heart ever since I can remember. We can always count on their unconditional love in this life no matter what. I wanted to make a difference in any small way that I could, and helping an organization like Linda's was a cause I wholeheartedly believed in. The alignment felt good, and it was just something I was compelled to follow through on. I was blessed with a wonderful opportunity to write a children's book, something I loved, and I wanted to give back. Rick and Linda have known each other for a very long time, and many of his fans support her. I just wanted to help make a difference.

"**Moms Big Catch** *came to my attention purely from Marla's love for animals, and she approached my charity, Linda Blair WorldHeart Foundation, with an open heart and a need to help. I can't tell you how refreshing it was that a book with such a positive message is in turn helping animals in need. Those reaching out for that message are helping give homeless doggies the chance they deserve all while going on a little adventure with their children. I hope there are more stories to come from Marla. Thank you for creating another positive in your already beautiful message. Many thanks!*" - Linda Blair

So, I built *Mom's Big Catch* and my message around "Baseball, Dogs, and Rock 'n' Roll," and I stepped up to the plate and swung for the fences. And that ball is still flying high…

Rick Springfield started as a fandom from my teenage years, and as I grew up, he turned into a mentor and human being I admire. His music is like a familiar friend traveling with me wherever I go. His lyrics are moving, inspiring, and brilliant, and so is his best-selling novel, *Magnificent Vibration*.

His authenticity, sincerity, and compassion are real. Over the last 10 years, I've had many opportunities to engage in some wonderful and inspiring conversations with Rick. At first, every time I'd see him, I'd say, "I'm Marla, I wrote the book your matching donations to for Linda." He'd respond, "I know." It took me a while to realize he recognized my face, knew my name, and he made the connection long before I figured that out. I don't believe, then, I knew the power I have within myself today. I will never forget one moment that was a pivotal and enlightening turning point in my journey. It was in Malibu, at the movie premiere for *An Affair of the Heart*, a documentary about how Rick has touched the lives of so many of his fans. I was thanking Rick, for what seemed like the hundredth time, for supporting my work, and he looked me right in the eye and said directly to me, "You're a writer." I can't even express the gift of those words from him and what they still mean to me. The moment was surreal, and I knew then and there that *Mom's Big Catch* would not just be a "one book wonder," but I would confidently move forward in the direction of my dreams. I AM a writer. I would write more books! *This* I knew for sure.

The World of Baseball

As *Mom's Big Catch* was released, I was introduced to a publicist. Not only did he promote books, but his specialty was promoting baseball books. He had worked in public relations for the Chicago Cubs. I grew up a Milwaukee Brewers fan, so I had to get over that rivalry. I had already reached out to the Brewers to see if we could team up together, but there were a few bumps and roadblocks; however, again the manifestation had been set in motion. I certainly was not giving up on the Brewers!

My publicist had the unique idea that we could customize *Mom's Big Catch* to fit any baseball team including: their logo, team uniform, colors, stadium, mascot, stadium food, pennant, and sponsor logos, etc. Anything was possible to make it *their* team book. So, we designed our play book and took our game plan to the Baseball Winter Meetings in Dallas that year. We pitched the customized version of *Mom's Big Catch* to the best in the industry. To date *Mom's Big Catch* has partnered with major and minor league teams for and including: the Milwaukee Brewers, Chicago Cubs, Pittsburgh Pirates, Toronto Blue Jays, Tampa Bay Rays, Oakland A's and other league affiliates. And more versions are on the way!

I dream of **Mom's Big Catch** *partnering with a national sponsor for all the MLB teams…and we know dreams can come true!*

Considering my publicist had the Cubs connections, he set up a meeting with their front office, and it seemed promising that a future partnership was possible. He then suggested I call Fergie Jenkins, Hall of Fame pitcher, and one of the best pitchers in Chicago Cubs history. He said I should go out to spring training in Mesa, Arizona, and sign a "Wrigley Field" version of *Mom's Big Catch* with Fergie. I thought, *sure I'll just call up Fergie Jenkins,* and that's exactly what I did. Fergie answered his phone and said, "Come on out to Arizona." For several years, I attended Cubs spring training for a few days and sat next to legendary baseball player, Fergie Jenkins, as we signed copies of the "Wrigley Field" version of *Mom's Big Catch.* Partial proceeds went back to the Fergie Jenkins' Foundation.

It took six years, but it finally happened. In, 2017, I officially scored my first major league baseball team for *Mom's Big Catch.* With the help of Fergie and his Foundation, we were able to place the official Cubs logo on the *Mom's Big Catch* cover. The book also sported the Fergie Jenkins' Foundation logo as well. Fergie is even spotlighted and illustrated as a character in the book. This partnership formed a great alliance in sharing a positive message for children along with teaching them the importance of giving back.

In recent years after meeting Fergie's personal assistant, I've had the wonderful opportunity to team up with Fergie at some of his Chicago area appearances. Fergie Jenkins is the real deal; he is genuine and kind, and his good-natured soul just shines through. I feel blessed to know him and call him my friend. I am so grateful to Fergie and his "team" for believing in me and treating me like part of their family. We have an absolute blast at the signings together. How did I team up with Fergie and the Cubs? *I just asked.*

Another poster which hung on my wall included my very favorite baseball player, Paul Molitor, and another favorite player, Robin Yount. The poster was titled, "The Batman and Robin," and featured the popular duo holding bats while posing next to the Batmobile. Through *Mom's Big Catch,* I've had the incredible opportunity to meet and have conversations with none other than, Paul Molitor and Robin Yount, and they have graciously connected me and *Mom's Big Catch* to their network of contacts. Now when Hall of Famers say, "I want you to look at this book," people listen. What an honor, and I am beyond grateful to them both.

The seeds have been planted and the manifestation is in motion.

The Milwaukee Brewers - Brewers on Deck 2015

After much perseverance and patience, *Mom's Big Catch* and I officially teamed up with the Milwaukee Brewers. I'd been talking to people at the Brewers front office and building the foundation for a strong partnership. After nearly four years, all of my hard work and determination paid off. At the 2015 Brewers on Deck, together, we promoted the "Community Book Drive." If fans brought in a new or gently used children's book, they received the "Miller Park" version of *Mom's Big Catch*. It was a huge hit, and we collected over 1,500 books for kids in the Milwaukee area. I will always be grateful to the Milwaukee Brewers for giving me the chance to team up together, just a dream come true. I couldn't have done it without the partnerships of the Milwaukee Police Department, Next Door Books for Kids, and the sponsorships of M|Group Holdings, Inc., Wellspring Personal, Financial Services, LLC., and Frett Barrington, Ltd., who purchased the books to be given away that special day. It was truly an amazing event!

"We enjoyed working with Marla and were all very pleased with the results of the Community Book Drive. With almost 1,500 books collected, we hope that the Next Door Books for Kids Program sees a significant benefit from our collective efforts."
- Rick Schlesinger, Chief Operating Officer of the Milwaukee Brewers.

"Brewers Community Foundation enjoyed having an opportunity to partner with Marla McKenna and one of our key community partners Next Door Foundation. Our fans, along with Marla's book, **Mom's Big Catch***, created a wonderful way to collaborate on encouraging and supporting youth and their families as they embrace the critical issue of literacy!"*
- Cecelia Gore, Executive Director Brewers Community Foundation

Sadie's Big Steal - 2015

Sadie's Big Steal, the second book in the *Mom's Big Catch* series was released. And our story continues…all the dogs in the neighborhood know about the ball in *Mom's Big Catch*, and they all want Sadie to steal the ball, but Sadie has to choose—should she do what the other dogs are telling her to do, or should she do what she thinks is right? The book reveals a parallel story as Julia's character encounters a similar situation at school with her friends. This book has an anti-bullying theme and focuses on kindness, respect, and true friendship.

Sadie's Big Steal remembers and honors a few of our loving, furry friends who have crossed over the rainbow bridge…Rosie who we loved and lost too soon, Gus who lived to his golden years and is loved and missed, and Gomer, Rick Springfield's dog, featured in many of his photos that his fans love. If you're a dog owner, you know the grief and sadness of losing your pet, a loving member of your family; it's devastating. I wanted these dogs to live on in *Sadie's Big Steal*, and now my sweet Sadie girl will live on forever in all of my books too.

*"**Sadie's Big Steal** is another great story from Marla. It has a personal touch for me with the addition of my sweet pal Gomer immortalized in ink. A great story and a great cause! XO"*

– Rick Springfield

Coming Into My Power

In 2011, I believe I experienced my first spiritual awakening, and I wanted to learn everything I could about tapping into my intuition more closely while understanding how to utilize its power. Prior to this, I had read the book and watched the movie *The Secret*, as well as received inspiration from Wayne Dyer, Joel Osteen, vision boards, and positive daily affirmations. But now I was introduced to an entire new world of intuitive souls who knew how to best use their special gifts.

A numerologist told me I was going to "come into my power" in 2015, and for many years life may be challenging. At the time, it concerned me somewhat not knowing what he meant. But I've learned that challenges birth opportunities, and opportunities cause growth. And you could say growth produces a sort of power.

In 2015, my life completely changed, and I believe I had to actually lose my power before I could completely take it back. Coming into my power meant I was getting strong enough to make some new decisions about the direction my life was taking, and for years even prior to that, fear held me back. Sometimes circumstances force us to move forward because we are stuck and can't take those steps on our own—toward the destiny God has planned for us.

None of us is perfect, in fact we are all imperfect people trying to do the best we can in this life.

Coming into my power meant I would have to deal with those challenges and adversities including the dark days and fiery arrows and daggers of manipulation, hypocrisy, betrayal, and judgement—all simultaneously unleashed on me. And I learned, people who judge really need to take a better look at their own lives, for when others judge it really says more about them and their character than it does about you. No one really knows what's going on in your life so they shouldn't act as if they do. Manipulation is a weak attempt to *not* take responsibility for their own mistakes and to make themselves look better. Those people who try to bring you down just aren't "your people" anymore. If God closes that door, don't try to keep opening it. This allows room for new people to enter your life, and for people who really care about you unconditionally through the good times and bad. These are "your people." People who believe in you, support you, and have your back. I am so grateful for these people.

So, I wrapped myself in God's armor, and I surrounded myself with "these people," my family and friends who love me. I held my head up, looked forward, and chose to take the high road. This was the better path for me. It's the better path for everyone. No one can take your power away unless you let them. Choose to be the better person, then relax—*karma* will do the rest.

Taking Back My Power
I'm A Secret Superhero - 2016

The entire book, *I'm A Secret Superhero*, actually came to me while I was a taking a shower. *Ask any writer how ideas and stories manifest, and their answers will be a story in itself.* Inspiration can set in at the perfect time or the most inopportune time, but any writer knows it must be seized at all times.

I immediately went to my laptop and typed the rhyming stanzas that filled my thoughts, and *I'm A Secret Superhero* was born! My illustrator and friend, Brenda Kato (katocreative.com), created her magic and the book took on a life of its own. Everything I saw in my mind was beautifully manifested in her brilliant illustrations. It was a wonderful and magical new partnership. *I'm A Secret Superhero* teaches children how we are all unique; we are all born with special gifts, our own superpowers. It's our job to find what we're good at, work hard, and believe in ourselves. Each page has its own beautiful illustration and stanza to teach children the importance of thinking positive thoughts, taking responsibility for their actions, giving love and being kind to others, cleaning up after themselves, and giving back.

The actual idea for the children's book stemmed from a book for adults I wanted to write titled, *Take Back Your Power,* which now has been shared in my story, *Manifesting Your Dreams,* three years later.

A Soccer Summer Dream with the Milwaukee Torrent - 2018

While I was promoting *I'm A Secret Superhero* in 2016 on *The Morning Blend*, a Milwaukee NBC television show, I met Andy Davi, the owner of Milwaukee's outdoor soccer team, the Milwaukee Torrent. Talking in the green room, before our featured interviews, he looked at me, gave me his business card, and said, "I want you to write a book for us." And that's how *A Soccer Summer Dream* came to life. Enter a new sport and the world of soccer.

I am so grateful to Andy and the team for this unique and exciting opportunity! As a bonus, nearly one year later, Andy and I were able to appear together on *The Morning Blend* and share how the book was inspired while, thanking the television show for introducing us. Milwaukee Torrent games are awesome! Check them out!

Our Last Day in Heaven - A Story of Tragedy, Loss, and Hope with Angels in the Midst - 2018 - *A Coauthorship for a Serious and Heartfelt Book for Adults*

I worked with Alex Hoffman in the mid-1990s in the corporate world; he was a banker and I was a marketing specialist. Years and time passed, and our careers took us in different directions. I had no idea what had transpired during his lifetime. A few years ago, we reconnected on social media when I contacted Alex with the hopes of him sponsoring *Mom's Big Catch*. Little did I know then, we would team up on a different book. But just like the title displays, we have angels in our midst. God had a plan. I began to learn more about Alex's story and that he wanted to write a book. Alex told me he lost his son, Shay, to a heroin overdose in 2012. I was shocked. Alex also told me how he was doing everything he could to help other families in similar situations. I introduced him to my publisher, Michael Nicloy of Nico 11 Publishing & Design, and together we wrote *Our Last Day in Heaven*. It was like nothing I've ever written before. This book is built on real, raw emotion, extreme heartbreak, loss and forgiveness, and even offers light touches of humor plus many blessings. The opioid crisis in America is a serious problem, one in which we can all learn from whether affected personally or from afar. Alex's work with government officials and leaders is impressive, however there is still more work that needs to be done. I encourage you to read this book and Alex's story. This project was a true gift, and I'm grateful for Alex's friendship and belief in me.

Manifesting More of My Dreams...

(Mom's Big Catch Spoiler Alert*)* – Sometimes it's hard to believe how a ball landing in a purse changed my life and career!

School Author Visits

My true passion is visiting schools with my children's books and teaching the students about the publishing, writing, editing, and illustrating process while focusing on the power of patience, positivity, and perseverance. We talk about character development, theme, word choice, and writing structure. We create and write a story together using our endless imaginations. I share my "behind the scenes" journey with the kids and encourage them to follow their dreams and never give up. I talk to them about the importance of embracing their special gifts, believing in themselves, and working hard for what they want to achieve in life. It's never too early to teach children about the power of a positive mindset and the importance of expressing gratitude.

I've enjoyed combining the sports themes in my books paired with kindness, friendship, and anti-bullying—engaging both boys and girls in the stories. Physical health and mental health are both important aspects for our children to learn about and understand.

It's been a true blessing for me to have visited hundreds of schools across the United States and to have shared my books with thousands of students. The letters, smiles, high-fives, and hugs inspire me and let me know I'm living my life's purpose, and I have more work to do.

I receive signs from God, the Universe, and my angels all the time confirming this...*but that's a story for another book.*

Marla McKenna Writing & Design is Established

More opportunities began to present themselves as I expanded my network to include more writing, editing, graphic design, and speaking opportunities. I have wonderful opportunities to work with clients locally and globally on:

- Ghostwriting ebooks/books for influential people making a difference in this world
- Editing books for Olympic athletes and professional athletes in baseball, football, basketball, and swimming
- Designing book covers and press kits for Forbes best-selling authors
- Writing press releases for national media
- Writing copy for and assisting with websites and podcasts
- Helping writers get published
- **The *Manifesting Your Dreams* book is born**

More projects continue to develop, and I couldn't be more excited for all that is to come!

Rick Springfield continues to support my work and match my donations to The Linda Blair WorldHeart Foundation. He has promoted my newest book releases on three of his fan trips including: Jamaica, Port St. Lucie, and the Bahamas at the beautiful Atlantis. Fans were even greeted with promotional pieces about my books in their welcome packages during these trips. He has talked about my books on stage during his concerts, on the radio, and in social media, and he continues to offer inspiration and belief in my work.

When a fan asked him at a Q & A after his show, what's the best way to break into the music business, Rick responded, "Don't Give Up! Don't Give Up! Don't Give Up!" Good advice to be heard and listened to for anyone wanting to achieve their dream, and it's encouraged me to persevere and keep moving forward.

I couldn't be more grateful to Rick for supporting my work over the years. I like to explain it to the kids I visit at schools this way:

"You know that favorite rock star or musical group poster whose pictures you have hanging on your walls at home or taped to the inside of your school locker?" They all look at me with their own level of elevated excitement on their faces and shake their heads signaling a *yes*. Then I add to the conversation and say, "Then imagine 20-30 years down the road your favorite rock star supports your work, something YOU did," and their faces light up with even more wonder and amazement. I explain to them, "That's exactly what happened to me!"

And they say, "Wow, that's pretty awesome!"

It is with much gratitude that I express my sincere appreciation and heartfelt thanks to Rick Springfield for believing in me and my work. *It is indeed pretty awesome!*

Don't Give Up!

It's important to note that for every "YES," I've received, there were and still are at least 50 noes. But the most important thing to remember is just keep moving forward in the direction of your dreams. Don't let the noes consume you, and some days they will; but remember, "You have places to go!" You may take one detour or several detours in your life, but you will eventually reach your destiny.

I've learned to just ask and take a chance. What have I got to lose? They might say no, but they just might say YES.

DON'T GIVE UP!

So, for now, I will end my chapter here...but my story isn't over... it's still unfolding. I can't wait to see what manifests next!

About Marla

Marla McKenna is a published author, speaker, editor, and graphic designer. She has written several fun and inspiring children's books as well as authored books for adults, ghostwritten ebooks, and designed book covers, and other creative marketing materials for best-selling authors.

Her passion for writing and sharing a positive message with children comes to life in all of her children's books. Young readers were first introduced to Marla's heartwarming story *Mom's Big Catch*, which has given Marla the opportunity to partner with baseball teams and create customized team versions. She loves visiting schools and teaching the importance of patience, positivity, perseverance, and giving back while encouraging students to believe in themselves and never give up.

Marla also loves working with other writers and helping them get their work published.

Partial proceeds from all of Marla's books benefit the Linda Blair WorldHeart Foundation, with special thanks to Rick Springfield for matching her donations.

Inspired by her daughters, Julia and Ashley, Marla continues to write books while living in Wisconsin with her family. For more information on Marla's work, please visit marlamckenna.com

My graduation from the University of Wisconsin-Madison.

Bascom Hall at the University of Wisconsin.

*With my mom and dad, Marlene and Jerry Czeshinski, at my **Sadie's Big Steal** book signing the day before the Brewers on Deck and **Mom's Big Catch!** event.*

With my beautiful daughters Ashley (left) and Julia (right), just following their dreams - Check out their YouTube channels: Ash Kenna and Julia Norma.

My sweet Sadie girl.

Sadie, the "Give a Dog a Home" logo.

Illustration of Julia, Ashley, and Sadie in **Sadie's Big Steal**.

With Rick Springfield on the red carpet in Malibu, California.

With the very sweet Linda Blair in Chicago, Illinois.

*With Rick Springfield and **Mom's Big Catch**, in front of Miller Park.*

Teaming up with the Milwaukee Brewers at Brewers on Deck.

With Bernie Brewer and the Miller Park version of
Mom's Big Catch *at Brewers on Deck.*

With the Brewers famous Racing Sausages at Brewers on Deck.

With Hall of Fame baseball player, Paul Molitor

Doug Davidson of **The Young and the Restless,** *reading* **Mom's Big Catch.**

With Hall of Fame pitcher Fergie Jenkins, signing together at PopCon, Milwaukee.

With Fergie Jenkins at Wrigley Field before our Chicago signing.

At the Cubs spring training in Mesa, Arizona.

*Presenting **Mom's Big Catch** at a school.*

Signing books during a school visit.

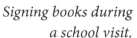

*With Rick Sringfield and **Sadie's Big Steal**.*

*With Rick Springfield in the Bahamas at Atlantis,
with **I'm a Secret Superhero**.*

I'm a Secret Superhero promoted on
the Rick Springfield fan trip to Atlantis.

*With my mom and dad at a **Mom's Big Catch** day at the ballpark.*

*With Andreas (Andy) Davi, kicking off the
Milwaukee Torrent season party.*

*With coauthors Alex Hoffmann and Michael Nicloy before a
TV interview for **Our Last Day in Heaven**.*

Mom's Big Catch *customized team versions.*

DONNA DRAKE

"Embrace the sky and realize all things are possible. If it has been done, you can do it. If it hasn't been done, it was waiting for you to do it. Invent. Create. Celebrate. Be open to the vastness of possibilities and make your contribution to the world. You will thrive and achieve—believe!"

- Donna Drake

My Dream in Color

The story of a girl from St. Louis, Missouri, who, during the second grade, sat in the second row, in the second seat, and knew that a compliment from her music teacher would fuel her journey as she embarked on manifesting a career in the arts. This musical moment, combined with a vivid dream during the night of December 28, 2008, launched Donna Drake's ability to create her own CBS talk show which allowed her the opportunity to meet celebrities, travel globally, and sustain her family.

On the night of December 28, 2008, I had a very vivid and detailed dream. I envisioned an entire television show in bright rays of color and brilliant sound. I pictured myself on the set as the host of that actual television show. I saw the angles of the cameras, felt the heat from the spotlights, and I heard and saw people darting all around me creating a whirlwind of activity. *That dream today is my reality.* What led me to this dream and my ability to "pull it off" has been an interesting journey. When serendipity smiled on me, I literally sold everything I owned, and invested in myself.

Here are a few pivotal moments along my path that have seasoned me to, at times weather storms and for the most part, dance in the sunshine. I faced big challenges including: the death of my mother while I was pregnant with my first child, a widow by the age of 38, and that frightening moment I had a whole $1.97 to my name. I have triumphed over more challenges than I care to count, and if I can do it—so can anyone. My joy and huge highlights include: interviewing celebs like Tony Bennett, Jay Leno, and Gloria Gaynor, traveling free to foreign countries, and being honored by the United Nations with a Global Citizenship Award.

From an early age, I knew I wanted to live in New York or California. I wanted to be "famous!" I wanted to be famous because I was bullied in second grade, and I had a deep desire to prove something to those bullies. Perhaps if I was famous, they would have "wished they had been nicer to me and were my friends." One day after recess, I was feeling a bit down, but my spirits were quickly uplifted. I was excited for music class. It was then that my inspiration took root. Although I can't remember what song we sang, I remember the moment my music teacher, Ms. Buegner, purposely stopped and looked at me and said, "Donna Marie, you have a beautiful singing voice!" My response was loud enough for the mean girls to hear me, and I said, "Thank you, I'm going to be famous." My teacher smiled at me. That one exchange fueled my desire and my eventual reality to work in the arts as an entertainer.

As the years progressed, I joined the patriotic singing group, The Futures of America. For 10 years, 1979 through 1989, I spent my Wednesday nights singing at rehearsals in the neighborhood as well as performing shows for veterans, the disabled, and the community families in and around Florissant, Missouri. We sang shows for the Special Olympics and worked with the Missouri School for the Blind. It was there I learned several valuable lessons I still apply to my life today, lessons of compassion and empathy. Watching a young man play wheelchair basketball while carrying the torch at the Special

Olympics, as he rolled his chair in a pride-filled circular motion is imprinted on my heart. Charities in my opinion are worthy of our time, our talent, and our treasure.

My first job in the entertainment industry resulted directly from my years singing songs from the 1930s to 1970s era. The songbook in my head held the perfect training and experience to acquire a job as the music librarian. This position required me to select music and sound effects for radio and television commercials, as well as corporate image videos. Some of my other earlier career moves positioned me as a manager of creative services for Barnes Hospital, promoting all of the clinical service lines as well as a stint as a creative talent providing digital graphics for the scoreboard for the St. Louis Cardinals. In 1994, my husband, two children, and I moved our family from St. Louis to New York. As the girl who always wanted to live in New York or California, my vision became clearer. Some of my jobs I had on Long Island were in the dinner theater, producing corporate videos and doing voice-overs, and that led to my break as the promotions coordinator for WLNY-TV. In 1997, I became a full-time employee at the TV station where my show, *Live it Up! With Donna Drake* would eventually be televised on April 9, 2009. It airs on the same station today.

Prior to my having a TV show on that station, I had various television related jobs and voice-over gigs. I also acted in small films. Then October of 2008, I went to Philly to work on a Melting Pot advertisement, and while I was there, I met Bernie who was Michael Douglas' original director. I felt chills as he walked me around the studio and told me how he had worked with Mike doing a three-camera setup for a talk show. It was this foreshadowing that transpired into an actual dream on the night of December 28, 2008. I dreamt the entire TV show in color, and I have been manifesting it ever since. We went on the air April 9, 2009.

On April 9, 2009, *Live it Up!* aired its first show! This was a major step for me because every day as I walked the halls of the station creating local sales commercials and promotions, that on-air dream seemed impossible. Personally, I struggled with low self-esteem; I felt my nose was too big, and I did not like the space between my teeth. The timing was profound as well, because all of the females on the station airwaves happened to be blonds—all of them. I was a petite brunette. I remember walking by a poster of Oprah Winfrey adorning the TV station wall, and I'd say to her picture in an empowering way, "If you can do it, I know I can as well. Thank you." I have been a fan since the beginning of her career. When WLNY-TV was sold a few years ago from an individual owner to the CBS Corporation, I was asked if I wanted anything as they dismantled the Long Island offices. I replied with just one thing, the framed poster of Oprah. My wish was granted.

On a more serious note, while working at WLNY-TV, I was the first person to report the events to the newsroom on September 11, 2001. Things in the world shifted. Not just for me personally but for thousands of New Yorkers. It was a moment of introspection and reflection that led me to transition from a full-time employee for someone else to instead strike out on my own as the president of Drake Media Network, embracing the idea of "Life is short, do it now, or don't do it at all." I embarked out on my own.

On a personal note, my love life also dramatically changed for the better, as a divorced woman I met my second husband soon after 9/11. My first husband, to this day is a wonderful man and a great father. We just grew apart due to the stresses of life. My second husband, Tom LaScala, and I met through Love at AOL and our first date was on Christmas of 2001. We married on December 28, 2002 ironically on the same date as my dream many years later. On February 8, 2004, Tom passed away; I suffered another tragic loss. My marriage to Tom, who was an engineer, writer, and composer, was wonderful. One of the songs he wrote was titled "Life is Only What We Make of It." The name of the TV show was specifically named after that song. The word "Life" from the song was turned into "LIVE" and the word "IT" from the song title stayed as "IT" hence, *Live it Up!* The reason December 28, 2008, the night of the dream was so important to me is that it would have been our wedding anniversary had I not lost Tom. So, the coincidence of that prolific dream has always felt as if the Universe gifted the TV show to me, and it is simply my responsibility to fulfill that dream. The economy took a dive in October of 2008 so by December when I wanted to create my own TV show, I simply liquidated everything I owned and invested in myself. It was a risky move based on the economic climate, but I focused on my vision and moved forward.

One key aspect I brought to reality on my show is the "dream set," my childhood black and white Zenith television that my parents received once they were married in 1964. It was one very powerful source of my childhood happiness. Never in my life did I think that one day I would still have my childhood TV on my "dream set." Once the plans for creating this reality started to unfold, I begged my dad to send me the TV so I could display it as a table on my brand new set. Although there were shipping struggles and time crunch issues with the TV's arrival, it made it just in time for my first shoot day in my new studio. My TV now sits on my "dream set" as a table on display for my audience to see. I am forever grateful for making and ultimately manifesting this dream into a reality, and my wish is for it to be my source of luck and happiness forever. *I embrace living life in color, and that is my mantra for all of you.* No matter where you are in the world, television helps bring us all closer and connects us through the perfect medium. Every day I am humbled by the fact that my dream became a reality and that I get to live it every day with the people I love and those who tune in every week.

I was truly a mom and an entrepreneur. Anyone who knows me appreciates my resourcefulness. My greatest successes were derived from networking and supporting the efforts of others in pursuing their goals. Patience, acceptance, and tenacity are a few of my other traits I possess. When I'm asked how I got my own TV show, that's pretty easy for me to explain; **I had a dream.** I literally manifested my dream to the best of my ability using the resources I had available at the time. I went to the TV station and asked if I could buy the time. They said, "Yes!" I formatted a show inviting friends to appear as my guests. One thing led to another, and I was asked to create celebrity interviews. Once a sponsor agreed to advertise on my show, others soon followed suit as did the celebrities.

Along my journey, I wanted to tell stories for the non-profits that aligned with my heart during my days in the patriotic singing group. I am a cheerleader for brands, people, and causes. Juggling my personal life and my professional life hasn't always been easy. How did I explain to my children Andrew, Elise, and Matthew, why

I needed to be out networking, and consistently attending charity events, or spending long hours on the computer? Nothing I did seemed like work, and my children, for the longest time, when they saw me struggling financially, wanted me to get a "real" job. It wasn't until I interviewed Mel Brooks, a name they all recognized, did they say, "Wow...now that's really cool, Mom!" Another fun moment and validation for me was when my youngest, Matthew, and his older sister, Elise, witnessed someone sing my praises and thank me. Matthew told Elise, "Hey don't ever tell Mom this, but isn't she cool?!" Of course, later that night, he decided to let her tell me. The television show has been going strong for a decade, and I have created over 5,000 interviews while visiting several countries. Our show was the prototype and the first to stream live on Facebook using the "SMACKDAB" platform putting content in the middle of the feed. This was an opportunity brought to me by networking at NATPE and meeting animator Mark Simon and Doug Stanley from Ridgeline Entertainment. Winning two National Telly Awards, honoring excellence in video and television across all screens, was truly an honor and a dream come true. When I won the awards, my mother, my angel, Judie Campana, a remarkable woman, filled my thoughts. She was steadfast, loving, progressive, dynamic, philanthropic, and devoted to her family and friends. I enjoy being a card-carrying member of SAG/AFTRA. I am a past executive board member of the Huntington Arts Council and a board member of the Long Island Film/TV Foundation.

Ten years since manifesting the dream, I continue to find new ventures. My recent partnership with SBTV.com and Footprint.tv, thanks to my Executive Producer, Lou Vaccarelli, not only allows the guests of my show to reach a larger audience than ever before, but through national syndication allows all to live it up on the recently launched newly named television show, *The Donna Drake Show.*

Due to timing, loyalty, and experience, people have gathered around me, from interns I have recruited to audiences for speaking engagements with the youth of tomorrow; I always find joy in giving others an opportunity to enrich their own lives and achieve their aspirations. In my travels, I continue to meet new people who never cease to inspire me and my work. My life's challenges have taught me that paying it forward is the greatest act of all. As I have once said, "I feel like I owe humanity this. It's my responsibility for the future." Many charitable causes are close to my heart, and while my show is a vehicle for shining a light on good news for my audience, as of this year, I'm participating in the ACLD's Limitless Luncheon, whose slogan is "Empowering a limitless life for all." Never forgetting my personal mantra – F.O.C.U.S. (Figuring Out Consistent Unique Strengths), I have been able to accomplish my vision for my very own show. I have found by approaching life this way, no dream is too small to become reality. So, what are you waiting for? Go out there and manifest your dream.

About Donna

Donna Drake is an international award-winner, television broadcast show producer, and host whose CBS TV show, *The Donna Drake Show—Live It Up!* brings experience in conception, production, and fiduciary management of a broadcast television show on broadcast television for 10 years. "Live It Up!" was one of the first hybrid shows with delivery over the air and on the web with a following in 25 countries and was the first show to stream via Facebook using the SMACKDAB platform.

Drake emcees corporate and charity events, and is hired as a motivational speaker. A highlight for Drake was sharing her first TedX talk, delivered in 2017 in Hilton Head, South Carolina. Drake's speaking platform uses the word FOCUS which Drake coined for representing the phrase, Figuring Out Consistent Unique Strengths. The talk is a combination of her "Live it Up Tips for the Day" with quotes from celebrities she has interviewed.

Donna is the head of Drake Media Network, Inc. Drake Media specializes in content strategy and video content production facilitating cross-platform media experiences for national and international brands such as Green Mountain Coffee, Coca-Cola, The Melting Pot, professional sports teams, and celebrities, resulting in negotiating and implementing flawless execution from strategy to deliverables in print, broadcast, promos, radio commercials, social media, storytelling, and events.

Ms. Drake is a former college professor having taught new and emerging media and broadcasting classes, a British Airways "Face to Face" award-winning entrepreneur, and has received the Goddess Artemis Award from the Euro-American Women's Council, and a Global Citizenship award from the United Nations. She also received two National Telly Awards for her coverage of a young woman who was bullied after Hurricane Sandy.

In addition to Drake's career, she enjoys spending time with her three children, Andrew Drake, Elise Drake, and Matthew Dunninger. She is an avid artist with the ability to paint in watercolor, acrylic, and oil. Her favorite art trip was to Italy where she painted landscapes en plein air. Recently Donna traveled to Nova Scotia where she learned a great deal about American history, and in particular the ancestry of the early settlements in New Orleans. With the recent ability to harness DNA information, Donna spends time on ancestry.com and 23 & me platforms. Highlights of her journey include: interviewing Tony Bennett, zip lining in Helen, GA, and singing at Wallt Disney World as a teen.

Contact information for Donna Drake:
Email: liveituptvshow@gmail.com
Phone: 631-432-0372
Website: liveituptvshow.com
IG: donnadrakeliveitup
FB: https://www.facebook.com/LiveItUpTV -and-
https://www.facebook.com/liveitupdonnadrake/.
TWITTER: @DonnaDrake
Linkedin: https://www.linkedin.com/in/donna-drake-613a95/

Donna Drake grew up in Florissant, Missouri, a suburb of St. Louis, and now resides in Huntington, Long Island, NY.

I've had the pleasure of interviewing (just to name a few):

Charlie Daniels

Tony Bennett

Michael Strahan

Jason Priestly

Jay Leno

Deborah Norville

Ozzie Smith

Howie Mandel

Evander Holyfield

MTV on-air VJs

Mike Tyson

MANETTE KOHLER, DVM

"You are the Michelangelo of your own life. The David that you are sculpting is you. And you do it with your thoughts."

- Dr. Joe Vitale

The Secret to Good Behavior

Thirty-one years ago, sitting in a large classroom as a first year veterinary student, feeling nervous, excited, inspired, and a bit overwhelmed, I listened as a professor explained how a veterinary degree could open doors. So many opportunities were to be had both within and beyond a traditional private practice setting, and we were all embarking on this awesome journey to finding ourselves, our passion, our mission, and our dreams. I remember looking around the room at my classmates, all bright and driven people, wondering what destiny awaited each of us?

I discovered early on in my career, as a private practitioner, that the behavior of my patients, be it good or bad (from the viewpoint of the owner) would ultimately determine their destiny. The sad truth was that more pets ended up in shelters because of unwanted behavior issues than for any other reason. Undesired behaviors destroyed the human-animal bond. It was really that simple. Animal behavior became my passion. Educating pet owners on why their pets do what they do, how to modify behavior if needed, and how to achieve and maintain strong, healthy, fulfilling bonds with their pets, based on trust, love, and good communication. This became my mission.

Behavior medicine was in its infancy when I graduated with only a handful of board certified veterinary behaviorists, and a behavior education in veterinary school was minimal at best. To follow my passion and move forward with my mission, I needed more education on animal behavior. As I furthered my veterinary experience in private clinic settings, both in Georgia and Wisconsin, I sought out everything I could find on animal behavior via conferences, seminars, webinars, online classes, and reading countless books, articles, and studies. The field of behavior was changing rapidly as we came to understand animals better and better, through countless hours of observation and groundbreaking studies, and I was determined to stay current.

While I enjoyed addressing my clients' behavior concerns within the context of yearly exams, it wasn't enough, and trying to educate clients on behavior and still stay within the 20-30 minute appointment time slot was frustrating. I didn't feel like I was really making a positive difference in terms of addressing behavior concerns or repairing broken bonds. I began feeling depressed and emotionally burnt out, and I couldn't see a way out of my current situation. I'd occasionally entertain the idea of starting my own behavior consultation business but would quickly push the idea aside. *Why would people want to seek out "MY" help?* I wasn't board-certified in behavior medicine. I wasn't one of the leaders in the field of animal behavior. *How could I really make a go of it with a behavior consultation business?* The fear of possible failure loomed, and I was consumed with self-doubt despite my continued passion for animal behavior and the welfare of countless pets on the brink of shelters.

Little did I know, 2006 was to be a pivotal year for me. My mother had just purchased and watched *The Secret,* a new film created by Rhonda Byrne, revealing the great mystery of the Universe, and she was so inspired and excited to share the film and its message with me. For a science-minded person, like myself, who desired hard "evidence" that a concept was legit, I was skeptical at first but decided to watch the film. I was more and more intrigued, and felt sparks of possibility and hope the further into the film I got.

So, what is *The Secret?* It is the "law of attraction." It's the most powerful law in the Universe. Bob Proctor, philosopher, author, personal coach, and contributor to the *The Secret,* describes it this way…

"Everything that's coming into your life you are attracting into your life. And it's attracted to you by virtue of the images you're holding in your mind. Whatever is going on in your mind you are attracting to you."

Wow, this seemed heavy. *Could it really be true?* Could the "law of attraction" help me realize my dream of having my own successful behavior practice? Little did I know, this film would send me on quite an educational and inspiring journey.

I embraced the teachings in the film and started to visualize what I wanted my reality to be, and things just started falling into place. I met people who were pivotal to my journey, and I met them at just the right times. The Universe laid it all out for me, and I was along for the ride. My job was to just continue to believe in the process and follow the yellow brick road, so to speak.

Interestingly, the events that kick-started my journey included a Lyme disease diagnosis and a tendon rupture in my wrist, both of which ended my career in private practice. As I healed, I continued to immerse myself in animal behavior. Looking back, this was the impetus to finally move forward. Free of my commitment to the clinic, I decided to take the big leap and started my behavior business, Helping Hand Veterinary Behavior Counseling. The mental image of a dog's paw gently resting in a human hand immediately came to mind and became part of my logo.

Key influential people and opportunities seemed to fall into my lap just when I needed them. With no background as a trainer and knowing I would need to teach pet owners how to work with their dogs, I knew I needed hands-on training myself. One night, at a fundraising behavior talk at a local shelter, I thought about what a good experience it would be to work with the dogs at the shelter. Before the night was over, I'd met the director of the behavior department for the shelter and arranged to become a volunteer. She had a unique program in place where a group of highly trained volunteers worked with the shelter dogs on their various behavior issues to help them find their forever homes. She was very excited to add a veterinarian to the group. This was perfect. I gained hands-on skills in training, leash handling, and behavior, and I was introduced to the concept of "intention" as I trained with the director. We were to set our intention for the time we had with a dog, and we were to do this before we even went to the kennel to get the dog out for training. This entailed visualizing the dog and how the training session would go, including seeing the dog enjoying the session, and progressing nicely with the training. This made sense to me because this was, in practice, the "law of attraction." This realization gave me goose bumps, and I knew then, I was on the right path to my dreams.

My time at the shelter overlapped with the launch of my behavior business. I knew I needed to get my name out there so I could retain referrals and the logical path was to reach out to vet clinics and let them know I was available for behavior consults. So I penned a letter and sent this, along with a flier, to all of the clinics within a 60-mile radius. Referrals slowly trickled in. This was great, but I still envisioned a thriving and successful behavior business.

I often passed a new and impressive looking veterinary emergency and referral center, and I envisioned myself working there. Self-doubt crept in, again, and I pushed those thoughts away. I knew these large referral practices typically hired veterinarians with board certification in their specialty, and I was not board certified in behavior. Despite this, I envisioned myself working there, and my visions were very vivid. I saw myself, attired in the typical veterinary lab coat, calling my next patient/client into an exam room, providing a thorough behavior consultation and sending the client home with a set of consult notes and a behavior treatment plan. While I had never met her, I knew who the owner of this referral center was, and I envisioned myself at a continuing education event, and introduced by her to various clinic owners and staff in attendance at the event. These daydreams or visions were vivid as well, including a banquet room filled with large diameter round tables adorned with white tablecloths and veterinary clinic owners and staff sitting at each of the tables.

Shortly thereafter, at a large pet expo, I met the referral practice owner at her exhibit booth. I introduced myself and gave her my business card. She was ecstatic to hear I had a behavior practice.

She'd been thinking of adding "Behavior" to her own practice. We arranged to meet for lunch to discuss the details and soon thereafter I was seeing behavior referrals at the center. This was so critically important for me since it got my name out to the referring clinics. Being associated with the referral center awarded me the credibility I so needed at that stage of my new career. I was included in all of the referral center's marketing promotions, and I was given a landing page on their website where I could share my business and educational behavior information.

Just a few months later, the referral center hosted a continuing educational event for all their referring veterinary practices, and I was introduced as their new behavior consultant. It was at this pivotal moment, I realized just how powerful the "law of attraction" really was. Right down to the details, it had all played out exactly as I had envisioned it, including the large diameter round tables adorned with white tablecloths and veterinary clinic owners and staff sitting at the tables.

Other aspects of my behavior career have also been touched by the "law of attraction." Writing has always been a dream of mine, and I longed to use this platform to educate and entertain pet owners about pets and animal behavior. The owner of the referral center arranged for me to write an article for a dog magazine she was a contributor for, which evolved into my own quarterly column. Also, at one point I set my intention to meet trainers in the area as I felt we could be valuable resources for one another, not only in referrals but also to learn from each other. Shortly thereafter, I received an email invite to join a group of force free trainers who held all of the same beliefs as me, and many members of this group have become great friends. We refer cases to each other, thus providing timely help to clients and their pets.

My own behavior business grew to the point where I had to finally step away from the referral practice in order to keep up with my private referrals. I am forever grateful to the owner of this beautiful referral center for making my name recognizable. Self-doubt rears its ugly head now and again, but I'm now quick to remind myself, while my time at the referral practice introduced me to the veterinary community, it was my successful behavior treatment plans I provided to my clients that built up my credibility and reputation. On a daily basis I am blessed to be able to help families understand their pet's better, repair damaged relationships, and form fulfilling, loving bonds with their pets through great communication, consistency, and building trust. Now, when I look back at my career and life, I am amazed and ever so grateful I was introduced to *The Secret,* and the stars aligned at just the right times, allowing me to pursue my passion and manifest my dreams.

About Manette

Manette Kohler is a writer and a veterinarian in Southeast Wisconsin where she provides animal behavior consultations for cats and dogs. If she could have one wish granted, it would be for all pet owners to have loving, trusting, respectful, and fulfilling relationships with their pets. She's contributed as a freelance writer and columnist for nationally recognized *Dog World* magazine and, currently, for Wisconsin-based *FETCH* magazine.

In August, 2018, Manette published her first children's book, *Bella's First Checkup*, a fun and exciting chapter book for young readers that teaches families how to raise a behaviorally healthy puppy, and gives readers an inside look at a veterinary clinic.

She speaks locally and regionally to veterinary audiences as well as pet owners and other pet professionals on animal behavior topics including: canine body language, dog bite prevention, the health and behavioral effects of stress, feline behavior, and dog park safety, as well as dog bite prevention talks for school and library groups.

When not working, Dr. Kohler enjoys spending time with her family which includes her husband, two daughters, two dogs, and two cats.

Contact Manette at: helpinghanddvm.com

Me and my soulmate dog, Murphy, for the launch of my
"Helping Hand Veterinary Behavior Counceling" website.

My first book,

Bella's First Checkup.

MARKOS PAPADATOS

"If you want to be the best, you have to do things that other people aren't willing to do."

- Michael Phelps
(Olympic gold medalist, swimmer)

Achieving Journalistic Dreams, Despite Adversity

After 12 years in the newspaper, magazine, and online media industry, with over 12,000 bylines to my credit, and interviews with the biggest names in entertainment, music, and sports, I have achieved multiple successes in journalism. These include being published in seven different states, two languages, and my articles generating over 50 million unique views in print, digital, and online formats; however, back in my early days in high school, as an aspiring writer, it was far from glamorous.

At Saint Francis Prep High School in Fresh Meadows, New York, I had always wanted to become a published journalist or author. Those dreams were short-lived when my high school newspaper, *The Seraph*, turned down every single article I had ever submitted. Even the faculty member moderating the high school newspaper suggested I call it quits. "Markos, you're a nice guy, but none of these submissions are good enough. Nobody is interested in reading about country music," he told me.

My main passion at the time was country music, and back in early 2001, country music was taboo in New York City, especially since they didn't have a country radio station in the area. As a result, none of my country music articles and features I had written then ever saw the light of day. Looking back, with the popularity of country music in the New York music scene, I always joke: "I was country when country wasn't cool," to quote the song lyrics and title of the classic Barbara Mandrell tune, "I Was Country When Country Wasn't Cool."

The rejections didn't stop there. They followed me through college, though Queens College was the standing point of my journalism career. For the most part, the staff of the college newspaper took me under its wing and gave me press access for the coverage of entertainment events that were held locally and in the Manhattan entertainment scene. While there was no money attached to it, I was able to see the films and Off-Broadway shows I liked, all for free, for a written review in return, and I was enjoying it since I was doing something I loved. My scrapbook started to develop from there. We helped build the college newspaper from a 12-page into a 96-page publication that had multiple sections including: News, Business, Music, Entertainment, Sports, Travel, and Features.

In June of 2009, one of my professors at Queens College asked the classroom of students on the first day of the summer semester to write two truths and a lie about ourselves on a piece of paper. It was used as an icebreaker activity, where the class would have to guess which was the incorrect fact.

I had written down "I interviewed Criss Angel" as my incorrect fact, in honor of the Greek-American magician, who happened to be one of my biggest heroes at the time. His hit television show, *Mindfreak,* on A&E was skyrocketing in the ratings back then. The other two statements I wrote down were "I interviewed Chuck Wicks" and "I interviewed Jake Owen," both of which were rising country singers, who most people in New York would not have known about. Aside from attending graduate school full time, I was a staff writer for the college newspaper, *The Queens College Knight News*, which was my first stepping stone in the field of journalism, which started it all for me.

When it was my chance for people to guess which statement was a lie about myself, many classmates laughed since they picked out the incorrect fact right away. They had no idea who the country singers listed were, that I had previously interviewed for my college newspaper, and they realized the name Criss Angel stood out as the obvious fact of unreality, or the "lie" in that situation.

The professor himself, who was also amused, responded, "I said to write down two truths and a lie, Markos, not two truths and a *dream*." At that moment the odds were against me, but after six years of nonstop hard work and perseverance, I proved everybody wrong. That fueled my fire.

Fast forward to 2015…I had the last laugh! I interviewed Criss three times in the same calendar year. This "power journalist" made his college "dream" a reality. My nickname in the music business was derived from my lightning fast turnaround rate.

To this day, when people ask me who "my favorite male interview of all time is," I instantly tell them Criss Angel. I always looked up to the magician's hard work ethic, perseverance, and ability to prove his naysayers wrong. I saw a lot of myself in him. Aside from being very genuine and humble, he is a master in his craft of magic. Angel has earned every ounce of respect, fame, and all the accolades that have come his way. He has set the bar high for Greek-Americans who wish to pursue their dreams. For me, it was never about how his magic demonstrations were done, what fascinated me most about him was how fast he would do everything, his top-notch presentation skills, and that he never gave up.

In my first interview with Angel, which dates back to January of 2015, Angel told me that it took him "18 years to become an overnight success," and that is a very true statement. The same holds true in journalism, especially in the beginning when I taught myself the tools of the trade. For every "yes" I ever received, I must have gotten at least seven or eight "noes" in return. I always had enough success to keep going, built my portfolio along the way, and established trustworthy connections with managers, publicists, and PR agencies, which were essential for growth in the field.

Meeting and interviewing Criss Angel always resonates with me, and as part of my 30th birthday celebration a few years back,

I honored him with my red velvet birthday cake which displayed my favorite photo with Angel. It truly was a "magical" moment, and a reminder that anything is possible in life as long as one focuses, perseveres, and works hard.

The ultimate honor and icing on a big fat Greek cake took place November of 2017, where I was inducted into the *Hellenic News* Hall of Fame, as part of its 30th anniversary. The induction ceremony was held in Cinnaminson, New Jersey, and I brought my mother, Effie, with me, which made the night extra special. In my humble acceptance speech, I had thanked everybody who helped me along the way, even through the hard times, which have molded me into the journalist and the man I am today. I thanked I.S. 25 (my junior high school), Saint Francis Prep (my high school), Waldbaum's (my first job ever as a cashier, which exposed me to customer service and the food service industry), and especially Queens College, where my journalism roots were firmly planted.

A special thank you went out to all the outlets in the Greek-American press I have written for over the past 12 years, especially the *Hellenic News of America*, the *Greek-American Herald*, *Greek Reporter*, and *NEO Magazine*. An equally big thank you went to *Digital Journal*, the online news publication, where I serve in the capacity of Music Editor-at-Large. "Thank you for giving me a platform to publish my work, and to share it with the rest of the world," I said in my speech. "A journalist is only as good as his reading audience."

I extended my gratitude to every publicist I had ever worked with in my life, including Ken Phillips of the Ken Phillips Publicity Group, as well as my mentor Professor Doreen Schmitt from the Anthropology Department of Queens College, Herman Canosa, Dan Romano of Frankie's East Side Gourmet Pizza, Alex and Olga Moschos of Neraki Greek Mediterranean Grill in Huntington, Christos Pavlatos and Spiro Markatos at GreeKrave, my church, the St. Nicholas Greek Orthodox Church in Babylon, The Paramount in Huntington on Long Island, Phil Smith and The 90's Band, Edvin Ortega and Larger Than Life, Mike DelGuidice and the Billy Joel tribute band Big Shot, Doug Gray and The Marshall Tucker Band, Jeff Timmons from 98 Degrees, Mulcahy's Pub and Concert Hall (especially Bobby Karounos, Ricky Cappiello and Tim Murray), pole vaulter Sam Kendricks, and everybody in the track and field community (including Bubba Sparks, Linda Prefontaine, and Daniel Mitchell), and of course, Criss Angel, and most importantly, my mother, Effie, without whom none of this would have been possible.

Another favorite male interview was one that I did in December of 2018, and that was with the ever talented Dan Reynolds, the lead singer and songwriter of the Grammy-winning rock group Imagine Dragons. They have been my favorite rock group over the last five years, and I absolutely love Reynolds' philanthropic work with his nonprofit organization, the LoveLoud Foundation. He is such an inspiration to all, and a musician whose heart is even bigger than his talent.

When asked about "my favorite female interview of all time," two come to mind. First, it would be Martina McBride, whom I've had the pleasure of interviewing on at least five separate occasions. She is my favorite female singer of all time and the reason I fell in love with country music in the first place.

Yet another proud moment was when I interviewed best-selling global music superstar Nana Mouskouri this past April. She is my mom's favorite singer, and we grew up listening to her music when we lived in Greece. She has recorded songs in over 12 different languages and has sold over 350 million albums throughout her illustrious career in the music industry.

Speaking of living legends, I celebrated my 10,000th career article this past Christmas Eve with a phone interview with seven-time Emmy Award-winning actor Ed Asner (known for his lead roles in *Elf, The Mary Tyler Moore Show,* and *Lou Grant*). Following the interview, I revealed to Asner that I accomplished a major milestone in journalism with that particular interview. "Oh God! You should quit while you're ahead," Asner said, jokingly, and in return, I responded as follows, "I can retire now, but I am having too much fun." Asner kept at it. "No, now you need to win the Pulitzer. You have spunk. I'm a spunk dealer," Asner exclaimed. In honor of this journalist's 10,000th career article, The Paramount in Huntington on Long Island, which *Pollstar Magazine* ranks in the Top 5 theaters worldwide in the "Club Venues" category, paid a tribute to this journalist with its marquee sign that read: "Markos

Papadatos, Power Journalist, 10,000 articles." That was a neat gesture and something very special, since this journalist would review shows there consistently, as well as interview the artists, bands, comedians, and magicians that it books, when they come to Long Island to perform.

Advice

I always believe in paying it forward and giving back. I share my 12 years of insights on how aspiring writers, reporters, and journalists can make it in the contemporary music and entertainment journalism scene. I offer my advice below.

First and foremost, it is essential for the writers to start early. Get your "feet wet" with journalism experience in your junior high school, high school, or college newspaper. Always keep a portfolio and a track record of the articles that you publish, whether they are printed or online, to show managers and publicists the events you have covered and the individuals you have featured. That will help to secure interviews, especially when it comes to submitting samples of your written work. Looking back, that is the best way to see your own personal growth as a writer, as well as becoming the lifelong, reflective learner. To this day, 12 years into my craft, I am still constantly learning and growing.

A major necessity in the media world is punctuality. Journalists need to be punctual, even if that is not always the case with the artists and musicians. For in-person interviews, always arrive 30 to 45 minutes in advance. This shows true professionalism, especially since agents and management frown upon journalists and interviewers who arrive late.

Also, it is essential to remember that if one travels long distance to provide coverage of an event, it is best to call the venue in advance, to verify that everything is still in effect. Events or concerts can change due to weather or last minute cancellations (such as performer illnesses).

Always email, fax, or snail mail a copy or link of the published interview/article/podcast to the person who set up that certain interview/review for you. Again, this shows true professionalism, and that one cares for his craft and for the relationships established.

Try to focus your interview on what that particular person is promoting at a certain time, whether it is an album, movie, tour, concert, or show, etc. Save other questions towards the end of the interview. Try to avoid hostile questions. Let *TMZ* ask those. For the most part, most people want to talk about the present moment, their latest endeavors, and the future, and not so much about the past.

As hard as it may be, try to get your interview or article written within 48 to 72 hours (two to three days) from when it happened. That way, it is still fresh on a journalist's mind. The longer one waits, the harder it is to write about it as accurately as possible, and recall all the facts.

If you are doing an interview over the phone, always ask for permission to tape the conversation; that will help you with the transcription process for accuracy, and if any quote ever gets questioned, you have proof that it was said, and remember it's the person's words, not yours. Most people are comfortable having their voices taped for transcription purposes at least 99 percent of the time.

Since technology does not always work 100 percent of the time, also take written notes during your interview, in case your audio recorder malfunctions. Always carry a notepad, pen or paper, and backup batteries, for the audio recorder or a camera. That way, you have backup notes of the conversation.

Always try to be gentle with your interview subjects. I treat the people I interview the way I wish to be treated. If one wants/needs to ask a difficult/sensitive/hostile question, always save it for last, since by then, one would have gotten everything else needed for the story. The worst thing that can happen is the interviewer won't receive an answer for that sensitive question. Other than that, the key is to treat the person with kindness. Any artist who didn't treat me with kindness never got a follow-up interview with me.

Try to go outside the box. Do research on your interview subject, and try to find a different story angle than your fellow journalists, since if one only goes by the artist's bio and fact sheet, most will have the same story, give or take. Always ask artists what inspires them and their artistry. Most of them love to open up about that. That makes your journalistic work stand out by a mile.

Be the empathetic journalist. I always tell people that I am the Anti-*TMZ* journalist. Try to be sensitive and aware of the fact that artists and celebrities are people too. Show empathy towards them and their feelings. Try to refrain from asking sensitive questions about their family members and former relationships (or anything that heeds gossip). Keep it professional. That way, they are more comfortable with opening up to you. Always try to keep the interview within the allotted time that you are granted by the manager, artist, or publicist (12 to 20 minutes max). Trust me, you can get tons of information in that time. That amount of time with an artist has always sufficed for me. Artists are busy, and journalists are busy. Be respectful and mindful of each other's time. With me, I am quick and to the point. The last thing I ever want to hear is "one more question" or "last question" from the agent on the line, so I do my best for it to not get to that point. I am done with my questions, way before the time limit.

As I had remarked in my *Hellenic News* Hall of Fame acceptance speech, remember that, "A journalist is only as good as his reading audience." Use language that is easy to read and understand (not too difficult vocabulary words in your articles), otherwise you will lose people's attention and their interest.

As hard as it may be, try to keep your journalistic writing as objective (free from bias) as possible, especially when it comes to topics related to politics. Try to narrate/write the facts as objectively as possible, as they occurred, without taking a certain side. Report the facts as honestly and accurately as you possibly can. If you feel a certain way about a topic, provide backing evidence (reasons and details). Integrity is what makes writers and journalists stand out.

If you want to reach out for an interview, go through the proper channels. Reach out to a publicist and a manager first, as opposed to the artist or their family members. They are the gatekeepers to the artists that they represent. The only exception is if the artist is independent and handles his or her own publicity.

For journalists who are also photographers, it is preferable to use the press photos the publicists send you, to avoid any conflicts with the artists and their management/PR teams. That way, their image is always presented in the best way possible. In addition, if you must use photos of your own, always run them by the publicists. Send them several photos you took at the event, and then, have them choose the ones they like best, for photo approval purposes. That way nobody gets in trouble, in the event that one does not like a photograph that was taken.

Best of Luck, and Happy Writing!

"To give anything less than your best, is to sacrifice the gift."
- Steve Prefontaine (American track and field legend)

About Markos

For the past 13 years, Markos Papadatos has been a vital part of the music, pop culture, sports, and entertainment community in New York. He has authored over 12,000 original career articles and has reviewed artists in the biggest and most exquisite venues. Each week, he covers anywhere from four to six live events.

As a journalist, reporter, and editor, Markos has interviewed some of the biggest names in music including: Aerosmith, George Jones, Merle Haggard, Dolly Parton, Emmylou Harris, Sheryl Crow, Dame Vera Lynn, Olivia Newton-John, Donny and Marie Osmond, 98 Degrees, Backstreet Boys, New Kids on the Block, NSYNC, Lee Ann Womack, and Martina McBride, among countless other noteworthy individuals in the United States and Greece.

In the film and television industry, Markos has interviewed Academy Award winners Jeff Bridges and Olympia Dukakis, as well as Academy Award nominees Lesley Ann Warren and Joan Allen. In the daytime television world, he has interviewed Emmy nominated and Emmy award-winning actors from such drama series as: *The Young and The Restless, The Bold and The Beautiful, Days of Our Lives, General Hospital,* and *The Bay.*

Aside from music and entertainment, Markos avidly reviews restaurants, and he interviews Olympic-caliber athletes (including swimmers, wrestlers, and track and field athletes), as well as magicians, with one of his biggest childhood heroes being Greek-American magician Criss Angel.

Markos serves as the Music Editor-at-Large of the online news publication, *Digital Journal,* and he is a Senior Editor for the *Hellenic News of America* (HNA), and the *Greek-American Herald.*

In 2017, 2018, and 2019, Markos won "Best of Long Island." At the 30th anniversary of the *Hellenic News of America* in November of 2017, Markos was inducted into the *Hellenic News* Hall of Fame and named "Journalist of the Year" by the *Greek-American Press.*

With my mother, Effie, at the 30th Anniversary of the Hellenic News Hall of Fame Awards, with the "Journalist of the Year" Award.

*Criss Angel and me after his show at the
Foxwoods in Mashantucket, Connecticut.*

*My 30th birthday cake. The photo of Criss Angel and me has our
slogans, "Are you ready" from **Mindfreak**, and #Powerjournalist.*

Marquee of the Paramount Theater in Huntington on Long Island, New York, celebrating my 10,000th article.

The Paramount presenting me with a Founder's brick for my 10,000th article.

With country stars Drew Baldridge, Canaan Smith, Michael Ray, and Jerrod Niemann at a country music festival on Long Island.

With multi-Emmy winner Ed Asner
(**Mary Tyler Moore Show** *and* **Lou Grant**).

With Rock and Roll Hall of Famer Roger Daltrey of The Who following my interview with him.

With country queen Martina McBride.

With world champion swimmer Michael Andrew.

*Interviewing Billy Joel at the Long Island Music
Hall of Fame in November of 2018.*

*Photo with the cast of the hit daytime drama **General Hospital.***

CONNIE F. SEXAUER

"Nothing happens unless first we dream."

- Carl Sandburg

My Metamorphosis

The above Sandburg quote is chiseled above the entrance to the University of Missouri—St. Louis Thomas Jefferson Library. It serves as a guiding force in my life—to live out your dreams and find a purpose that allows you to transition from a dream to a state of action. Locate the courage, take the risk, and bring your reality to your dream. It involves a willingness to change. That isn't easy for most as that doesn't always feel safe and could well lead to even more troubles. Be bold.

Catalyst for change is a unique experience occurring at different stages in life. As I reflect on the changes in my life, I see unimagined dreams led to a metamorphosis, like what a caterpillar experiences when transforming into a butterfly. I changed from an immature adolescent into a mature adult. The change did not emerge until I was in my thirties, rather late in life by most standards; but thankfully I came to love and respect the new me more than I ever did the one I left behind.

I see myself as a turtle in life, slow moving. The journey of change for me took years. The "aha moment" that triggered the biggest change for me came one evening in a marriage counseling session. That meeting focused specifically on my life and me.

I was close to 40 years of age when I experienced this profound life-changing moment. The doctor guided me on an examination of my life, asking me to reflect on events and experiences that led to where I was. I discussed my past life for close to 45 minutes. During a five-to eight-minute wrap up, the doctor confronted me with some penetrating, stark realities. As I sorted through each stage of my life I slipped in, "My parents never gave me a college education." Dr. G. enlightened me that if I were 19 years old, he might let me get away with that statement, but at my age, I needed to understand a few things. One was that no one ever gives you a college education; you earn it. He also advised if I really wanted a college education I should go after it.

I was upset with that answer. I wanted to be listened to but also coddled and supported, with my simplistic, juvenile answer. After we left the office, my husband was eager to address this topic. He commented, "Well, the doctor certainly put you in your place." He was quite pleased that I had been the one on the hot seat. Both men hurt me. Yet, I began, for the first time, to seriously think about the option of attending college, not necessarily to pursue a degree, just to see if I could pass a college course.

In 1945, I was born into a working-class, Catholic family. I was the third daughter. My father had a sixth grade education and my mother finished 10th grade. Both worked. My maternal grandmother lived with us and ran our household.

The prescribed role for white, middle-class women during the 1950s and 1960s, and the dream of my mother and grandmother, was that girls would not have to work outside the home. We would marry men who would "take care of us for the rest of our lives."

That dream was instilled in my youth through school training, church sermons, books, and newspaper and magazine articles, as well as radio shows, movies, and television roles. Domesticity was all part of the "American Dream." The preordained roles of men were as "breadwinners" and the women as "homemakers."

I never questioned that position. In fact, I embraced it. Early on, I looked forward to fulfilling my role and leading a happy life, free from the turmoil of the outside world. While in high school, I participated in speech and drama and got along with others. My

Catholic high school divided the students by a track system (A, B, C). A track students were geared for college, B track students were geared for office or retail jobs, and C track students were expected to get retail, factory, or housekeeping jobs. I placed on B track.

My grades were acceptable. A few of my teachers noted my talent in speech and theater and encouraged me to apply for scholarships at Fontbonne and St. Louis University. I did, but to no avail. My social studies teacher and drama coach encouraged me to go to college. University of Missouri, a state school, opened a branch close to my home and by all standards the tuition was affordable. I talked it over with my folks, and Dad was quite enthusiastic about the opportunity, but he also noted that we needed to discuss it with Mom. We did. She did not support the idea since she claimed they had not given my two sisters the same option and she wanted to be fair to all her children. So, I graduated from Mercy High School, got an office job, and set about fulfilling my role of finding Mr. Right.

I accomplished that goal in 1969 when I married my sweetheart. We worked together for a defense industry. I was a keypunch operator, and he was a college-educated programmer. Everyone thought I had landed quite the catch. He was good looking, charming, fun to be with, educated, a good provider, and to top it off, he was Catholic. He got along well with my family. Everything seemed perfect. My life was set.

For the next 15 years or so I lived what appeared to be a contented life of marital bliss in a nuclear family and played my prescribed role as the stay-at-home wife and mom. The unstated rules required me to support my husband's career by catering to his every need, entertaining in my home, and accompanying him to social functions. I also helped with car pool, volunteered at my children's school, served as a room mother, Brownie leader, and softball coach. My life seemed the ideal dream for a woman of the 1970s.

I devoted myself to being what my husband, my family, and society wanted me to be. We lived the best material life of anyone in my family. I never thought of challenging my beliefs or questioning my decision. Yet sometimes life has a way of awakening us.

As luck would have it, sometime in the mid-1970s, my mind opened to another world. I turned on my television set at 9 a.m. on a weekday morning and caught *The Phil Donahue Show*. Little did I realize, that experience would eventually change my life.

Most of the daytime programs at that time were either game shows or soap operas. Donahue's show was innovative with audience participation and a talk show format. Donahue challenged me every day, to step outside myself and learn new things, things I never knew existed. I eagerly tuned in every morning without fail.

Raised and schooled with a Catholic education, I conformed and made decent grades by following rote memorization. Thinking outside the box, forming one's own ideas—especially if they questioned the Catholic Way—was not permitted. Consequently, I did not have analytical thinking skills.

Donahue's controversial program was my College 101. Watching these shows and challenging myself to new ideas, I began to see the world differently. I began to see myself and my life in a fresh new way; however, this recognition did not happen overnight. It took years of watching, learning, absorbing, and questioning for me to grow into a deep, critical thinker. It was through the process and habit of connecting to these new ideas that I began to think analytically, not only about the world, but also, even more importantly, about who I was and what my place in life was.

Before the exposure to this show, I never questioned anything in my life. I was trained to be a good dutiful daughter, a Catholic woman, and a kept good wife who knew her place. That path seemed natural to me. There might have been times I wanted to question my role in life, but it would not have benefitted me to do so since I had no other route to pursue.

Donahue introduced me to new ideas. He presented important people, movers and shakers from many different fields. I had never heard of most of these folks. In the newspaper each day I read the sports page, the lovelorn columns, the entertainment section, and the comics. Front-page news went right past me, and I don't ever remember reading the editorial section. My magazine subscriptions consisted of *Better Homes and Gardens, Good Housekeeping, Ladies Home Journal, Redbook*, etc. All the articles reinforced and educated me on my dutiful domestic role. Except for my mother, I did not associate with women who worked outside the home, and I was happy I did not have to stoop to such a level. I was guarded and protected in my home, sealed away from any outside worries.

Some of the people I met through *The Phil Donahue Show* were recognizable from the entertainment industry, but his guests also came from many different fields. There was Madalyn Murray O'Hair, an atheist; Milton Friedman, an economist; Malcolm X and Jesse Jackson, civil rights activists; Gloria Steinem, Betty Friedan, both modern feminists; Ralph Nader, Eldridge Cleaver, political activists; Margaret Meade, a cultural anthropologist; and Fr. Andrew Greely, a Catholic priest and sociologist who challenged the church hierarchy. Donahue had been raised Catholic and attended Notre Dame University. He pitted liberals and conservatives against each other. He openly challenged ideas of Catholic faith and doctrine. I never knew one could do that.

Phil sided with the audience. He was a sensitive male who tackled important social issues of the day incluing: belief in God, money matters, race issues, women's rights, gay rights, and the role of the Catholic Church. He strongly supported concerns for women and wanted to enlighten them on all issues. In his friendly, casual manner, he made women feel important and believe what they thought truly mattered. He was a breath of fresh air. His confrontation of the prescribed role for women took on society. Each day I came to the show bright with excitement for what he would present.

Slowly, over the years of watching this program, I began to realize I had a brain and free will. I could think for myself. I had opinions and deserved the right to express them. I found logic and understood I could challenge contradictory evidence rather than deny it. Donahue assured me that I could critique the world, even society. I had the power to question and reach conclusions other than those fostered on me by others.

One of the first ways I successfully questioned my role in life was to recognize that I was not 100 percent happy in my chosen life as a domestic goddess. I wanted more out of life. I began to see that while I lived a "good life" and was financially well cared for, I did not feel content nor at peace. I faced the fact that I lived in a dysfunctional relationship. My husband ruled not only our household but also my overall life and my place in it. I wanted to remain married, but

I wanted my life to change. I wanted my husband to change and respect me as an equal partner.

We lived in the suburbs of St. Louis. Over the years we moved further away from family and lifelong friends. I became more isolated. I came to see our relationship as abusive in that he was condescending and said things designed to make me feel worthless. I had no one to talk this over with. He made all the major decisions in our life, and for a long time I believed that was the way it was supposed to be. Once I began to examine my life, I recognized he controlled all aspects of my life, and that I did not have a say in any part of it, or that the say I did have had to do with where I grocery shopped or what to serve for dinner. I realized that not only had my voice been taken but so had my decision-making and the overall right to speak against his wishes. He was jealous, even of the attention I gave our children. I did not attend social activities without him. If we had an engagement planned and at the last minute he decided we weren't going, I made up lies (i.e. one of the kids was sick, etc.), so no one knew he just didn't want to be around whomever it was for that day. Behind closed doors he ridiculed my family, friends, and our neighbors. He was demanding, controlling, and verbally abusive, especially when I began to find my voice and to speak up. He tormented and belittled me.

Together we put on a show of domestic bliss. For the most part ,no one, not even me at first, realized what a submissive life I led. He was a bully and had a dark side. Over the years I began to realize I was married to a Dr. Jekyll and Mr. Hyde personality. He presented himself as one person to the world and a different person once he retreated to our home.

I think if he had physically abused me or acted that way all the time perhaps I would have found the strength to leave, but he played with my emotions. We lived a seesaw relationship with loving behavior for a time and then suddenly out of nowhere there would be outbursts of rage. For days he could be fine, and then the slightest thing would throw him into a fury. He wanted perfection. I was expected to be a mind reader and know what he wanted. His weapons were his words, his moods, and control of the purse strings.

During the first years of our marriage, he convinced me that I was the reason he became angry because I did not take care of his needs and cater to him. I was confused, off-balance, and made to feel stupid. He was never wrong and consequently never showed remorse. He never apologized, and he controlled when or if he would accept an apology. He froze the children and me out with his silence. He attempted to play the four of us against each other. I learned to rehearse things I had to talk to him about and try to predict his reaction. When he traveled for business, our home was open and fun. When he was in town, people needed an appointment to drop by for a visit, and those of us living there walked on eggshells.

I stayed in my marriage for 25 years. That is a long time, a lifetime. When I began to question my life, I realized I stayed each year for a different reason. It took me a long time to discuss my life with anyone and then only a select few. Of course, my kids lived this life along with me, but most of my family, nor my husband's family, knew the life we lived behind closed doors. I discussed my frustrations with few. I was insecure. I feared no one would believe me. I did not want to embarrass myself or endanger his career. I did not want to lose the love of friends and family. I feared his overall control and position, believing he could take my children from me or leave us without financial support. I wanted respect and believed the adage I had heard in my own home growing up, "You made your bed, now lie in it." For the most part, in my circle of friends and family, we knew no one had divorced or left the church.

I attempted to find support through my faith, but instead was guided by my confessor that my role in life had been set for me, and I was there to support my husband. I was instructed to pray to be an instrument of peace, return home confident that I could be the wife I was meant to be through the grace of God. This was the real kicker I received, "You were married in the church and know the Lord will always guide you."

In addition to continuing to watch the *The Phil Donahue Show*, I began to read more thought provoking, in-depth works, many by the people who I became acquainted with on Phil's show. I found my way to books by those I mentioned earlier, as well as spiritualist Wayne Dyer, and sex therapists Masters and Johnson. Gone from my reading list were fiction books. I embraced non-fiction, especially biographies and self-help works. I soaked up this new knowledge. I let go of my reliance on the control of the opinions of those close to me and searched to question everything I had been taught.

Thanks to the enlightened advice of our marriage counselor, I took a reluctant step. In fall of 1985, I took my first college course. I decided on an English writing class because in high school one of our teachers explained if you could not pass an introductory English course, you did not belong in college.

I was not aware of it, but evidently, I was harboring doubts about daring to think I belonged in college. A dear friend, who had a degree in math, was very encouraging and asked me about a week before classes how I felt about attending school. At first, I ignored the question, but when she pursued the line of questioning I responded, "I am fine."

She would not let it go. She asked, "How do you really feel?"

Again, I assured her, "I am fine." That would not do. She kept it up, and finally I looked at her and said, "I am scared."

She inquired, "Of what?"

Exasperated, I looked at her and replied, "I am afraid I won't know what to wear." Today I laugh at that response, but she didn't.

She replied, "Well you will go the first day and look around at what others have on. Then go shopping and buy what you need to fit in." She continued, "What else are you afraid of?"

I opened up and revealed, "I am afraid they will ask me things I've never learned before, and I will fail."

She assured me that would not happen, but even if I failed who would know? I explained, my husband would. Her clever reply was, "Not if you don't tell him." I didn't think that was possible, but of course, she was right.

Over the years I changed. College solidified that change, accelerated it, as well as reinforced it. I found professors who encouraged and supported my efforts. On the last night of my first semester my English teacher gave me sign-up information for honors courses because he thought I would appreciate the challenge. Truthfully, I never planned to take another course. I took that class to prove I could pass college. Now though, with that encouragement, my journey was set. The next semester I took sociology and psychology.

I loved the way that material helped me to evaluate society and to examine my life. I decided to earn a two-year degree.

I enjoyed learning and, over the years, improved my self-esteem and self-confidence. People I met at school believed in me, thought I was smart, and looked for my opinion. It was a powerful feeling, and I found myself looking forward to my time in class. Before long, I decided perhaps I would pursue a degree.

My classes opened me to new ideas and new ways of learning. I constantly read, attended out-of-class lectures, studied, worked in groups, interacted with others, and discovered a new sense of self. This experience helped me to step outside my prescribed role and myself. I began to place myself into society at large and contemplated who I was and where I fit into the vast world. I learned to appreciate not only myself and my capabilities but also others within society. I expanded my world and looked for ways to continue to learn. I found the confidence to dream that I could change and improve my circumstances.

Education changed my entire life. I found my path to individuality and the courage to change into someone other than what others expected out of me. My favorite times were found when I was in the classroom preparing for my classes. I met interesting and exciting people. I became friends with other nontraditional students, the younger students, people from diverse backgrounds, as well as the faculty. I came alive on this academic journey. Slowly I emerged as a completely different human being. Oh, believe me I did not note that change myself but others, especially those within my inner circle, experienced a different Connie.

While this was an exciting time for me, the path was not necessarily good for my marriage. I found my voice and began to stand up for myself and my kids. I did not simply roll over and allow my husband to completely control our lives. My plan, when I began this journey, was never to become separated from my marriage and responsibilities. That was why I had signed up for professional help. I wanted my marriage to last, but I also wanted it to work. I enrolled in college because I wanted to experience that challenge, but something unexpected happened on this journey.

I found self-respect. I began to truly love myself and believe I deserved to live a life that I had chosen. I opened myself to every new opportunity to grow and develop all aspects of my life. Each year as I became stronger as a woman with confidence in my abilities, my husband became more controlling and demanding. Certainly, this was something I had never anticipated and was not prepared for. To me, my education was not a threat but a way to enrich my life as a wife and mother.

My academic path threatened my husband and his control over me, as well as the direction of not only me but of our family. I did not see that and continued on my merry way. We stayed together, and in our own sick way tried to hold our marriage together. I believe we both loved each other but not in a healthy way. We both had been programmed to live the life of societal expectations, and I changed all of that. I changed, and once I changed it fostered change in the whole dynamic of our relationship and the overall direction of the family dynamic. I have seen other relationships survive and thrive when change appears, especially on the academic path, but that was not our life.

Over the years we discussed the changes occurring, mainly through heated arguments. As I developed strong analytical skills and questioned my place in the world, I grew stronger in my desire to be an equal partner not only in my marriage but also especially in the decisions of my own life. I recognized I could not change him, but I could change myself. If he would not or could not accept the new me, then I wanted freedom—the freedom to embrace change. I had a new sense of commitment to a new life trajectory for myself. I talked divorce. He didn't want that.

At first when the topic arose, we both expressed our love for each other and that we did not want to upset our children's lives, but eventually he fell back on the fact that our marriage was a business, a company, and financially we could not disband, as it would not benefit any of us. Not exactly the loving plea I had hoped for. As the kids got older, I realized one day they would all leave his abusive ways, and I would be the only one left. When the girls moved out and our son was in military school, it dawned on me, I was correct, I *was* the only one left. I made the decision that I finally respected myself more than I did my husband, and out of that respect I sought my own peace.

I found myself as I developed analytical thinking skills, and I synthesized the diverse parts of my life. I concluded that I was a productive and worthwhile person who deserved to have a complete and fulfilling life. That life for me included the path of a devoted and loving wife and mother but also embraced a woman who was capable of finding a fulfilling life outside of those demands.

Over the years I earned a Ph.D. in history and a tenure position with a respected university. I truly believe I entered that marriage undeveloped mentally and emotionally. The awakening for me, through *The Phil Donahue Show,* the diverse works I read, and the ultimate decision to attend college, was life changing, and I believe life saving for me. I do not propose it is necessarily the life for all women of my generation, but I found a complete fulfillment in developing my own unique self. I learned to love and respect myself as more than a mere image-maker for others.

I don't think I really recognized the full, unconscious control others had on my life until I passed the threshold of earning my Ph.D. The day I graduated and was hooded, I was so ecstatic that I simply could not help but smile continuously. When my adviser and I crossed the stage to receive my hooding, remarkably, somewhere out of my past, came an experience I had not given thought to in 35 years. Suddenly I heard my high school sophomore PE teacher tell me, *You are a quitter and will never accomplish anything in life.* WHAT?! Where did that come from; who was that voice of my past? Well, that woman was another influence in my life, and one I never even realized had any control over me.

When I was 15 years old, I was a busy girl. I babysat, worked as a busser in a cafeteria, and was involved in speech and drama at school. I was recruited by my PE teacher to play track and field and participate in our school's first Catholic School Olympic Program. I was surprised and honored to be asked. I did not express athletic prowess but evidently because I was 5 feet 9 inches tall, the woman believed I would benefit our track and field program. This invitation flattered me, but as days wore on I began to examine my overall schedule and realized something had to give. I talked this over with my mom. I simply could not see how I could keep up with all the commitments I had. She wisely pointed out to me that I needed to review my schedule and choose what I wanted to spend my time on. So, over the weekend, I looked over everything and decided I needed money, so the jobs were paramount. I loved the theater and drama work and had already committed myself to those projects. The thing to eliminate was the request of the PE teacher. I was not turned on to that project, had not pursued it, and felt the easiest decision was to let the PE teacher know I could not continue to train for the high school Olympics. Now mind you, I was only less than one week into my commitment. I went to the teacher and explained my dilemma. She was furious with me. That is when she decided to berate this young girl and explain to her if she did not compete for the teacher's dream then the young girl was a loser who "would never accomplish anything in life." I tell you this story because, of course, for me all these years later this was enlightening, but also for you to understand that while the opinions of others may influence you, they are not who you will become. That woman was wrong. We become winners when we achieve our dreams, not those of others.

I strongly urge anyone to find a dream and manifest it. Take personal responsibility. You will grow in ways you never imagined and will find fulfillment beyond measure. Don't be afraid to explore the journey you were set on earth to explore. Success for you is what you envision, and your success will fulfill your life goals and your life's purpose.

About Connie

Dr. Sexauer taught U.S. History and Gender Studies at the University of Wisconsin–Marathon County for 16 years. She is a graduate of the University of Cincinnati with a specialty in urban history. The main focus of her primary research is the role of Catholics in the 20th century and the importance of faith in their lives. Her works include articles on Catholic Civil Rights action, and the study of Charles V. Vatterott, Jr., a St. Louis real estate developer during post-World War II. She argues that "faith makes a difference in a person's life." The subject of her latest book, *From a Park, To a Stadium, To a Little Piece of Heaven* brings together her love of history, cultural studies, social change, and changes in sports. This book was released summer 2019 by Nico 11 Publishing, Mukwonago WI. Dr. Sexauer has published articles and delivered national papers on these exciting topics of research.

Connie's contact information is csexauer@uwsp.edu

PAULA H. MAYER

"Never, never, never give up."

- Winston Churchill

Beyond the Three Walls

I had to pinch myself as I walked alone down the narrow cobblestone streets of Prague, spring of 1992. I was taken back by the bullet holes and artillery damage still left in the beautiful pastel facades. It's as if time stood still from the end of World War II. Days before, I was at Checkpoint Charlie where the Berlin Wall had come down 2 ½ years prior. It was in 1987 that President Reagan had said, "Mr. Gorbachev, tear down this wall." Little did I know that the chain reaction and ramifications of the effect of the Berlin Wall coming down would later impact my family's life.

Shortly after my husband Rick and I were married in 1987, we desired to start our family. Ultimately, whether we had children biologically and or through adoption, it didn't matter. I was in Prague in the first place, because after many years of struggling to start a family, my parents thought a trip would be a good diversion. A failed cycle of In Vitro Fertilization (IVF), followed by a failed open adoption prospect, and failed foster care prospect, had taken a heavy toll on us. My husband and I both had good careers that led to corporate relocations to three major cities in less than three years. Moving from state to state was an obstacle in forming a family. Walls seemed to pop up wherever we had moved. Regardless of barriers, I was not going to give up on my dream of adopting children to form an international family.

Psychologically, walls go up in our minds too—mental road blocks. Figuratively and literally, walls are a vertical testing point of proving our grit and determination to climb over them or break through them. Ancient and modern man have built them to divide. Walls are controversial. Mankind has dreamt of building walls, and some have dreamt of pure perseverance to scale them for a better life or in my case, to break through them literally and figuratively.

My career goal of beginning in the commercial insurance industry started off by obtaining my sales license. Next, I acquired my state insurance adjustor's license, and then landed a coveted position as a senior commercial insurance underwriter. I ended my career working in risk management. Little did I know the underwriting position that required analytical and legal thinking skills while paying attention to fine details would help in the near future. My skills would transfer into the understanding of building several international dossiers for my husband and I to travel to remote parts of the world to adopt our precious children.

Spring of 1995, Rick and I were crammed into a large passenger van with other American couples we had met a few days earlier in Beijing, China. We had just left the Wuhan Airport that had one small terminal for the city the size of Chicago. Peasants from the rural areas watched foreigners with curiosity. They still were wearing the gray Mao pant suit clothing. I was nervous while sitting next to Rick, as I realized we both had money belts strapped to our waists, as did all the other American couples, as we headed to see our precious babies. There was thousands of dollars in that van. What if we got stopped at gunpoint because we were foreigners? I quickly remembered, from all my China readings, that criminals are sometimes executed in their town squares; and thus, the crime rates are extremely low.

I remember when I was thirteen years old, I learned about the Great Famine in social studies class. American parents told their children to eat all their food on their plates because of it. It was in 1972 when President Nixon made an unprecedented trip to China, and it changed the world. I remember watching the images coming out of China on TV. In all my wildest dreams, I never thought that a time would come when I would cross the barrier of the Great Wall of China via a trans-country airplane flight to Wuhan, China to adopt my first child.

In 1992, China implemented a law enabling foreigners to adopt its orphans as a result of China's one-child policy that started in 1979. The orphanages were primarily made up of female infants and handicapped males. China had developed an imbalance in the population, with more males to females. In the news, Americans began to hear about the documentary called *The Dying Rooms*, filmed by a few journalists posing as American relief workers inside China's orphanages. The abuses in the orphanages were not for the faint of heart to view. Eventually, the Chinese government was encouraged to ameliorate the situation.

Two hundred and six orphans were first adopted by foreigners in 1992. China's Ministry of Civil Affairs, in charge of the orphanages, did not have a centralized formal adoption program, and they left the process up to the provinces. It wasn't until a few years later that the Ministry of Civil Affairs centralized and established a formal adoption program with appointed foreign adoption agencies. Prior to the centralization, all the immigration permits were issued at the American Consulate in Guangzhou, China where foreigners were to exit the country with adopted children. Both China and the United States regularized the procedures between the two countries. The next year the adoptions doubled.

Fall of 1994, Rick came home one day from work and told me the story of an adoption possibility in China. *When the light is green, go!* Rick's colleague had a relative living in Beijing, and he was an American attorney working at the Beijing Dragon Law Firm. The attorney, Edward Lehman, along with his wife, would periodically over a two-year period have babies left at their doorstep. Word must have gotten out amongst the Chinese, that possibly this American couple could find safe havens for their abandoned babies. It's illegal to abandon a baby in China. What were these desperate Chinese to do? They chose life and a future for their babies versus the unthinkable.

The compassionate Mr. Lehman and his wife quickly found

orphanages and care for these babies. Mr. Lehman worked with the Ministry of Civil Affairs and couples found help in an official, referred to as Madame Lu. Mr. Lehman and his wife reassured Madame Lu that they would find vetted American parents willing to adopt Chinese baby girls. Mr. Lehman's sister in the United States would match babies with American couples after they completed an independent home study in their county and prepared their extensive dossier required by the Chinese government. This needed to be notarized and apostilled at the state level by adoptive parents. And then finally, they needed to complete their extensive U.S. immigration paperwork. In 1994, outside of the Lehmans, there were maybe a few U.S. adoption agencies working with China.

Rick and I were considered trailblazers in the Chinese adoption process because we did our Chinese adoption independently on our own. It was difficult to find a social worker in the Milwaukee area where we resided. I found an experienced and reputable social worker after several phone calls. Our social worker was affiliated with an established Milwaukee adoption agency, but they had never worked with a couple planning to adopt an infant from China. The agency was intrigued and excited to do our home study. Edward Lehman's sister was our "child finding source" and our connection to get all our vast paperwork to the Beijing Dragon Law Firm where Mr. Lehman would present our paperwork to Madame Lu. Then Mr. Lehman's sister would select an infant baby girl who was considered to be thriving, but with little medical information. Mr. Lehman processed dozens of adoption petitions for infants with Madame Lu while she worked as an official with the Ministry of Civil Affairs. It wasn't until a year or two later the Chinese formalized an adoption program.

After our van traveled a narrow and chaotic highway through a city of six million people, we arrived at our high-rise hotel. It was one of a few high-rises we could see along the Yangtze River. Rick was excited to see they sold Milwaukee Pabst beer at the hotel. The only place foreigners could shop was at the Friendship Stores. Before we spent the night, we were told to prepare for tomorrow to visit our child's orphanage.

In the early morning, the van drove us to an orphanage that

was not of Chinese construction. We found out the building was built by missionaries before the Boxer Rebellion during the turn of the century. It was a very old Euro-American building that had a crumbling facade. There was so much excitement amongst us to see the babies. We had received a thumb print picture of our daughter, whom we named Madeline. I was attached immediately to the picture we received a couple months after we were assigned our child, Zhen Li, by Mr. Lehman's sister. While inside the orphanage, we were immediately greeted by mainly women dressed in white coats. We all thought we would soon see a glimpse of our children, but we were told they would bring our children to us tomorrow at the hotel. Our entourage was quiet as we walked on marble floors into the infants' room. We did not say a word as we saw dozens of cribs, each with two infants laying on their backs all swaddled in tightly wrapped bundles. There was no heat in the facility, and it was chilly. I noticed the appalled faces on our other American friends' faces, and we noticed the dirty walls and soiled cribs. Most of the infants had crackling coughs—upper respiratory colds. We held some of the bundled babies to comfort them and realized the orphanage workers did the best to care for the children with the limited resources they had. We all wondered how our six-month-old infants were doing. We were told our children were taken home at night by foster parents, and that was comforting. But how could we not worry about the future of the infants we held?

It was a heartbreaking experience. Thank goodness a part of our adoption fee included a donation to the orphanage.

The next morning, our destined bundles of joy swaddled in traditional quilted layers of clothing were brought to us at the hotel. They placed the babies in the mother's arms while the husbands held their wives. When Rick and I received Madeline, I was so giddy, full of joy and happy tears. We soon took our bundles of joy to each of our rooms. Rick and I laid on the bed with Madeline in wonderment. It all felt like a labor delivery. The paperwork was like our pregnancy, but it was only a five-month miraculous pregnancy and delivery! Our daughter was absolutely beautiful. My younger thirteen-year-old self never would have imagined going beyond The Great Wall of China with her husband to adopt a baby girl. Our dream was manifested by the prayers of many.

A few years later, in 1997, I found myself nervous and hanging on for dear life as Rick and I rode in the back seat of a common utilitarian Russian Trabant car. Our assigned driver was speeding and weaving through traffic effortlessly as I was jerked around bouncing off of Rick because we had no seatbelts. I thought as we headed to the orphanage for the first time, I didn't want my infant in this car. The infant seat we brought with us was in the trunk. Rick didn't seem to be rattled. I asked the young driver in his late twenties, who actually spoke good English if we were late, and if he was in a hurry? It ended up he was a fighter jet pilot from the Russian Afghanistan Conflict, and that explained his driving.

We were in Ekaterinburg Siberia, east of the Ural Mountains, which is considered to be Asia. The last royal family of Russia, the deposed Tsar Nicholas II and his family, the Romanovs, were executed by the Bolsheviks in 1918 in Ekaterinburg, named after Peter the Great's wife. The city of one and a half million was made up primarily of your typical communist square, bland, box buildings. I felt as if Rick and I were in a movie; it all seemed surreal to me because I grew up during the Cold War, and never imagined going beyond the Berlin Wall of communist rule to adopt a baby boy with my husband.

In 1992, Russia formalized its international adoption program. Rick and I were hoping to adopt a boy, and, for some reason, boys were more plentiful for adoption. *When the light is green, go!* The Frank Foundation of Washington D.C. was our child-finding source. I had read about the humanitarian foundation online and started investigating the organization because of their adoption assistance program. If George Schulz, former U.S. Secretary of State's daughter was assisted by this organization in an adoption, then it had to be good enough for me to pursue. I found out that the organization's founder, Ronald Fraase, had spent years as a diplomat working for the U.S. Wheat Exchange dispersing grain to Russia. He saw first-hand the plight of the orphans in Russia and wanted to do something about it, so he formed Frank Associates (now only the name exists with a distant adoption agency).

Adoptions in Russia by the U.S. were just beginning to be

formalized in 1992, and U.S. adoption agencies were starting to establish their own programs with Russia in 1993. Again, Rick and I took the independent route since we found a child finding source with the Frank Foundation and retained our social worker who was beginning to become familiar with Russian adoptions. She was more familiar with the well-established Korean programs. She had some reservations at first for us because of high fetal alcohol rates amongst births. I quickly started the immigration papers, home study, and dossiers late March of 1997 as the petitioner, and I told Rick, I feel like I'm pregnant again! Although it actually ended up being six months from start to finish to finalize our adoption to bring home our precious six-month-old baby boy, Zachary.

It was a beautiful autumn day in Ekaterinburg when we pulled up to the large yellow with white trim stucco, two-story building, referred to as Baby House Number One, although it also housed toddlers too. There was an unoccupied, small, gated playground. We did see some grandmas walking with a group of bundled-up toddlers even though it was mild outside. Excitement was building up inside Rick and me as we were told we would be able to meet our son for the first time. Other American couples were arriving at the same time.

The night before, we were hosted by a single woman and her son in a typical communist-style, 700 square foot flat. The outside of the building was in ill repair with some graffiti on the metal doors, but our host had turned her flat into her little palace. It was nice to eat her Russian cuisine. I did walk out to her little balcony, and I snooped around and opened a little burlap sack which contained various root vegetables, some rotten. I realized we were eating out of the bag; her version of a root cellar. Although we were so anxious to see our child, we slept well in her little bedroom. I didn't see a crib. *We were to come back with our child to her home the next day with no crib?*

We entered the orphanage and walked into a large conference-type room and took off our coats. We proceeded on our tour and immediately went to a large room with sofas. Everything we saw was clean, bright, and cheery, a far cry from Madeline's facility. We were told to sit, and they would bring our children to us. We were adopting children under twelve months old. We had received a picture of

Zachary when he was a few months old along with a brief medical history. We had taken our adoption medication history to our pediatrician to review. It had been translated for us into English. Our prominent Milwaukee pediatrician hadn't seen any medical referrals from Russia but did his best to interpret the findings to us. Russia labeled all institutionalized children with various developmental delays.

When I saw the picture of Zachary, I immediately fell in love with him. Did we care if he had motor delays? Not at all! I joined a group of Russian adoption parents on the Internet, and every single medical report listed "developmental delays" in infants under 12 months. What would you expect from institutionalized children? My doctor was appreciative to have the important head circumference measurements at intervals, birth weight, and length, plus a head shot to look for fetal alcohol syndrome, which was ruled out. But still, it's not for the faint at heart to adopt with many unknown facts on top of the institutionalization factor. Nonetheless, Rick and I, regardless, felt somewhat equipped on a second international adoption, and in our hearts, fell in love with Zachary. I had thought, whether you give birth or adopt with an unknown medical history, there is always a risk when bringing children into the world or adopting under our circumstances.

The mothers were first presented with their children. I waited with Rick, and here came Zachary in a yellow fleece, zipped suit. I was filled with joy to hold our darling son with curly, sandy-blond hair and beautiful hazel eyes. He was chunky; wonder what was in his formula? His birth certificate said Tatar in the race/nationality box, which translates into Asian. Rick and I could see his Asian features in the shape of his eyes and broad face at the time. Later at home, a blood test confirmed he was a trait carrier for a disease common in the Asian race. And the doctor said he appeared to have biracial features. I loved it!

It was painful to leave Zachary in the orphanage until the court date. We visited Zachary for a few days. I had grown fond of the fact that classical music was played while the babies laid in their cribs during parts of the day; at least I knew this was stimulating to their brains. Years later, our son developed a strong passion for music playing multiple instruments and singing. I wonder why?!

Our court date finally arrived, and we had Zachary with us. We were greeted with a judge in a black robe who appeared Asian. Our hearing for the adoption approval went off without a hitch. The judge shared he was a Baptist when he realized we were evangelical Christians, which I thought was touching, but bold considering we'd heard of incidences where Russia still persecuted Christians. Imagine all that work behind the dossiers, immigration paperwork requirements, and home study had almost come to a closure. We completed the adoption in less than six months which was rare as was with our Chinese adoption too! All we had left to do was board a plane to Moscow and get a health check approval for Zach along with his visa and passport.

We had a little time to sightsee in Ekaterinburg and more time to visit the Red Square area in Moscow. We spent our last night with our gracious host, and it ended up that she put two cushion armchairs together to form a crib. Somewhere along the line Zachary developed dreaded scabies in Russia, and he had an outbreak when we got home. It took a while for Zachary to be diagnosed, as scabies is not common in America. Our dream had come true; I went beyond the communist wall, Iron Curtain, with Rick, and I brought home our son.

Little did Rick and I know we would be traveling to exotic Kazakhstan nine months before 9/11 to adopt again, but not without experiencing a traumatic situation. I caught word that the Frank Foundation was operating a child assistant program in Kazakhstan and children were available for adoption starting in 1999. Rick and I were hoping to adopt our third child, maybe a fourth (twins). *When there is a green light, go!* So, I started the home study in late spring of 2000, and Rick and I felt comfortable this time adopting a toddler. Ethnic Kazakh children and toddlers were more available to adopt versus the Caucasian Russian children which were also available for adoption. We were told our adoption could go quickly because our home study stated we wanted to adopt a toddler versus an infant under 12 months old. For us, the sex didn't matter, and we also would accept a Kazakh child.

Stalin had relocated thousands of White Russians to the Steppes of Kazakhstan after World War II. Kazakhstan was on the Silk Road and it had a melting pot of ethnicities including: Mongol, Tatars, Turks, Chinese, and ethnic Kazakhs, of course. So, we would have a Han Chinese, a Tater, and Kazakh Hun (Mongol). The Hans (Chinese) built the Great Wall to keep the Huns (Mongols) from invading China. It's a beautiful thing to think our children's ethnicities would be connected by the Silk Road. The Lord answered my prayers as I had dreamt of having an international family through adoption.

In the second week of December 2000, we arrived in Astana, Kazakhstan, via an overnight in Moscow. We were in the Steppes, the flat land of Kazakhstan, that thousands of miles later, eventually fed into the base of the Ala-Tau Mountains leading into the Himalayas. As of 1997, Astana became the new capital of Kazakhstan. Islam is the primary religion at 70 percent, and the rest of the population is Russian Orthodox. During our stay, the temperature was below zero. The capital was filled with newly built garish high-rise structures due to oil money flowing into the country. The gaudy architecture felt cold and sterile, with little, if any landscape planning. Elaborate ice sculptures and ice palaces were constructed all about the city by the locals. Everyone wore fur coats, even the toddlers. I remember being in a local meat market and seeing a gorgeous woman wearing what I thought was a tiger fur coat; coats were status symbols in this culture.

Our program coordinator, Svetlana, had met us and a few other American couples at the Astana Airport and then took us to a hotel. We met a new American couple who had seen our daughter, Gulmira, the day before. They said Gulmira was assigned to a little gated play area called a pod, with 13 other toddlers ranging in age from 16 months to two years old. She was memorable they said because she ruled the roost! Their son, a white Russian, was also in the pod, and they told us he had bowed legs due to rickets, but this could be corrected.

The next day, we finally entered the orphanage waiting room where we would meet our children for the first time. Our precious Gulmira, or Mira as we renamed her, was walked in by the hand of a caregiver wearing a white medical coat. Mira was stunning, with big, wide brown eyes and rosy cheeks. She appeared tall and confident. She was brought over to us, and she backed into me wanting to be held. I was overcome with joy as she sat on my lap, face out with Rick next to me. We were warned by the staff, the children do not take warmly to the husbands because there is not any male staff present at the facility. Mira saw Rick hug me, and she was a little standoffish to Rick at first.

We spent a week visiting Mira daily only to take her off the premises for terrifying health checks, passport pictures, and immunization shots in order to exit the country. We were amazed how well the toddlers were developing with their potty skills; they were taught to sit on a potty seat at a year and a half. Also, their dexterity skills, handling a spoon, was well developed in that they could eat their porridge better than most three year olds. I guess it was a matter of survival if they didn't use the spoon and get every last drop; they could possibly go hungry. It was emotionally painful to have other toddlers in the gated pod approach us with enthusiasm, wanting to be picked up and held.

It ended up we would be delayed getting to the American Embassy in Almaty, Kazakhstan with our children to process immigration paperwork and then flying to Moscow to exit for the United States. One afternoon after visiting Mira, we went to the hotel lobby for dinner. We were interested in watching the U.S. election count returns. We found a TV in the lounge. The chads had to be retallied in Florida in order to determine the presidential winner between Governor George W. Bush and Senator Al Gore. The TV had no picture but audio only. While watching the fuzzy gray screen, we found out that Al Gore conceded the win to George W. Bush on December 13. The American couple who was with us watching TV had adopted a beautiful, blond boy with rickets. That day they told us they took a taxi to the Kazakhstani Presidential Palace, got out, took tourist-type pictures, and machine-gun clad guards detained them along with their Kazakh escort who happened to be carrying their dossiers. They were let go after the guards explained the law of not taking pictures of the palace. The Americans said, "Well, we can take pictures of our White House." They pleaded ignorant.

The scary thing about the detained couple by Astana guards, was that the husband was a U.S. Air Force One-Star General and his wife was employed by the CIA at the Pentagon as a nurse. Had the guards gone through their paperwork, they would have been detained for a long time. By the time they returned to the hotel lounge, they were downing a few beers!

Svetlana told our small American group the next day, December 16, we would fly out of Astana with our children to Almaty, the old capital of Kazakhstan. Almaty was a spectacularly beautiful city with the snowcapped, Ala-Tau Mountains in the background that fed into the Himalayas. After leaving with Mira and saying our goodbyes to the dear orphanage staff, Mira clung tightly to me for comfort. Mira sat the entire time on my lap during the flight. After arriving at the Almaty Airport, we were all placed in a communist-built four-story, box apartment complex, in various vacated flats. The residents had rented out their tiny flats for us to reside in while we were in Almaty. Svetlana hired workers and drivers who would drop off our food on a daily basis. We were given keys, along with a daily itinerary, and we could use the landline for emergencies. That late afternoon, Rick and I walked around while I held Mira. We found an outdoor market in the cold, and as we walked around we stumbled across a local town square, where we were stared at up and down by the locals. It was an eerie feeling because we were in a strange land and no one spoke English. I found a deck of cards for sale, and we were able to negotiate money in order to purchase it. We went straight back to the apartment to eat and go to bed with Mira sleeping in a crib! We went stir crazy a few days cooped up in the 500 square foot flat with little communication. We were told we could exit Kazakhstan with Mira December 19 or later. Somehow, we needed to get word back to our family regarding a delay. We thought at one point we would possibly arrive home after Christmas and miss spending the holiday with Zachary and Madeline. The next day we were taken to the U.S. Embassy in Almaty to process our paperwork. We actually were escorted by the security director into an employee's common area where Santa arrived on a camel delivering gifts via U.S. mail bags to employee's children. It was fun to witness this tradition. Post 9/11, that wouldn't have occured.

A Kazakhstani *Mira-cle* occurred, on December 22, 2000. After a grueling trip, we arrived back in the U.S. with our precious dreamt-for gift, Mira. Prior to our arrival, Rick had been detained at the

Almaty Airport. When the guards escorted Rick to a nearby room, I went along with a terrified and traumatized toddler climbing up to my head with all of her adrenaline. The guards motioned me away and I said a firm, "NO." Don't mess with an angry mama bear. Soon a wall separated us from Rick while he was detained by intimidating machine-gun-carrying Almaty airport guards. Our flight was being held on the runway at 2 a.m. I tried to listen through the wall and then the door. *Why did they want Rick? How did we find ourselves in this position?* Then another American adoptive father was escorted in with Rick, and I had my ear next to the wall while praying no harm would come to them. It ended up that when the other American friend entered the room, Rick spelled, "S-C-A-M." That word put the American at ease.

Rick and the other American were being shaken down by corrupt guards for U.S. dollars and wanted $300 from each of them, and they said, "NO." They were behind a wall of corruption. Rick said the name Svetlana over and over again, and it got their attention when he used a Russian name. Meanwhile, I approached the guards at a desk nearby and laid down an Almaty U.S. Embassy card from days before that clearly displayed the head of security on the card. It seemed to get their attention, and they knew their guards, holding the Americans, would be in trouble. Rick and the American walked out of the room, and we called Svetlana. The security guards rushed to stamp our passports and visas and sent us out to the dark tarmac to board the plane to Moscow. Shortly, we would be beyond the wall of corruption.

We arrived home a few days before Christmas, and we were all reunited with an anxious and excited Zachary and Madeline. After two days of traveling, Mira had finally fallen asleep…underneath our Christmas tree. Best Christmas present ever!

"Every good and perfect gift is from above, coming down from the Father of heavenly lights, who does not change like shifting shadows." - James 1:17

We are now living in a new era with tension developing with Russia. In 2012, immediately after the Magnitsky Act passed in the senate and was signed into law by President Obama, Putin was angry and wanted to inflict pain to America. The law bars Russian officials suspected of human rights abuse from entering the U.S. and bans their use of the U.S. banking systems as well as freezes any assets held by U.S. banks. As a result, in December 2012, Russia's Duma proposed a law that would permanently ban adoptions of Russian children by Americans, and it passed. Kazakhstan also put a hold on American adoptions. Putin used marginalized Russian orphans as pawns to retaliate back at Americans. There were American couples in the process of finalizing their adoptions while in Russia. Putin hurt his precious orphans, and many needed surgeries in America. He brought grief to hundreds of Americans. Over the two decades prior to the ban, Americans adopted nearly 60,000 orphans.

I have to pinch myself sometimes when I realize that Rick and I created a family through international adoption after *following the green light* in three countries. It took two decades to accomplish my dream of having a family, from my early twenties before I was married to my early forties—when the last adoption was completed at 41½ years of age. I was pushing age 36 with the first adoption, as "timing" was everything in planning the adoptions—three children in six years. At the beginning of our journey to parenthood, it took guarded optimism and the ability to overcome loss while never giving up.

"For as he thinks in his heart, so is he." - Proverbs 23:7 (NKJV)

I decided to become passionately involved in pursuing what was beyond the three walls, our children.

Our now-adult children are fully Americanized. Rick and I were blessed to have the contacts and grit which enabled us to go beyond the three walls, that at one time in the past, historically banned foreigners. Or in one case, a corrupt government detained my husband with intimidation behind a wall to separate my daughter and I while shaking him down for money. Sometimes I have to remind myself that all three of our children's ethnicity: Han, Tatar, and Hun/Kazak are all connected by the Silk Road due to Marco Polo.

Today, they vote and are American through and through. I was able to manifest my dreams by building my family going beyond the three walls, inspite of the unknown.

"Now faith is being sure of what we hope for and certain of what we do not see." - Hebrews 11:1

To impart hope to families considering an international adoption, please visit the informative U.S. Department of State's Intercountry Adoption website at: https://travel.state.gov/content/travel/en/Intercountry-adoption.html

About Paula

Paula H. Mayer is a published short-story author, speaker, an almost licensed Chaplain, and Young Life board member. After graduating from The Ohio State University, the Rocky Mountains lured Paula to hike and start her decade long commercial insurance industry career in Denver. She married her best friend, Rick, in Colorado in 1987. In their adventures together, they traveled to the remote corners of the world where they were trailblazers at the time, accomplishing three independent international adoptions; they adopted their now-adult children from China, Russia, and Kazakhstan. Paula is a survivor of three cancers and a recipient of a donor bone marrow transplant in which one doctor gave her the title of a medical "outlier." It's hard to believe a few months before being diagnosed with her first aggressive cancer, a 13 cm wet, sloppy, non-Hodgkin's lymphoma tumor had been brewing in her chest cavity, as she was out climbing Long's Peak (14,259'). The mountain is a Class 3 climb in Colorado.

She became what she calls an amateur writer after surviving her bone marrow transplant. A doctor and others asked her, "When are you going to write your book?" She surprised herself and contributed a chapter, "It's Not Over Yet, People!" to a successful, anthology collection, an Amazon best-seller!

Her mother had always told Paula to stay encouraged by developing her talents and dreams because artist Grandma Moses was in her seventies when she first started her career. Paula feels the freedom to take a risk in middle age and go for it! She's in pursuit to obtain a Master's Degree in Theological Studies to become a board-certified Chaplain. Paula enjoys her northwoods lake cottage, reading, Germantown Life Church, bible studies, and art.

When you have a weighty determination to live daily, life becomes more focused. She resides in Mequon, Wisconsin.

Paula desires to impart hope to others through her unique life-stories. Contact her at paulahodappmayer@gmail.com.

I want to dedicate this short story, Beyond the Three Walls, to my husband, Rick, as I love our blessed alliance.

Kauai, Hawaii, 2019, celebrating my birthday!
(Left to Right) Mira, Madeline, Rick, me, and Zachary.

PENNY TATE

"In search of my mother's garden,
I found my own."

- Alice Walker

Nancy's Light of Hope

Written in dedication and remembrance of my mom, Nancy.

Mom,

You are at the heart of every word I write. You are my guiding light, and my story isn't complete without acknowledging the profound love I feel from you every day. Thanks Mom, for the wisdom you've shared with me, for your tremendous and unconditional love, and for continuing to find ways to show me you are still present in my life.

With love in my soul, courage in my actions, and HOPE with you in my heart.

Manifesting. If you Google the word, chances are you'll find multiple ways to define this concept. But, I believe you need to think long and hard about what this word means to you. As I perused the Internet, trying to discover how this term has resonated in my life experience, I found three descriptions that connected with me.

First, manifesting is the art of cocreating with the Universe.

Second, everything happening in your life is a reflection of what is happening inside of you.

Third, as best-selling self-help author and motivational speaker, Dr. Wayne Dyer, shares in his work, that to manifest your reality, you create a new concept of yourself.

First, manifesting is the art of cocreating with the Universe.

Talking with others, I've learned that most people come face-to-face with the Universe when death enters their lives. Whether you're contemplating death or have lost a cherished loved one, death and dying are concepts that so many struggle to grasp. There's no way of really knowing what the Universe holds—a sense of wonder and amazement, whether you believe in an afterlife of some kind, or perhaps believe there's nothing. An internal conversation about your personal belief system may unfold in your mind. You may question your faith as you examine what exists, and what is yet to come.

The death of my mom opened that door for me—an unimaginable pain that held no answers. I had a new heightened sense of awareness, as I tried to desperately find those answers to questions that only faith can answer:

Was she at peace?
How do I live now without my mother?
Will I see her again?

I could no longer pick up the phone and talk to her, laugh with her, or hug her. I was so lost without her; I found myself searching for her in other forms of communication or signs…a song on the radio, a deer crossing my path, or a stranger suddenly uttering a phrase she often said. I needed that connection to her, to a higher power, and to the Universe.

Tragedy Enters My Heart and My Life

In 2008, my parents began their year happily retired, spent time with our family, traveled, and celebrated 40 years of marriage. My mom was part of our daily lives as she helped care for my two daughters. As an only child, I was incredibly close to my mom. Her health was always important to her, and due to a history of heart disease in our family, she scheduled an appointment with her cardiologist that spring. It was recommended she stop hormone replacement therapy (HRT), as she was told this could increase the risk of complications. She had been on HRT for several years since the onset of menopause. She stopped the hormones and with this change, her chemical balance quickly shifted.

She began to suffer from anxiety, as well as depression. She sought out treatment and began therapy. She was diagnosed with clinical depression that fall and was placed on several medications. When one prescription was not effective, another was added, or the amount was altered. In her case, the medications seemed to worsen her symptoms. My dad and I had a difficult time determining if her depressive symptoms were a side effect of the medications or her core diagnosis.

She was placed back on HRT, with no relief. Within months, she became a shell of herself in contrast to the bright and full of life personality she once possessed. And, as much as I tried, I couldn't connect with her. I compare her depression to a thick window of glass parting us…we could see one another, but we couldn't reach each other. It was devastating to us both. She spoke of her tremendous pain, but everything she did to try to heal that pain…failed. *She fought with all she had, and she loved with all she had.*

This was her silent battle. She blamed herself for not feeling better, and she described herself as "damaged goods." She didn't want family and friends knowing because she felt ashamed and as if she was a burden to us. My dad and I respected her decision for privacy, but with this decision, she was isolated and forced to fight to appear "normal" on the outside. This took an incredible amount of energy which eventually waned. My mom was such a light, and as we watched her flame snuffed out by depression, it was heartbreaking. In just under a year, our family lost her to suicide. My world was forever changed on October 19, 2009.

I felt helpless during her struggles, and I was completely shattered when I had to face life without her. Because I had a graduate degree in clinical psychology and because I was her one and only child, she had asked for me to be her advocate. I felt I failed her. Over the next several months, I experienced deep grief and was engulfed in guilt, and began to lose hope for my own happiness to ever find its place in my life again. I missed her terribly, and it felt like my life couldn't possibly go on without her. I was going through the motions for my own family, but I wasn't really "present."

I prayed and prayed to God. I would have done anything to have her here with me, but I had complete faith that she was finally at rest from an arduous battle. I've had people make comments such as, "How could your mom do this to you, to your girls, to your family?" This is where our society has a long way to go in understanding depression and suicide. I have never placed blame on my mom. Her battle, along with so many others suffering from the grips of depression, can seem incomprehensible without understanding it. After all, what is this immense pain that leads anyone to take their own life? I wanted so desperately to teach people how to understand and to help. I didn't want anyone else to go through this type of loss or suffering. But, I was completely engulfed in guilt for not saving her, not taking further action, and failing her. My pain and grief masked any sign that my part in her care and in her death could be forgiven. I, too, was now suffering in silence.

Second, everything happening in your life is a reflection of what is happening inside of you.

God works in mysterious ways. My life takes a magnificent turn here, and it may seem like I'm veering way off track, but I promise I am not. The moment I'm about to share led me to find the forgiveness I so desperately needed for myself. I felt that God was watching over me and showing me the way. I also felt guided by my mom.

On the morning I lost my mom, I was feeling mentally exhausted from the months of worry. I knew something sounded off in her voice when we spoke earlier, but I didn't call her back immediately. My dad and I were in constant communication regarding her care, except for this day. We each had our own understanding of what the day held. I was also under the weather with a chest cold and headed to the doctor's office in search of an antibiotic. Although she sounded strange, my mom's last conversation with me involved telling me to get to the doctor, to rest, and to feel better. She was concerned about ME. Thinking she was safe with my dad, I figured I would call her after my appointment and decided instead to crank up Rick Springfield's music on my drive to just escape for a little while.

All my life, I have been a Rick Springfield fan. If I was ever in a place where I needed a little pick-me-up, one way of doing it would be to listen to his music. His songs were my hands down "go-to" playlist. His music has been with me my whole life. I danced and sang with him as an eight-old-girl. My mom took me to see him as my very first concert. I remember having to stand on the armrests of the seat to see the stage. She always encouraged my love for his music having known firsthand the incredible emotion and excitement experienced from seeing your favorite band or musician in concert. She saw her favorite band, The Beatles, four times. She truly understood the power of music and its influence. I've never forgotten the joy on her face seeing me jump up and down giddy, just 10 years old at the time, when Rick Springfield first took the stage. The love continued as I went on to college, blasting his music from my college dorm room, getting ready to go out on the town. And later in life, I happily hummed along to those favorite tunes while making dinner for my family.

Back to my drive, during this "escape" time, my mom ended her life. And I had to face the real music—that I chose caring for myself in that timeframe over calling her back. When I did, it was too late.

After that tragic day, hearing Rick Springfield's music brought nothing but pain, not the joy I once embraced. Songs that once brought so much happiness led to anger. I was ashamed of my own selfish decision. Listening would haunt me and carry me back to that morning and the tremendous guilt leading me to question "what if" over and over again. *Would she still be here?* I stopped listening and turned off his music. My soul was silent and in agony over decisions made along the way. I questioned everything we did or didn't do when it came to my mother's care, and I wondered if anything would have changed the outcome. But this decision and the phone call I didn't make hurt the most.

One year later, I was watching a morning news program, and Rick was being interviewed on the release of his new autobiography,

Late, Late at Night. He started out by sharing that he had experienced a lifelong battle with depression and had attempted suicide at a young age. I couldn't believe what I was hearing. He was "with me" in my most awful and tragic moment, and here HE was talking about depression? *If the Universe was going to give me a sign, this was one not to be ignored.*

One week later, he came to my area for a book signing, which happened to be one day after the one-year anniversary of my mom's death. I decided to go by myself. I wrote a short letter about the loss of my mom and expressed my gratitude to him for shedding light on such a difficult topic in the public eye. I didn't share with anyone that my main reason for going was to deliver this letter.

When I arrived at the signing, there was a camera crew present, and they were interviewing several fans who were sharing their personal stories. I didn't know what it was all about, but I felt a strong urge to say something. I can be pretty shy, but this was different. I wasn't speaking for me. I was speaking for my mom. I felt I was her voice, telling him "thank you" for speaking up about a topic most people don't want to touch due to stigma. He had shared the message to those who may be suffering in silence, to hold on, and know that time changes things. Listening to him on the news a week earlier helped me hear her again. I found my voice for her. I met Rick Springfield for the first time and shared my letter. I signed a release for the footage shot and walked away with a business card from the interviewers.

Once home, I panicked. Doubt and fear crept in, making me worry others would mistake my words as a way to get close to the rock star I loved for so many years. I placed the card aside and returned to my daily life.

Two more years went by, and I was still lost. My hope diminished, and I accepted the possibility that the pain would never end. It had been three years since my mom had died. I thought often about death. There were times when I thought I might find peace if I joined her. Frightened by this, I went into my daughter's room and prayed. I prayed and prayed for help and guidance. I needed to heal for myself and for my family.

"Hope is hearing the music of the future.
Faith is dancing to the music now." - Caroline Pitre-Oaks

Just days later, I received a phone call. It turned out those words I felt compelled to speak at the book signing were included in *An Affair of the Heart*, a documentary about Rick Springfield and his fans. The producer called to ask me if I would be willing to speak to the staff at *The Dr. Oz Show* regarding my story. I would travel to Times Square and appear on the show with Rick, who would be talking about his depression. She informed me they had been searching for me for two years—they could not locate my release form with my contact information.

I was bewildered and filled with emotion. *Would I find the right words to honor my mom's memory? How would the rest of my family feel about my speaking publicly? Would talking about her health and resulting death define how she lived? What can I say to help someone else? Why me? Why our story?* And of all things…after heading to New York City, I found myself with the musician who happened to be "with me" three years earlier in my darkest hour now talking about depression, suicide, but—above all—HELP AND HOPE. I now had hope too.

Unfortunately, changes were made, and time constraints kept me from being interviewed on stage during the show, but I was in the studio audience when they shared the footage from my visit to the book signing. It was surreal. I saw myself for the first time speaking on the screen, which was located behind where Dr. Oz and Rick sat. It was overwhelming, and yet I managed to stay fairly calm, trying to take it all in. I traveled home and reflected on why this was all happening.

I began to feel light in myself again for the first time. I could finally hear and feel my mom in my heart louder than the sadness and despair. She would want me to find joy and friendship. She would want me to sing and dance. She would want me to take my experience, her experience, and use it to make a difference. Most importantly, she would want me to forgive myself. Knowing my mother, I saw this as a wink from her delivering this message to me via Rick Springfield. It was the connection I needed and had been so desperately seeking.

It was an amazing gift, and it did not end in New York that day. One of the supporters for the documentary was a nonprofit organization called iFred (International Foundation for Research and Education on Depression). The organization provides education on prevention and treatment resources available for depression, with a focus on hope. And they do noble work to grow public awareness about depression. Their symbol for hope is the sunflower—to create a shift in society's negative perception of depression through positive imagery and branding.

> *Third, best-selling self-help author and motivational speaker, Dr. Wayne Dyer, shares in his work, that to manifest your reality, you create a new concept of yourself.*

I began advocating for iFred. Their mission spoke so loudly to me, I knew I had to be a part of it. Within the year, I crossed paths with iFred's founder at a Rick Springfield concert! In our conversation, she told me about a new program they were launching called "Schools for Hope," now known as "Hopeful Minds." The curriculum targets youth and gives them tools they may use to build and maintain their hope, which supports brain health and wellness. I expressed my gratitude for their work and my interest in supporting this program. Within a short time, I was hired to join the organization as the program manager for Hopeful Minds.

The Hopeful Minds Program allowed me to use my knowledge and experience to give back to others and promote the importance of mental health from an early age. My work with the organization opened up opportunities to engage with many gracious people and brilliant minds who continue to inspire me to do all I can to change how our world views depression.

I have been blessed to honor my mom's memory in a positive way. Perhaps in a world where she knew she would not be judged but supported, she would still be here. In the past few years, here are just a few of the iFred projects I have been proud to be part of as a project manager, consultant, colleague, and advocate. I attended and presented the Hopeful Minds curriculum and research at the Children's Mental Health Conference. I helped bridge a partnership with Catholic Charities LOSS Program (Loving Outreach to Survivors of Suicide) and iFred. The LOSS program offered me tremendous help and provided grief counseling at a time when I needed it most. During their Blossoms of Hope Brunch in 2015, iFred sponsored the blossom as the sunflower. The room was filled with hundreds of people who had lost their loved ones to suicide. Each table was adorned with sunflowers symbolizing hope for these families and friends in attendance. iFred has supported, with tremendous efforts, the World Health Organization and the United Nations, bringing global leaders together for mental health care reform.

Hopeful Minds has now touched the lives of children across our nation, as well as internationally, bringing hope to children in Ireland, Malaysia, Nepal, Suriname, and Uganda. This organization has been a true gift in my life.

Along with supporting iFred, I have been presented with additional pathways to educate and offer hope. My days have included supporting children in our local school district who struggle with academic and behavioral concerns. In the past two years, I joined two international organizations giving me the experience of virtually teaching children in China and supporting global education here in one of our high schools. I had the incredible opportunity to travel to my state capitol with the American Foundation for Suicide Prevention to advocate for suicide prevention initiatives. These initiatives led to four critical bills being passed into law in my state, created an Office of Suicide Prevention within the Department of Public Health, and mandated a 2020 update to the existing Suicide Prevention Strategic Plan. No matter what current project heads my way, I follow what is dear to my heart.

Years later, I have formed beautiful friendships that have grown from being a Rick Springfield fan. I attend concerts, and sing and dance again. I've been blessed with precious moments to personally thank Rick for all he has done to help others. He shared his story, which ultimately led me to share mine. He is more than a rock star to me. He has been an inspiration, and I will forever be grateful to him.

Manifesting my dream to offer support and hope to those suffering from depression blossomed from tragedy. I learned that in our deepest darkness, there is always light. It can be found in the most unexpected and surprising ways. With this lesson, I try my best to share this light by being present for others. I listen to those who feel comfortable to reach out to me, and who just need a friend when they are struggling.

It brings me healing.
It brings me compassion.
It brings me strength, joy, peace, and love.

I feel my mom's spirit with me in every moment. I know now that by giving hope, I will always find my own.

"All that I am, or hope to be, I owe to my angel mother."

- Abraham Lincoln

About Penny

Penny Tate is a devoted mental health advocate, educator, volunteer, and business professional. She began her career as an inpatient child and family therapist, providing individual and family counseling services. She has presented on topics such as dating violence, substance abuse, self-esteem, and suicide to parent education groups, schools, and communities. In 2009, she lost her mother to suicide, which fueled her passion and dedication to eradicating the stigma associated with depression and mental illness. She has been honored to aid in the mission and programs for the International Foundation for Research and Education on Depression since 2014—first and formerly in her role as program manager for Hopeful Minds, and today continues to be a consultant and advocate for this and similar causes. Penny is the director of operations for Silver Tree Communications and enjoys teaching in her local school district. She loves spending time relaxing with her family and friends. She lives in the suburbs of Chicago with her husband, two daughters, and her sweet dog, Lola.

For more information on the following programs, please visit:

Hopeful Minds Program
hopefulminds.org

International Foundation for Research and Education on
Depression (iFred)
ifred.org

American Foundation for Suicide Prevention
afsp.org

Catholic Charities Loving Outreach to Survivors of Suicide Loss
catholiccharities.net/GetHelp/OurServices/Counseling/Loss.aspx

Suicide Prevention Lifeline
1-800-273-TALK
suicidepreventionlifeline.org

Mom and me enjoying lunch together in Lake Geneva, Wisconsin, in 1997. Looking back, I treasure the special mother/daughter moments we shared. This is one of my favorite photos of us.

*This photo was taken at Anderson's Bookstore in Naperville, Illinois, in 2014. It holds a special place in my heart because it is where I first met Rick Springfield four years earlier, gave him the letter about my mom, and was interviewed for the documentary, **An Affair of the Heart**.*

Illinois State Capitol Day with the American Foundation for Suicide Prevention: In March of 2019, I joined my fellow advocates to meet with our state legislators. These efforts resulted in four suicide prevention bills being signed into law.

*Children's Mental Health Conference in 2015 in
Tampa, Florida, with Former Congressman and
Founder of The Kennedy Forum, Patrick J. Kennedy.*

*Loving Outreach to Survivors of Suicide (LOSS Program/
Catholic Charities) Blossoms of Hope Brunch, 2015. iFred
sponsored sunflowers as the blossom for the event. Attendees
were encouraged to plant seeds in their communities to raise
awareness and build support for depression treatment.*

Pictured with Kathryn Goetzke, Founder of iFred, and Reverend Father Charles T. Rubey, Founder and Director of the Catholic Charities LOSS Program. Photo credit: Kathryn Goetzke

*Milwaukee Film Festival with Producer, Melanie Lentz-Janney, and Director Sylvia Caminer of the Rick Springfield Documentary, **An Affair of the Heart**.*
Photo credit: Yellow Rick Road Productions

*This image captured a clip from **An Affair of the Heart** shown on the Dr. Oz Show.*

My dad and I formed Team Nancy and completed our first American Foundation for Suicide Prevention Chicagoland Out of the Darkness Walk. Our family and friends have been so incredibly supportive throughout the years, and for that, I am grateful.

With my loving husband, Dan, and my two beautiful daughters,
Abby (pictured on the left) and Adalia (pictured on the right).

BRENDA E. CORTEZ

"Those who are happiest are those who do for others."

- Booker T. Washington

A Purpose Becomes a Passion

I was 33 years old and married with two children when an opportunity was presented to me—an opportunity to save another mom's life. My heart strings are easily tugged at, so when this mom told me how she was searching for a kidney I knew I wanted to help. I immediately asked her what was needed to be a kidney donor, while in my mind I put myself in her shoes.

Blood type was the first requirement to be considered when donating a kidney, and I was the blood type match she needed. I offered to get tested, but it was at that moment a peaceful feeling came over me, and I knew I would be a match for this mom. Our daughters were in fifth grade together while our sons shared second grade. We were both moms who volunteered a lot at school, and we chatted occasionally, but other than that we didn't really know each other very well.

A couple months later, after several blood tests, it was confirmed I was indeed a match. My physical and mental health were both examined over the next two months, and then a surgery date was finally scheduled. "My purpose" was about to happen although I didn't know it at the time. I already thought I was living my purpose as a mother and a wife, but little did I know the direction my life would take. I was truly doing for someone what I hoped someone would do for me if I was in need.

The kidney donation surgery took place Wednesday, March 23, 2005, and it was a successful transplant. My kidney had a new home, and it functioned as it should. My family visited me at the hospital every day and offered their unconditional support. I was released four days later.

For the next six years, I spoke about organ donation and my decision to become a living kidney donor. For many years, I didn't even know anyone else who had donated an organ to save another life. I don't really know why I felt different and isolated, but looking back I think I was bursting at the seams wanting to share my story to help others. The right opportunity just hadn't presented itself yet.

It turned out my daughter gave me the inspiration I had unknowingly been looking for. Six years after I donated my kidney, my daughter, Kailey, wrote an essay about my kidney donation for acceptance into college. She wrote how scary it was to see her mom in the hospital...she was 11 years old at the time. She said I had inspired her to want to be a better person, to help others, and to pursue a career in the medical field. When I read the essay, I immediately knew what I needed to do. I would write about my kidney donation to help other kids understand what surgery and kidney donation is all about. I wanted transplant centers to use the book as a helpful tool, and give it to living donor families with younger kids. It took a few years for my children's book, *My Mom is Having Surgery—A Kidney Story* to get published, but it was exciting, and I had a lot of support from family and friends. The transplant center where my surgery was performed purchased several books to give to future living donor families.

I decided partial proceeds from my new book would benefit Donate Life America, an organization supporting organ donation awareness. It was the perfect group for me to align with. Donate Life is a slogan and logo used and recognized in the transplant community. There are many groups and foundations dedicated to raising awareness for organ donation but Donate Life America is all-encompassing including all organs and tissue.

Did you know one person can save up to eight lives through organ donation, restore sight for two people with cornea donation, and heal the lives of 75 people with tissue donation?

Even with advances in medicine, the need for organ donors still greatly exceeds the actual number of donors. A kidney is by far the most needed organ, so thankfully a kidney can come from either a living or deceased donor, but realistically we need more donors. Hopefully my story will inspire others to consider donation.

Many suggested I should reach out to children's hospitals about using my first book, but I really didn't feel it was the right choice for kids in the hospital. I decided I should write something for a child who is going through a transplant, but I wanted a cute character a child could relate to. Around that time, the slogan YOLO (You Only Live Once) was all the rage, and while it's a good saying it wasn't a call to action. I wanted a saying that would inspire people to be kind and help others. *Help Others With Love*™ popped into my head. It was the perfect slogan! I kept thinking about that phrase and what I could do with it, when one day it just clearly came to me. It spells HOWL™ and rhymes with owl. I love owls! My character should be Howl the Owl™! I researched a stuffed animal version of an owl and decided what he would look like. And what is better than an adorable plush owl? Who wouldn't want a snuggle buddy to cuddle with while reading a book? Eventually, I found the perfect plush owl but wondered how would people know his name and the special meaning? The solution was perfect. Plush Howl the Owl™ would wear a shirt bearing his name HOWL™ and the words Help Others With Love™!

Now that I had my adorable character for kids to love and relate to, it was time to write a book to help children understand organ donation. I knew I would need more than just one book to accomplish my goal since there are so many facets around organ donation and transplantation, and it can be a "heavy" topic for children to comprehend. *Howl the Owl*™, *the Organ Donation Series* seemed appropriate, and the first book would help those kids who were in the hospital waiting for a transplant or already had one. Since I had already written a book about kidney transplant I wanted to choose a different organ. I thought back to a story a friend shared about her nephew and his heart transplant.

Around this time, some stories were circulating on social media about donor families meeting the heart recipient their loved one donated to, and they were able to listen to the heart beating inside that recipient. How amazing! I chose a heart transplant for Howl" and wanted to portray this profound, life-saving miracle for children and their families by incorporating a lifelike feeling of what really happens when a child is sick and waiting for a heart. I also wanted to show the excitement yet nervousness of receiving that new heart and getting back to a normal life, but still needing to take medication for life.

As I mentioned earlier, the ending would incorporate that amazing moment the donor family meets the person their loved one saved, and listening to the heart beating inside the recipient. I wrote the first draft of *Howl Gets a Heart* in an hour while I sat in a Wendy's restaurant eating a salad for lunch. The story just flowed onto paper, and it felt right. Even though I hadn't personally met a child who needed or had received a heart, I really felt the pain and urgency of needing that miracle and then the excitement of receiving it. My heart was filled with hope that this book would serve its purpose and *Help Others With Love™*. I wanted it to bring comfort and healing to those in need and also raise great awareness for organ donation. The book came to life with amazing illustrations of an adorable owl on his journey to receive a new heart that would save his life!

My wish for my book to help a child who had been through a transplant came true when unbeknownst to me, my friend Ellen came to my book signing and bought the *Howl Gets a Heart* book along with the plush Howl™ and sent it to a family from her church who had moved to North Carolina. Their little girl, Autumn, was five years old and had a heart transplant when she was a baby. That family had just returned from the hospital, a four-hour trip for them, for a routine checkup. I was able to see how my book had truly helped them when my friend Ellen was tagged in this post: "A member at our old church sent us a children's book about organ donation along with tattoos and a stuffed animal! We love it! I read the book to the kids and all of them continued to say, oh, that sounds like us...like what our family went through...Oh, this is JUST like Autumn." My heart was full of joy as I read how the book and Howl™ did exactly what he was meant to do…Help Others With Love™!

While the heart book was in the illustration process, my next story in the series unraveled. I knew I wanted to write something to help children understand when a loved one who is an organ donor passes away. This would be a book with a very specific purpose to help children and their families in a time of grief and to hopefully bring comfort, but I just didn't have the storyline quite figured out yet.

Let me circle back a couple months to June, 2016; I attended my first ever Transplant Games of America in Cleveland, Ohio as a Team Wisconsin supporter. I met many wonderful people at this spectacular gathering of transplant recipients, living donors, and donor families who met to compete in fun games, show their resilience and appreciation for a second chance at life, and honor those who gave that amazing gift.

One family, however, stood out to me—Jessica and her husband, Chris, and their little girl, Bella. They had recently moved to Wisconsin after the death of Jessica's mom who was a donor. They were at the games in honor of her memory. We had a connection because they lived near our weekend cabin, and I really adored little Bella. Two months after the games, an email went out to Team Wisconsin that Chris had unexpectedly passed away, and he was a donor. My heart sank, as I felt so much empathy for Bella and Jessica. She had just lost her mom six months ago and now her husband. Poor adorable Bella was only a five-year-old and now without her dad and grandma.

What could I do to help them? This could be the storyline I wanted to write about to help children when they lose a loved one. I didn't know any details of what happened to Chris other than he passed away at work. I didn't want to reach out to Jessica because her pain was too fresh, and it wasn't appropriate to talk about a book at this time, so I went with what was in my head and wrote the first draft of *Howl Helps Bella*. I needed to address the sadness of losing a loved one, but redirect that sadness toward the joy of their loved one saving lives like a superhero while living on in others. I wanted to honor Chris, and all the superheroes and their families who truly *Help Others With Love*™ with the greatest gift of all.

After a few months, I finally reached out to Jessica to let her know I had written this story but I could easily change it if she wasn't comfortable. I was grateful when she shared how honored she was to have a book like this written in Chris' memory, and what a wonderful gift it would be for Bella and other kids. I met with Jessica and Bella a couple months later to show her the story and make any adjustments according to what really happened.

The day we met happened to be the one-year anniversary of her mom's passing, so I knew it was both difficult and healing for her. We decided we would incorporate her mom, Bella's grandma, in the story too. As the book moved forward, I consulted with Jessica on the edits and illustrations and then finally the finished product. *Howl Helps Bella* was published in November of 2017, and has brought healing comfort for Jessica, Bella, and many more families alike who are donor families. I was honored when I was invited to have a booth and sell my books at the Transplant Games in August of 2018 in Salt Lake City. Jessica and Bella were in the booth with me, and Bella was so proud to have a book about herself and Daddy! Bella even signed the books people bought like a true star. I am happy to say this book is serving its purpose and being used by Organ Procurement Organizations (OPO's) in their aftercare program. The positive feedback from people at the Transplant Games was amazing. Many commented they wished these books would have existed years ago. My heart was full of joy knowing my passion for helping others and writing about organ donation is serving its purpose. I realized my kidney donation was not just meant to save one life, but rather lead me to this greater purpose of spreading awareness about organ donation which means more lives saved. My purpose as a kidney donor has led to a passion for writing, helping others, and inspiring others to do the same. I'm also addressing difficult topics for children and families in a way they can relate to and understand.

My fourth book, titled, *Howl Helps Others* focuses on kindness and helping others, while touching on transplants, autism, and bullying. This book is meant to reach younger children and is great for preschool to third grade. The third book in the organ donation series (my fifth book) was released a while ago and is titled, *Howl Learns about Dialysis*. This book circles back to kidney donation but a bit differently. It is meant to teach children about dialysis, and what it means to search and wait for a life-saving kidney. It addresses real-life scenarios using social media and vehicle advertising to find a donor match.

As I sit and write this chapter I am proud to say my sixth book has just been released. This book is titled *Howl Goes to the Races*, and as the title suggests, it's about racing but still connects to organ donation. Howl was invited to the races for Organ Donation Awareness Day by race car driver, Joey Gase. Joey is a big supporter of organ donation since his mom was a donor and saved other lives. Howl is thrilled to be at the race track and learn the ins and outs of racing. I am honored to partner with this NASCAR® driver and continue to raise awareness for organ donation while getting kids excited about racing!

I am truly blessed to have found my purpose in life which has led me to this wonderful career as a children's book writer and strong advocate for organ donation. I have also had the opportunity to meet wonderful people including Marla McKenna, who I have consulted with on many of my books for editing (the mastermind behind this book you are reading), and Mike Nicloy, the publisher of *Manifesting Your Dreams*, (and all of my Howl™ books). Mike happens to be a kidney recipient from a living donor, and I believe it is by no coincidence our paths have crossed. I have met so many amazingly brave children and their families who have been through so much, and I've been able to educate others with school presentations and community-based events. I am also blessed to be a living kidney donor mentor at the hospital where I donated.

In case you are wondering, my kidney recipient is doing great and was recently told at a clinic appointment that "our" kidney is functioning as if it was her own native kidney. Wonderful news! Life had a calling for me, and I am grateful I listened and followed the path that was set before me. While being an author and saving someone's life had not initially been a dream of mine, I can truly say that being able to do this is a dream come true. Like you, I will continue to dream and excel in the things I am passionate about. Maybe one day my dream and vision for Howl will become a reality. That dream is for *Howl the Owl*™ to be a household name like Winnie the Pooh, and for him and his message—*Help Others With Love*™ to be known and recognized for generations to come.

About Brenda

Brenda is a living kidney donor and children's book author, who has a passion for helping others. She was inspired to write her first book, *My Mom is Having Surgery*, after her daughter entered her college entrance essay about Brenda's donation and the inspiration she felt from it. Brenda is now a strong advocate for living donation awareness. Because of this advocacy and her passion for helping others, Brenda came up with the slogan, HOWL: Help Others With Love™. Learn more about *Howl the Owl*™ and Brenda's organ-donation-focused children's books at howltheowl.com. If you are inspired to register as an organ donor, please visit registerme.org

Mascot Howl the Owl™.

*Plush Howls with an illustration from **Howl Helps Bella.***

With Howl the Owl™ and my friend Jonna.

With NASCAR® driver Joey Gase at our book signing.

KYLIE MCGOWAN

"Keep smiling, because life is a beautiful thing and there's so much to smile about."

- **Marilyn Monroe**

Spreading Smiles

When I was younger, I was always surrounded by happiness. It was as if problems didn't exist. Sadness wasn't real, or at least I hadn't experienced that emotion yet. The worst thing that could have possibly happened would be a crayon snapping in half while coloring a picture. Although, that was an easy fix—just grab another crayon out of the box. I didn't realize it at the time, but not every problem was solved as easily as a broken crayon.

As I grew older, I realized not everything in life was as happy as I always thought it was. I experienced the most noticeable change during my freshman year in high school. Lessons and units became more challenging to understand. Tests became more important. Sometimes, teachers seemed to care less about making sure everyone received passing grades and more about giving us busy work just to pass the time. We were constantly told that if our grades suffered, so would our future...everything happened so fast. We were being prepped to start thinking about college and our life outside of school, which was something most of us had never thought about before. We were almost adults, and I don't think many people handled that change well. I watched as my childhood friends grew into relentless and rebellious teens. The parties, the drinking, the smoking—it was all too much. Some days I saw people at school walking down the halls clutching their aching, hungover heads, mumbling about how they didn't want to get up that morning. Other days students would pass me during lunch, wearing dark sunglasses hiding their red, bloodshot eyes and heavy, fruity perfume, masking any alluding scents. I never understood why someone my age would ever want to do that, to put themselves through that. I always assumed it was just because they *could*. They had the opportunity to get high in the middle of the day or they found a bottle of booze to drink, so they did it because they thought it would impress their friends. That was my understanding, but it wasn't entirely correct. Though that reasoning applied to some people; it didn't apply to everyone. It broke my heart to find out how unhappy some people were. So unhappy, in fact, they allowed themselves to engage in temporary distractions, like an escape, and drinking and/or smoking was a convenient way to do that. Some of my friends I'd known since grade school turned into people I could no longer associate with due to their bad choices.

When people experience a heartbreak, it's usually by a romantic partner. These heartbreaks I experienced weren't like that; I separated from people I knew my entire life, and sometimes, it would tear me apart inside. I mean, I know that I'm young and relatively new to the world, and there are probably far worse things I will experience in my future, but going through this sadness was like torture.

I hated it. I hated not being able to understand what they were going through. I hated not being able to help them. I hated not being able to make them feel better. I needed to do something about it.

And then it hit me. A feeling rushed through me, not like small, lazy waves, but more like enormous tidal waves. Making people happy quickly became my ultimate dream. Forget traveling the world or buying that really expensive purse. I didn't want that anymore. If happiness is what people needed, I was going to help them feel that joy any way I could.

Brainstorming ways to get something started was one of the more difficult parts of this seemingly nonstop process to make people feel better. I needed something big enough to grab people's attention, but not so big that it would scare people away. I couldn't just blatantly say, "Okay, if you have problems then come find me!" Obviously, that wouldn't help anyone. I somehow needed to convey the message that I would help with whatever issue they were having at the time, without making them feel pressured or nervous. It didn't matter what the problem was—anxiety, arachnophobia, family issues, pestering teachers, or even relationship problems. I didn't care, and I wanted them to tell me—no matter what. I just needed something to get things started. Thinking about this brought up a ton of memories, some harder to deal with than others. My mind raced with my own issues, and how I tried to deal with them. I wanted to compare my problems to questions about what other people were feeling and what made others happy, just to see how I could personally relate to it. Vivid memories of a project I participated in when I was a bit younger started to give me some ideas.

During my seventh grade year, one of my friends sparked an idea that would eventually change the way I thought about other people's feelings. It would give me the ability to really read and understand people and get to know the wide range of emotions that exists beyond what I had personally experienced.

It was a simple idea to *spread smiles*—small and thoughtful; we planned to type hundreds of compliments and stick them on every student's locker for them to find the next day. My insides began to tingle with excitement and anticipation, but that wasn't the best part. Our name was going to be "Anonymous Angels," and we would be a secret. Nobody would know who hung the compliments, which was the way we wanted to keep it. We didn't need any recognition, and we didn't want it. The point of this project was to show that anyone could make someone smile and gain nothing for it. We thought, *What's the point of being selfless only to be congratulated for doing so afterwards?* The point was to make others happy, not to make ourselves appear as anything more than what we already were.

With that in mind, we discussed our potential plans. After a little while of talking, I didn't hesitate to become part of a two-man team. It would be a lot of work, but we believed it would be worth it. I wanted to start right away, and luckily my friend did too. We began preparing the very next week. We started by going around the school and discreetly began asking people how they were feeling. Not in a weird way, of course, but as subtle as a seventh grader could. We just wanted to get an idea of what people needed to hear to make their day better, and most of them sounded like they needed a confidence boost, or just something to make them laugh. After gathering all of our information, we began to come up with little "catch phrase" or compliments to be typed and printed out.

I went over to her house almost every day, and together we worked for hours, the constant writing and typing slowly killing our fingers. We didn't care much though—we were having too much fun. We came up with some ridiculous compliments, like "You're the gravy to my mashed potatoes," and some more genuine ones like "Don't you know how beautiful you are?" This nonstop compliment flurry continued through the next week over countless slices of pizza, a liter of orange-flavored soda, and at least two pans of brownies. Day after day, hours passed like seconds as we worked on these simple gestures. Typing, cutting, gluing, and stamping…I never thought we'd reach the end of the rainbow paper pile. When we were finally done, we admired our work. We ended up typing over 400 individual compliments, which we then cut into small rectangles, glued them onto different colored paper, and stamped them with our logo, a pair of beautifully detailed angel wings. The funny thing was as much work as we did, we enjoyed it all! You would think after spending that much time together an argument was inevitable, but one never occurred—no fighting or arguing, not even a disagreement. I believe that besides loving to spend time together, we always kept our goal in mind.

I remember walking into school on that Thursday and thinking, "Alright. How the heck are we going to pull this off?" The pit of fear resonated in my stomach while I waited, but fear wasn't the only emotion going on inside of me; I was the most excited I had ever been. The plan was to attend our usual classes during the day and wait after school, until everyone was gone, and then hang up our compliments without anyone being there to see it. Trying to get through the day with our secret was extremely difficult, especially when my friend and I would share a knowing smile during class or when we passed each other in the hallway. The end of the day couldn't come soon enough.

When it was finally time, we got straight to work. We had to cover two floors and over 400 lockers in our school, not including the ones we left on teacher's doors. Every hall we went down in the building was soon bursting with vivid and colorful compliments, including ones we put on our own lockers (to keep our identities safe, of course). The angel wings added a nice touch to the compliment cards, wrapping everything together. About one or two hours later, we finished hanging up the cards. Taking a moment to look at our hard work, we walked the hallways to check over everything. By the time we arrived back at our finishing point, I was smiling so much that my cheeks hurt. We were giggly, bubbly, and full of endless amounts of excitement. I couldn't wait to get home and go to sleep, knowing I'd wake up the next morning to see the colorful atmosphere in school.

My friend and I texted that entire night and the following morning, wondering what it would be like to walk into the building. I arrived at school and met my friend inside. As soon as we walked in, the whole school was buzzing. When we made our way to our homerooms, every single person had a smile on their face. Nobody had their head down with headphones blocking out the noise of the busy hallway. Nobody looked tired or like they wanted to go home. Nobody was in a bad mood. Everyone appeared to be so curious about the mysterious notes that were left on their lockers. It was truly amazing!

Not only were students comparing their compliments, they were complimenting other people with the compliments they received. A few people even stuck their card onto their shirts and wore them throughout the day, proudly puffing out their chests whenever anyone asked to see it. It was unbelievable. The reactions were nothing like we ever thought they would be. It was funny to hear people guess who they thought set all of this up or to hear the conspiracies of how everything was accomplished in seemingly no time. A few of my friends at the time would come up to me and asked if I knew who did it, and I would always reply, "I don't know. I think it was by a group called Anonymous Angels or something," casually shrugging the question off while biting my tongue to keep from laughing out loud.

My friend and I met our ultimate goal, making people smile

without being recognized. It couldn't have gone better. Just seeing the smiles made it all worth the hours of hard, time-consuming work. To this day, it is still one of my biggest and most gratifying accomplishments.

Together we managed to keep our project going strong for the next two years of middle school, with the help of parents and our principal. We began experimenting with our cards by adding candy kisses or candy canes in cute bags around the holidays. Everyone continued to enjoy them, and more than that, people started to understand and spread our message. At one point, we were called into the main office and met with a journalist from our city's newspaper. She wanted to dedicate a few pages on what we accomplished in our school. We agreed to it under one condition; our names would not be presented in the article. We would remain anonymous and go by "Angel One" and "Angel Two." The interview went smoothly, and by the next week the article was floating around our city, even gaining a little bit of attention. The whole experience was beautiful, and truthfully, I sometimes wish I could go back to those days just to relive the feelings of compassion, love, and excitement. People rarely feel that sort of feeling now, or at least, I don't see it.

I should really thank my friend for bringing "Anonymous Angels" to my attention at the beginning of it all. If she had never approached me with the idea, I'm not sure if I ever would've even thought about other people's smiles in the same way I do now. I now know that smiling can be hard when you're not happy on the inside, which is why portraying happiness on the outside can be almost impossible. Because of our project, I constantly think about how people are feeling. This has saved me from saying the wrong thing more times than I can count. If anything, it has taught me—you never know how someone is feeling or why they're acting the way they are, so you need to be mindful of what you say. You don't know what's going on in their life, so don't knock them down any further than they already might be. Instead, give them something to smile about. And hey, it'll make you feel good too.

***

Reminiscing about our old project, reminded me of how much I loved the feeling that would come after I've successfully made someone's day better. This was only pushing me to do something bigger and more powerful. The more people I could get to smile, the better. I just needed to consider how hard it was going to be to actually encourage people to talk about what they were feeling, especially at my age. It's one of the most difficult things, to come out and say what's on your mind openly and with little to no hesitation, and I couldn't think of a way to convince people I could help them. I thought the only way to get an answer was to try and figure out how I would want someone to help me with my biggest problem—self-confidence. If I could figure out how to help myself, helping others would be a little easier. With that in mind, I began experimenting. I started researching different ways to share feelings and get them out into the open. There were many ways that were recommended, but the two options that were most successful (according to everything I looked at) included one-on-one conversations and expressing your feelings through some sort of art. Since I was trying to see what would make me feel better, I tried art first. I love to paint, and I do it fairly often. *How could this be any different?*

Art has always come easy to me, so drawing or painting every day was supposed to be natural. I never have to think about what I'm creating, it usually just comes out. As I began to draw with a somewhat difficult purpose, the more distant I felt towards finding a solution to my problem. When I first started painting, it relaxed and calmed me, but after a while I couldn't think straight. All that ran through my mind were questions of whether or not painting was fixing anything. I couldn't express my emotions and feelings in my art without feeling like I had to hide what I painted. When I channeled my feelings into a picture, I never painted "happy scenes." They all turned out to be dark and gloomy, so unlike my personality that it confused me. I had accidentally turned my favorite pastime into a nightmare, and I stopped almost immediately. I didn't want to accidentally ruin the concept of art for me. In that moment, I realized that I was just distracting myself. Painting how I felt only worsened my confidence because all I wanted to do was throw away my work. I didn't want anyone to see what I created or what was going through my mind when I painted it. Maybe it was fear of judgement, or maybe anxiety about what people might ask me if they saw what I made, but something pushed me to throw away every single piece I painted. And so I did. I never felt that conflicting emotion before. It was scary. My problem couldn't be solved by painting a picture, and that was scary too. I decided it was best to switch directions to solve my issue.

I wanted to talk out my problems, but who could I talk to? Parents are the first thought, but like most stereotypical teenagers, I felt like I couldn't tell them what was going on. I'm sure that was never the case, and they would listen and give genuine, helpful advice, but I could never bring myself to say anything. I looked to confide in others, like school counselors and teachers I really liked, but that didn't seem like something I wanted to do either. I finally understood that nothing compared to telling a friend. I felt supported in a way I really never felt before. After talking to two different friends and getting their opinions on things, I went forward with what they said and tried to change myself for the better. Over time, I continued to talk to them while they supported me. I took baby steps, and they pushed me just enough. When we would go to the mall, my friend would grab a bunch of clothes, make me try them all on and take my picture afterwards. Sometimes they would make me go talk to boys I liked, even when I practically spazzed out right before even opening my mouth. Little by little, I gained my confidence back. It didn't come all at once. It took a lot of time and tons of support, and eventually I started to feel better about myself.

Then, I got it. I cracked the code. I began to finally understand what people needed. It was two important elements—someone who would *listen* and *time*. They needed to slow down and talk to someone. If they had a problem, all they needed was to let it out. They could cry, scream, or simply just be old-fashioned and talk if that's what they needed. And I wanted to be there for them. Once I realized this, I knew exactly what to do. I started researching peer counseling programs that could be implemented into our school. It was the best idea and action plan since "Anonymous Angels." My mind was already reeling with ideas and concepts of what I could do to help. After the idea came to me, my principal, a few teachers, and a couple friends encouraged me to test my idea in our school. With little hesitation and with extreme confidence, I did!

***

I guess my message to all of you is that any dream is a worthy dream. I've been told that my dream couldn't possibly be to make people smile, that it wasn't a "real dream." But who defines your dreams? I feel like whenever someone talks about achieving their dream, it always involves making or spending money, or gaining something superficial. I've learned that it never has to be something like that. You don't *have* to dream to be an astronaut or to buy an island. If one of those happens to be your dream, then great! That's perfectly fine to want to achieve that sort of thing. It's also okay to dream for something as small as knitting a fluffy blanket or paying for someone else's coffee on Monday mornings as you head to work. From personal experience, and in my opinion, the smaller dreams are not only more achievable, but they mean more. Sure, it's nice to ride on a private jet or buy a really expensive designer dress, but it feels so much better when someone laughs for the first time in weeks because I said something funny. Or when my mom smiles because I made her french toast in the morning. I can't really explain it, but every time I make someone feel good I get this warm, tingly feeling in the bottom of my stomach, and I lose all of the air in my lungs, but in a good way. I've never felt like that when I purchased a new makeup palette or bought a new shirt. It's an irreplaceable sensation, which just makes it all the more special.

I believe the strongest dreams are the little ones—the ones that anyone can achieve with however limited their resources may be, the ones that are so special they stick with you forever. You can dream and achieve anything, so don't let anyone tell you otherwise. Any dream is worth being called a dream. Mine just happens to be spreading smiles.

About Kylie

As a seventeen year old, Kylie McGowan knows what it's like to be a teenager in the 21ˢᵗ century. Communication has become a lost art, and nobody can talk about their feelings anymore—not unless they're using a phone anyway. Although she keeps herself busy with school, photography, painting, and other artsy activities, Kylie strives to remain true to her biggest goal—to make people happy. With the Internet slowly breaking people's honesty, Kylie realized the importance of a smile, and how hard it can be to find one. She began trying to make people happy in small ways, whether it be a written compliment on an index card or sitting down and listening to a friend. She believes making people happy is a simple goal and one that anyone can achieve. It's small and may seem a bit ridiculous to some, but it's worthy enough to be called a dream.

VIDAL CISNEROS JR.

If a fellow isn't thankful for what he's got, he isn't likely to be thankful for what he's going to get.

\- Frank A. Clark

How Gratitude Got Me Through

"My life will not end like this. My family needs me, and I have to follow my dreams and start now." That's the promise I made myself one evening years ago. I was sitting in my work truck on a road construction site that was the culmination of my dead-end career. My dreams had faded to nothing, my marriage was stuck in idle, and my daughters only saw the remnants of the father they'd once known, when they saw me at all, which was seldom.

Riding on the power of that decision, I left my financially comfortable, soul-destroying construction career behind. I jumped into a success mentorship program, quickly discovering the power of personal development and opening myself to the idea that my life was in my hands. I believed I had embarked on a journey that was waiting just for me. Then the unexpected happened.

I was quickly building momentum and learning the principles of building a successful business when my wife of seven years began to change. She had gone so far into her new reality that it took all the courage she had to confess it all. "I'm seeing someone," she finally admitted.

All of the momentum I'd been building crumbled under the

devastating blow as she hesitantly said, "There's more." A long pause, and then, "I'm pregnant."

At that moment I felt 100 percent shattered. I grasped for a straw of hope. "It's mine, right?"

One word blew that straw away. "No."

I still wanted her as my wife. I held on to that thought and tried desperately to make it work and win her back, but it was hopeless. As much as I prayed for a miracle, I had to accept she wasn't in the relationship with me anymore. It was time to let her go and move out.

Almost overnight, I went from new success to new distress. That year I spiraled into a deep depression and found myself sitting at bars and drinking more than I ever had. The rage I was trying to suppress came out one night in a drunken bender. In a high-speed chase one hopes to see only in a movie, I eluded a deputy sheriff twice, finally losing the officer but causing an accident and totaling my Jeep. While thankfully no one was severely injured in the accident, I was a mess. Unsurprisingly, I was placed under arrest.

I'd worked with deputy sheriffs on construction sites, and I had always respected the law. This behavior was out of character for me. I had to ask myself who I had become.

Sitting in that cell for four days straight not only sobered me up but also woke me up to the reckless way I was living my life. I hit rock bottom sitting in that cell, locked up with people who were on trial for awful crimes.

In those four days of incarceration I went through a wide range of emotions, but what I found was clarity in my mission and the passion that would pick me up from the deep depression I was in. I prayed. I fasted. I found inspiration in others' stories. Most of all, the light was beaming brightly out from me again. I realized that I needed to forgive if I was going to move forward with my life.

Praying for everyone, especially for those who had created my nightmare, softened my heart and made things turn around faster than I'd imagined. Words, I learned, have power, and the ability of grateful prayer to change your life should never be underestimated.

I had fallen prey to alcoholism and depression. But now I held fast to my new vision. I would be grateful and wish everyone the best, including my enemies. I prayed for blessings for my ex-wife, her lover, and their unborn child.

Unfortunately, the day following the arrest, my name was plastered all over the news as a suspect in a high-speed chase. I was sentenced to six months for "Driving While Intoxicated and Reckless Driving."

I saw the emotional effect my sentencing and conviction had on my family, and it was devastating to face six months behind bars away from my daughters when they most needed me. Although I thought this was the last thing I needed, looking back I realize it was, in fact, the best thing.

Those six months helped clear my mind from the nightmare and gave me the courage to accept professional therapy and get refocused. Most of all, it awakened my heart to a new relationship.

Before serving time, I had become friendly with a woman at work. Unbeknownst to me, she was also going through betrayal and divorce. The similarity in our situations was eerie, and it was obvious to us that our becoming friends was no coincidence. I began to write her daily, and the closer we became the more she was my ray of light in the storm I was living through.

She brightened my days with her letters and visits. She gave me hope, and it inspired me to keep going.

In the outside world, the life I once knew was being pummeled to dust. But in my incarcerated world I found contentment in writing, drawing, singing in the choir, and inspiring others to chase dreams.

I learned something powerful—being incarcerated doesn't mean being unhappy. I learned that though life takes us through dark places that we can choose to believe in something bigger and have faith that our journey will take us to better circumstances when we serve a greater purpose that involves others.

When my six-month sentence was over, traveling on that bus back to my reality was surreal. I was returning, but with a new level of awareness for life. Learning from others' stories gave me insight into how powerful the principles I learned from my mentors really were.

I've learned that we all have the same 24 hours each day to sow seeds of abundance. And we can't receive greater gifts if we don't let go of the past ones.

It became obvious that I had been blind for many years to the power of visionary gratitude. I had taken so many things for granted for so long, including achieving my dreams. But by intentionally envisioning and being grateful in the now, it gives way to abundance in the future.

When I'm asked to speak to audiences about my story and how I persevered in spite of circumstances, I talk about the power of words, forgiveness, and blessing others through prayer, and why holding that vision of gratitude for what you have so that greater possibilities become real.

I've also been fortunate to see life from a new perspective through the program of Alcoholics Anonymous. Learning how to live a 100 percent clean and sober lifestyle one day at a time has brought greater joy and impactful fulfillment, and I'm more than grateful for all I've learned from A.A.

Through the hardest moments, I focused on my faith and this mantra, *"Instead of waiting for the light at the end of the tunnel, be the light that sparks everyone on fire."*

About Vidal

Vidal Cisneros Jr. has been featured in *Chicken Soup for the Soul: Think Possible* and also has been featured in *The Huffington Post, Entrepreneur* Magazine, *The Good Men Project,* NBC's *The Morning Blend,* and book talks at Barnes & Noble Booksellers locations.

Vidal hosts a top-ranked iTunes podcast which features TEDx speakers, best-selling authors, world-renowned consultants, and inspiring entrepreneurs who share their story of tragedy to triumph. For more information, email vidalcisnerosjr@gmail.com and go to vidalcisnerosjr.com

Vidal Cisneros Jr. and family.

Vidal surrounded by the women who have his heart.

MARY MARKHAM

"To the world you may be one person but to one person you may be the world."

- Dr. Seuss

The World is Our Classroom

This was no ordinary Tuesday, nor was it a typical golf game. It was a teacher and a lesson that would change my life forever.

I was fortunate enough to belong to a stay-at-home mom's co-op group and exchanged tickets for my adult time away, without having to pay for a babysitter. We each earned tickets by babysitting each other's children, and I accumulated enough tickets each week to join a golf league. Our Tuesday morning women's golf league consisted mostly of teachers on summer break, but for me it was my adult getaway.

Luck was in my favor; my golf game was going well and, unbeknownst to me, the day was just about to get better. As I walked to the next tee box, I overheard one of the women saying, "I know, I need to get out more often, but my schedule is too busy."

As she got closer, my friend introduced me to this busy stranger. As the busy stranger and I continued our walk to the tee box, our conversation unfolded like two friends who hadn't seen each other in years, catching up on life. There was a definite connection and divine reason why we met. Since most of the women on the league were school teachers, she naturally thought I was as well. So, she asked the inevitable question, "What do you teach?"

"I'm not a teacher; I'm just a stay-at-home mom," I answered.

I should have said, *I'm not JUST a stay-at-home mom, I AM a teacher...to my own children! I read to them, plan daily activities, and I'm constantly teaching them something new.* But that is not what came out of my mouth; *I'm just a stay-at-home mom were the words I spoke.*

The busy stranger not only taught at an elementary school, but she also taught fifth grade religion classes on Sunday mornings at my church. With her demanding schedule, she thought team teaching the class might allow her some freedom by alternating every other session, once a month, since the students met every other week. She looked at me and said, "I think you'd be great at it! What do you think?"

How did she know I would be great at it? We never met before, and she knew nothing about me; although, we did connect like we'd known each other our entire lives.

All of a sudden, I felt this strong, yet calming sense, and excitingly said, "Yes! Absolutely...I would love to!"

I had a little over a month to prepare for my first day. I was very excited to do so. It felt right and comfortable. Although I thought I was calm, cool, and collected during my preparation, I became a little nervous walking into that classroom the first day. I had always wanted to be a teacher, and I couldn't believe my dream was coming true. The classroom was very diverse, and I believed I learned just as much from the students as they learned from me.

Creating a "Headline News Story" was my favorite lesson; "If you could make a difference in the world, what would you do and what would it look like?" And of course, as the teacher, I had to create a sample story to show the class. My headline read: *No One Is Homeless This Thanksgiving.* I envisioned all the homeless people sitting together in a large banquet hall, tables set with beautiful white linen tablecloths, nice silverware, and each person would have a uniquely patterned plate, representing our differences—one family under God. And, of course we would eat family style. That was never a real headline story, but everyone was impacted by the message. We are all unique in our own way and have our own special stories to share. That lesson created discussion around our differences, and how we should leave our judgements at the door. We just need to be the people God created each and everyone one of us to be.

That year went fast and by team teaching, the busy stranger was able to free up her time. The following year, she wanted her full-time teaching position back. It was not only a dream come true for me, but an opportunity to experience and share my gift from God. That busy stranger changed my life.

Life's changes are inevitable, and years later, my life changed faster than I was prepared for. I knew I needed to head to the one place for guidance, answers, a message, or even a sign; that one place was my church. Whenever feeling scattered or scared, praying and attending church services always centered me. I felt at peace about whatever I was going through in life. This particular Sunday, the church was packed...standing room only. At the end of the aisle I heard, "Everyone please move closer so we can have more people seated!" Under normal circumstances, we may have felt squeezed in like sardines, but this was different. It was almost as if the closer we were to each other, the more comforting it became. We were all connected as one family in this big Universe. Although we were all believers, we needed to hear messages from the Teacher; His parable lessons helped us understand what we were going through. While waiting for the service to begin, I gazed over the crowd and reflected on my gratitude. I was grateful for having two beautiful healthy children, a roof over our heads, food on our table, and an opportunity to provide these things due to my administrative assistant corporate job, especially going from a stay-at-home mom to a single mom. Suddenly, I was startled by a gentle touch on my right leg. I quickly turned my head and saw the sweetest smile and a look of mixed emotions. *Was she trying to tell me something? Was she scared?* It was as if we were all there for the same reason. We were coming together as a community, a church, and one nation under God. This gently smiling, elderly woman, leaned towards me and whispered, "I bet you're a wonderful teacher."

I wish I was a teacher.

I said, "I would love to be a teacher."

Again, she leaned in and said, "You're a great teacher and students love you!" Her eyes sparkled while her face lit up. I'm sure the wrinkles on her face held a lifetime of stories. It was as though we were connected in a different way, at some deeper level, and I longed to sit down with her and hear all about those life stories.

I smiled and quietly said, "Thank you, but I'm not a teacher." *How did she know what I really wanted to do? She was definitely adamant about my being a teacher. It was something I could never do as a single mom. I could never leave my great paying job with great benefits.*

I couldn't stop thinking about it as I walked up to the alter and received Holy Communion. When I returned back to my seat in the pew, she was gone. Gone so fast my head spun in every direction trying to find her. I couldn't see her walking away in any direction. *She was right there next to me! How could she be gone so quickly?* I know the church was packed, but she was elderly and frail looking; there was no way she could have ran out of church that quickly. So many questions raced through my mind but my focus remained on searching the church with my eyes frantically looking for her. I had never known a person from her generation to leave the church so abruptly.

Why did she tell me I was a teacher?
What just happened?
She was right next to me and real!
I felt her touch.
How could she disappear and walk away so fast?

She planted a seed, and from that day forward, I questioned what I was doing with my life. *Was I really happy being an administrative assistant in the big corporate world?*

Reflecting back, I was often told by friends and neighbors I would make a good teacher...just like the gentle push I received from the busy stranger I had previously met on the golf course when we team taught the religion class. And the fact that I was already a "structured mom" made me feel like a teacher to my own children. I loved teaching them new things, encouraging them to use their imaginations, and never stop dreaming.

Our weekly routine consisted of making breakfast together, having a morning activity at 10 a.m. (making a craft, going for a walk, going to the library, playing in the sandbox, going to the park, making cookies, or pulling out the "dress up box" so they could use their imaginations with old clothes, shoes, and jewelry. Then we had lunch at noon, story time afterwards, naptime, an afternoon activity, and then while I made dinner, Michelle and Nik would pretend to cook with their bowl of flour and water. There was very little TV time.

To my surprise, a coworker at the pharmaceutical company asked if I wanted to take night classes with her. The company encouraged furthering education, so it was a perfect opportunity. I thought, *maybe someday my dream of becoming a teacher would manifest.* I stayed up late after my children went to bed, completed homework, researched, or wrote papers. I hadn't realized how hard I had been working until I received an invitation to an induction into a Phi Theta Kappa ceremony, sponsored by my English teacher. She was the engaging type of teacher I wanted to be. It didn't matter the age of the students in her class—whether 18 or 80. *Yes, I said 80.* There was an 80-year-old taking classes because she loved to learn. She was my inspiration.

While continuing night classes and another year as an administrative assistant passed, I received a call from my friend Lorene, who at one time was my son's preschool teacher. Lorene said there was a new charter school opening across the street from the elementary school my children attended, and they were looking for a Pre-K teacher. She continued, "I know you have a job, but I think you would be perfect for this position. We could work together and team teach. Think about it, and get back to me."

Team teach? That sounded familiar! I thought, *an interview couldn't hurt, RIGHT?!*

I agreed to go for the interview and had a very important decision to make. I made my pros and cons list: a huge pay cut, less benefits but closer to home, more time with my children, AND fulfilling a dream I thought would never come true.

While I prayed to make the right decision, the light bulb flickered on and my heart was filled with joy. The Holy Spirit got my attention, LOUD, and clear! I remembered the elderly woman who sat next to me at church before the new millennium, who told me I was a teacher. I also remembered the 80 years young woman in class, who told everyone, "You're never too old to make your dreams come true." There was my sign.

I spoke to my boss and told her about my difficult decision. She gave me her best advice and said, "Never live with regrets." She added, "If you don't take the teaching job, would you be okay with your decision staying here, setting aside the money and benefits?" Although she didn't want to lose me, she said she didn't want to hold me back from fulfilling my dream. She taught me many lessons, professionally and personally. The calming and peaceful feeling confirmed I needed to take a leap of faith and walk away from the corporate high paying, great benefits job, to embark on my new career as a Pre-K teacher. It was a dream come true for me. While my corporate world door closed, and I mentally prepared myself for the next chapter in my life, my thoughts exploded like a meteor shower inside my head…a beautiful sight to see but shooting from all directions.

While focusing on the next steps of my new life chapter and my thoughts no longer shooting in every direction, I was startled, when my cell phone rang, and my team teaching friend needed my help. There was a parent meeting at the charter school but she had a family emergency. She could start the meeting with me but had to leave before it was over. I replayed what I would say to the parents over and over inside my head as I continued to drive from my last day at the corporate job to my new job. *It doesn't matter I hadn't started my new job as a teacher yet, RIGHT? And, I didn't know what I didn't know, nor what to expect or was required of me. I could do this. You've got this Mary! Let go, and let God. You took a leap of faith for a reason.* I encouraged myself.

I walked into what was going to be my new classroom, and it was filled with parents. Lorene gave a quick introduction and then said she needed to leave for a family emergency, but they were in good hands with me. Under normal circumstances I would have stood there frozen or speechless, or furious and scared to death, but I was actually calm. I was doing what I was called to do…to be a teacher and make a difference.

Surprisingly my days never felt like work, especially when initially this team teaching position turned into the lead teacher position having a paraeducator helping me with the students. I loved teaching, and going to work every day was a gift. I was making a difference and teaching those little ones with their sponge-like minds, soaking up every lesson plan. They learned and recited weekly poems and history projects; they sang songs and played musical instruments. They enjoyed learning colors and counting to 10 in both French and Spanish. They loved one-on-one writing and coloring time, and had fun in their group sensory, craft, and puzzle centers.

Teaching wasn't a job; it was a way of life for me. I had already been doing all of this with my own children, as I told them, "Every day is a school day." We all learn something new every day, whether in school or not. And, now, I was sharing this knowledge with my students. The difference I was making in their little lives enhanced my drive to make an even stronger difference moving forward.

While I was sharing my gifts and just doing what came naturally, to my surprise, my good works, words, and actions were apparently making a difference and not only in the classroom; it was carrying over into the student's home life as well. Parents came into the classroom and said, "Whatever you're doing, keep doing it because my daughter is so excited. It's making a big difference at home."

It's a Match

Not only was I making a difference in the classroom, but my love and compassion to help others was evident to my pastor friend and neighbor. He and his wife witnessed the love and compassion I shared so they asked me if I would be interested in mentoring.

I felt honored to be called to the ministry of being a mentor through a Christian organization called MatchPoint. Each mentor was required to apply, have a background check and if approved, assigned a case manager, not only for everyone's safety but to find that perfect mentor/mentee connection.

Although the sun was scorching hot, well over 100 degrees in Arizona, where you could fry an egg on the cement in seconds, my life was beaming like sunrays from heaven. No comforting air-conditioned home was better than what I was about to experience. My case manager picked me up, and we drove across town, to meet my MATCH. We drove into an older rundown trailer park with each home placed close to the other, similar to closeness of the house I grew up in, when I was a child. There was no sense of privacy. I initially felt sad, yet somewhat peaceful. I had so much, even an air-conditioned home on this hot day, and these families were trying everything to survive the unbearable heat. As we approached the door, we were instantly greeted with a warmhearted, genuine smile from a mom holding a little baby boy, full of life, yet too young to walk. We sat at the small, square kitchen table, getting to know one another, waiting for my possible mentee to come home from her friend's house. The door opened and immediately our eyes connected. You could tell she was her mother's daughter, as they shared the same warm smile. It was an instant connection. She was so excited; she grabbed my hand and led me down the narrow hallway toward her bedroom. It was a very small room, and she enthusiastically pointed out each of her cherished collectable items. Then, she excitedly said, "This is where I sleep." Her bed was a small mattress which laid on the floor. This was her life and all she knew. We then went for a short walk outside, talking, sharing, and briefly getting to know each other. I asked her if she would be okay if I was her mentor. Her smile grew bigger than the initial one when we first met. I teased and said, "By the size of that smile on your face, I would say that was a big 'YES!'"

We began our two-year commitment and a new chapter in our lives. My mentee was a very thin eight-year-old, the same age as my son. She had long, sandy blond hair, and was just as beautiful on the inside as she was on the outside. She had three siblings, two of which were also in the program.

The mentor guidelines stated that we needed to establish a relationship for three months before introducing her to my family. Once a month we participated in a MatchPoint group activity and met weekly doing different activities, (going to parks, talking, drawing pictures of things she liked and/or wanted her world to be like, having ice cream, or sharing lunch at her favorite place, Sonic.) She always ordered the same thing, a foot-long chili dog and tater tots. I initially thought, *WOW, how does such a little girl eat so much?* Then, each time, she would only eat half of her meal and wrapped up the rest. When I asked her why, she said she wanted to share with her little brother. I admired her tenacity for her family. In my experience, people who had little to none shared more with others than people with plenty.

After three months, she finally met my family. They welcomed her with open arms and connected like they were family since birth. Once in a while, my own children would participate with my mentee and me through our MatchPoint activities. It was a match made in heaven for all of us.

Time together flew by so fast that before we knew it, our "contracted time" ended. We kept in touch and continued to see each other on occasion which was no longer through MatchPoint but an arrangement her mother and I agreed upon.

Not only was there closure through *MatchPoint*, but my life in Arizona would soon be ending too, as an opportunity to relocate to Colorado was about to change all our lives. We made the move, and once we were all settled in Colorado, I received a call from my mentee's mom asking if her daughter could live with us, or if I could possibly even adopt her? "She would have a 'better' life with you," her mother said to me.

I told her, "You are the best gift you can give to her, just love her unconditionally." It was an opportunity to mentor my mentee's mom and see how God made us all different for His purpose; we all have special gifts to share. I continued, "Take all the lessons you've learned and continue being the great mom that you are! You gave your children an opportunity to be part of such a wonderful organization. You don't need 'things' to love your children unconditionally." We are all different, and everything happens for a reason in God's timing, and for His purpose. We are not here to judge or compare. We all have a purpose.

Teaching and mentoring were stepping stones in my life. God put that busy stranger in my life on that golf course, many years ago just as He put that angel in my church pew to tell me I already was a great teacher. God continues to put people in my life, at the right time, for the right reasons, to either teach me or guide me in learning a lesson. And when you see your future self in the present just like others saw me, the dream is easier to manifest. We are all gifted teachers, and the world is our classroom. Enjoy the journey. Every day REALLY is a school day!

About Mary

Mary Markham is the founder of Inspirational Visions LLC (a small business with simple and powerful messages on various products). She is the author of *In God's Hands* and published poetry, as well as a contributing author of the best-selling book *The Miracle Effect*. Mary is a mentor, facilitator of Divorce and Beyond and coordinator for Family Promise of Waukesha County, a nonprofit organization helping homeless families with children.

Mary enjoys encouraging others to never give up hope, by sharing her personal stories and God-inspired messages; "Let go, Let God," "I AM," and, "Broken Not Shattered." She enjoys her quiet time writing while soaking up God's creations all around her, as well as spending time with her family, friends, traveling, biking, and gardening.

Mary and her husband, Craig, reside in Wisconsin, and between them they have four independent and successful children.

Contact Mary Markham at:
Mary@inspirationalvisionsllc.com
or inspirationalvisionsllc.com
Instagram: inspirational_visions_llc

INSPIRATIONAL *visions* PODCAST

WITH MARY MARKHAM

With my husband, Craig, at my book launch for **In God's Hands**.

In God's Hands *book release, March, 2019, with my friend and editor, Marla McKenna.*

MARIE SUMNICHT

"The thoughts I told myself daily kept me in a cycle of defeat and bad feelings. I learned that I needed to challenge and confront my wrong assumptions and be willing to disrupt my thinking to find the peace I longed for."

- Marie Sumnicht,
Beyond Broken

Dreams Shattered...Purpose Ignited

I saw life and death in a new way after my daughter's death. Overcoming the lies to uncover the truth would be the heart of my journey.

What if you had a 21-year-old daughter who had dreams and goals and a future before her, and suddenly her life was taken through the careless and selfish actions of a stranger?

One item stood out at her funeral.

We displayed a large poster that had been found leaning on the back wall of her bedroom closet, a project she had made for a college class in the month prior to her death. Photos had been arranged into groups and showed her likes, dislikes, views of herself, and dreams for her future.

"My likes" was printed in a pinkish purple color above a group of photos that included her dog Ceci, a dance pose from a high school dance team event, a high school graduation pose, a bowl of fruit, a pair of running shoes, the face of a llama, a headshot of Brett Favre, a French phrase "L'adore," and, placed in the center, in large black letters, the word "Bible."

In the bottom, a collection of photos depicted her "Dreams for the Future." A map of the state of Florida, palm trees, and a large sun —these images made up half the collection. The other half included a group of dogs (she had great compassion for animals), wedding rings with the word "married" above them, and a girl working at a desk with a laptop.

"The one thing that you have that nobody else has is you. Your voice, your mind, your story, your vision. So, write and draw and build and play and dance and live as only you can." - Neil Gaiman

I shot up from a deep sleep and stared at the clock. It was 10:48 p.m. "Dan, please come down with me. Someone's knocking on the door, and I don't want to go alone."

My husband followed me down the steps. We saw police uniforms through the window to the left of the door. With trepidation, Dan opened the front door. Two policemen stood on the porch. One of them asked, "Is Julia your daughter?"

Dan replied, "Yes." They asked if they could come in.

The four of us walked through the study into our den where we nervously sat down. As we walked, I felt myself getting tense. *Maybe Julia was in jail or some kind of trouble?* I thought. The police officers sat in the two chairs across from us. I sat on the smaller couch, and Dan was adjacent to me on the larger couch, just a few feet away. I wasn't prepared for their words.

As soon as we made eye contact with the police officers, one of them said, "We found your daughter's body."

Those words would change my life forever.

"Courage is not having strength to go on. It's going on when you don't have strength." - Napoleon Bonaparte

My heart, soul, and mind instantly froze after I heard the words from the police officers. A dreadful feeling gripped my heart and soul. A deep ache combined with fear settled in my being. Somehow, as her parent, I must have done something to cause her death. *If I had been a better parent, she wouldn't have gone to Florida and died.*

My mind flooded with questions.

I didn't know how I was going to live with myself. My lack of foresight would haunt me for years. The guilt was unbearable, and in that moment, I understood why people commit suicide. I didn't want to live with that kind of guilt.

I just wanted Julia to be happy. In my desire to respect her and give her dignity, I gave her freedom to make her own decisions.

Not recalling falling asleep, I awoke from the couch as Dan made coffee, and I said, "We have to tell the kids, and I have to call my school to get a substitute teacher for my students today."

The world I thought I knew had just been blown apart. The sense of dread would fill my being for months after.

How does anyone living in this nightmare move forward with a broken heart and make sense of life after the sudden loss of their child?

The question that plagued me the most—*Could I have done something to save her*?

Shock and numbness had penetrated the deepest parts of my being. I felt caught in their grip with no way to escape. My emotional state seemed stuck in time since I'd heard the news. Even my brain circuits felt "fried" and unable to process the reality of my child's death.

None of my life experiences could be used or compared to help me through this. I had nothing to draw from or recall that might give me direction and hope in the blackness. Now and then Bible verses came into my mind, but I found no comfort in their meaning.

It was a week from hell. I had to plan for my daughter's funeral, figure out sub lessons for my classroom, make accommodations for relatives coming to the funeral, and cope with an ongoing nightmare.

Psychologists call life after loss the "new normal." But "normal" didn't fit. There was nothing normal about the horrific months following my daughter's death, and there was nothing normal about the way I was living either.

Watching the pain of our living children while going through our own pain from losing a child is an unimaginable situation that no parent should have to endure. *Why did I have to attend my daughter's funeral?*

The Funeral

We were asked to find photos and other collectibles that represented Julia and display them in the church lobby before the funeral. *Wasn't it just a few years ago that we displayed these same items at her graduation party? How could this be happening?*

A large blue recyclable container stood at the end of a table, representing her passion for the environment. A coworker had told me that Julia was known to round up all the bottles and cans at work and take them by bike, for weeks on end, just so they could be recycled. A soft, white baby blanket was another memorable item. It was shrunk, frayed, and worn. There were knots, and it had lost some of its "whiteness." It was 21 years old.

As I walked to the open doors leading into the sanctuary, I stopped and stared across a large room filled with chairs that had been arranged at different angles, all facing the altar. In the front of the room, near the altar, was a coffin. I stared at the coffin. I questioned what people meant when they talked about closure. *How could seeing the lifeless body of your child bring closure? What did closure mean anyway? All I felt was pain and numbness.*

Life is unpredictable. It is easy to take our life for granted until we are confronted with the fact of mortality. It does not feel natural to bury a child before their parents or two of their grandparents. Yet, there are no guarantees with our birth certificate that we are owed a certain number of days.

Investigation

It wouldn't be until a year later that I would learn about the involvement of two suspects and circumstantial evidence leading to the cause of her death. Not having heard anything in the first year after her death, a private investigator was hired by relatives from the Sumnicht family in hopes of getting some answers to the cause of Julia's death. In a few short months, the investigator would find out more than we wanted to know.

He reported:

"Detective Kenny Matthews ran through a summary of the case and said the case had been hampered by the delays of a cause of death from the medical examiner's office. He said it wasn't until September, six months after her death, that he received the toxicology report."

The cause of death was determined to be a lethal dose of a date rape drug called GHB. Our investigator also showed us data revealing that Julia had no alcohol in her blood. So, Julia died solely from a tasteless, odorless, and clear drug that was most likely placed in a water bottle she carried with her.

The investigator went on to interview family and friends, finding out that, "Julia was universally loved by everyone she knew. She was a wonderful, outgoing, and caring person who was so fun to be with. She was not a drug user and cared about her body. She was also smart, as is attested to that fact that she was not drinking the night she was taken away."

It eventually became clear, in 2012 and 2013 that the Miami Beach Police Department (MBPD) was going to dig their heels in deep and not work Julia's case. My belief is that it would have been disastrous for the MBPD if Julia's case ever went to court, considering their malfeasance.

For unknown reasons, the MBPD detectives neglected to follow some of the standard operating procedures (SOP) that are expected to be done at the scene of an unattended death. For example, they had not collected a water bottle laying by her bed nor had they canvassed the scene. They could have walked just a couple blocks over to the place where they knew she had been last. A sloppy investigation in the first 48 hours became the reason for a police department and legal system to derail our hopes of justice.

Fast forward to Christmas Day eve when I was online trying to research the standard operating procedures (SOP) of the Miami Beach Police Department. Every time I put in SOP, the name Joe Matthews would appear. Clicking on his name, I would discover an expert cold case investigator who had not only solved numerous cold cases such as the Adam Walsh case but had actually worked in the MBPD homicide department for 29 years before retiring and becoming a cold case investigator. Looking to Joe initially just for confirmation that I had been wronged, Joe eventually agreed to help me get the MBPD to work Julia's case. Using Joe's 50-page analysis of Julia's death investigation, we were determined to get the support we needed to get to the bottom of who drugged Julia and get the MBPD to do their job. But once again, it became clear that no matter what we did or said, the MBPD, and even the Florida Department of Law Enforcement (FDLE) and Miami-Dade attorney, would resist our efforts.

Going on Living

"The soul is healed by being with children." - Fyodor Dostoyevsky

The days blurred together, and Julia's absence hung over me like threatening black clouds. I decided going back to school would be a needed distraction from the continuous gloom. I'd never had a chance to say goodbye to Julia, so I was determined to finish the year with my special class of students. But first, I would reacquaint myself with them and try to explain my new world with a brief visit.

I entered my classroom in mid-April, greeted with smiles and hugs from my students.

It felt strange as I faced their sweet and innocent faces, all unaware of the turmoil in my soul. But I wanted these nine and 10 year olds to have some sort of understanding of loss.

"I want to tell you what it's been like for me to lose my daughter. Imagine a tornado had ripped through the middle of your home, leaving everything destroyed and strewn about the ground. Imagine yourself standing in the middle of the destruction and wondering where to begin piecing together whatever could be made whole again. That is what it's like," I said.

I then gave another analogy, "How would it feel to have your thumb cut off?" They all agreed it would really hurt. Then I asked them, "Could you still function without your thumb?"

One of the kids raised his hand, "Yes, but it would be hard."

I said, "Yes, but you could still learn to do things with the rest of your fingers, and would it hurt less as time went on?" They shook their heads, yes. I told them that I could function without Julia, but life would be very challenging for me.

Driving home, I decided I needed to go back...but slowly.

I started teaching half days. During my first week back, a student said something funny and I laughed. Shortly after I laughed, I thought to myself, *I laughed! I hadn't laughed since Julia's death.*

My school was like family, and I knew the classroom was where I needed to be. Teaching provided the right stimulus to refocus my energy in a positive direction and away from the constant sadness.

Hope Emerges

In the months and years after loss, sleep couldn't come quickly enough in the evenings. In the mornings, I unwillingly dragged my body out of bed, with the cruel reminder of death and loss gripping my mind and heart. As I sipped my coffee in the early morning hours, I opened my Bible to the page where I'd left off from the morning before, determined to understand God, life, and death.

Why did God allow her to die?

Philip Yancey, in *The Jesus I Never Knew*, gave me some perspective I needed in those dark moments. He showed me there was no mistake or sin too big for God's grace. I had allowed feelings of pain and regret into my heart, feeling judged, and indignation toward others. I had gone to Africa, engaged heavily in teaching, and pursued ways to feel whole again, yet the negative feelings persisted.

Nothing seemed to help. All I wanted was contentment and peace for a brief moment. I struggled with my failure and sought God's grace. The brevity of my life confronted me, and I was tired of wasting my days in gloom. All I wanted was to feel peace and hope.

From 2008 until June of 2014, I had fully invested my time as a fourth grade teacher at the Wisconsin International School (WIS) in De Pere, Wisconsin. Tragically, due to poor leadership, the school unexpectedly closed in June of 2014. Its closing was a tremendous loss to both the teaching staff and families of students who had attended WIS. Since teaching had consumed most of my life, I now struggled to find my purpose.

It was in 2015 that I was introduced to a young financially free couple. Since Julia's death, I had watched my oldest son Stephan grow in wisdom and business success while I was stuck in negativity and despondency. All I knew was that he had been part of an entrepreneurial mentorship opportunity that seemed to be making a positive impact on his life. I wanted not only another avenue of income after my school closed, but desperately wanted to feel the hope and peace that my soul longed for and the emotional stability I saw in my son.

After going through a process of education and trust building with my future business partners, I received an offer into mentorship. The offer was contingent on my agreement to integrate partnership responsibilities into my daily life. Reading and internalizing self-development and leadership books by great men such as John

Maxwell, Stephen Covey, and Napoleon Hill played a large role in shifting my mindset. In addition, listening to audios of successful men and women who overcame great adversity in their own lives and associating with like-minded people who made choices to follow their dreams and goals impacted my life in powerful ways.

Hope emerged from the dark shadows in my heart.

As my life changed through mentorship, I wanted to "pay it forward" by reaching out to others. I began to network and look for people who not only sought entrepreneurship, but desired personal and leadership growth as well. In the process of seeking to give value, I have been able to connect and share with many people from various backgrounds, even some who have had loss. Julia's death gave me the daily urgency of living fully and selflessly.

"Abraham Lincoln worked diligently to improve himself, developing self-understanding, discipline, and strategies for support that would become the foundation of his character." - Joshua Wolf Shenk

Life Truths

We have preconceived notions of God that may or may not be accurate; negative beliefs that hold us back, a misunderstanding of the grief process, "good" that can come out of tragedy, the ability to change, and freedom within forgiveness.

Weighted by my belief in a judgmental God, I finally saw a God of grace and love. Immediately after learning of Julia's death, I had believed it was my fault, and I deserved punishment; but I discovered a God of unconditional love.

Believing I had failed Julia, I lived in gloom. Searching for truth, I saw that in my grief; I wrongly blamed myself. I learned to release the guilt by accepting that I always had love and the best intentions for Julia, and that no parent is perfect.

While my soul was afflicted with pain, I saw life and death in a new way. I asked God in a prayer, *Why did you have to use Julia's death to teach me truths about life and death?* Just months after she'd died, I told my husband that her death seemed a sort of "terrible blessing." I saw God using her death in people's lives, even in the midst of my pain and confusion. I learned that life's most powerful truths are found in adversity.

My usual upbeat nature had been severely tested, and I was done being defeated by negative emotions. Noticing the effects of personal growth habits since September 2015, I made a New Year's resolution on January 1, 2016—to focus on self-development. I found that just as daily training had improved my running, consistent habits led to a positive mindset.

I saw the power of daily intentions as I experienced personal growth and true change. I learned that I needed to challenge and confront my wrong assumptions and be willing to change my thinking to find the peace I longed for.

Daily inspirational reading, positive habits, and serving others helped to free me from the bondage of guilt. As I sought truth, the lies I believed were exposed. Living with renewed purpose enabled me to forgive myself.

I believe that you also can break out of bondage, but only if you truly *want* to be free.

Understand that the journey to freedom might be the hardest work you'll ever do but will give you the life you seek.

"Understand that your life has been severely disrupted by loss, and your thought process needs disruption to break free. Realize that if you developed a thought pattern of wrong assumptions, you're closing yourself off from healing and change. Understand that it takes courage, guts, and discipline to change; but losing the battle to healing is far more painful than paying the price to overcome."
(P. 155, Marie Sumnicht, author of *Beyond Broken*)

I believe it is in suffering and hardship that we can reach our fullest potential and emerge as a butterfly from a dark cocoon. I finally believed that I needed to live as Julia did, leaving a legacy that changed lives.

I remember her zest for life and all things around her. And I remember her not having one mean bone in her body and ALWAYS welcoming everyone she encountered with open arms. I remember her confidence and her always making us laugh—she didn't care what people thought. It was admirable.

"And though Julia's time here on Earth was tragically shortened, she made a deep impact on each person who crossed her path. I know she taught a group of us girls what it meant (though we were young and

naive college-aged gals at the time) to live life to our fullest potential and go after what we want. And that's one heck of a message to be remembered by." - Kelli, college friend

"And the God of grace, who called you to his eternal glory in Christ, after you have suffered a little while, will Himself restore you and make you strong, firm and steadfast." - 1 Peter 5:10

"Not only so, but we also glory in our sufferings, because we know that suffering produces perseverance; perseverance, character; and character, hope." - Romans 5:3, 4

I learned that I wasn't meant to stay in brokenness. I finally understood that brokenness was the way to wholeness and purpose. The beauty in spiritual brokenness was found in where it brought me, to a place of humility and openness to all that God has for my life.

What was I waiting for?

About Marie

Marie Sumnicht—educator, athlete, author, and entrepreneur—was born and raised in Appleton, Wisconsin. One of six children, she became a "tomboy" who followed her two older brothers. Competitive games during her childhood years set the stage for participation in sports, eventually having one of the fastest high school times in the state for the 880-yard dash in track. She also enjoyed playing a year of women's basketball at Valparaiso University. Marie likes downhill and Nordic skiing, hiking, and swimming in lakes. At 41 years of age, she became an elite marathoner, running 26.2 miles under three hours.

After her marriage in December of 1984 to Daniel Sumnicht, they had their first child—Stephan—in 1986. In approximately two-year increments, her family grew to four, including Julia, Johanna, and Andrew. As a mother who deeply loved her children and desired to instill in them Christian values and a love of learning, she chose to home school for most of their elementary and middle school years.

On the evening of March 15, 2010, Marie and her family would experience unexpected devastation through loss. Struggling through the pain in the aftermath of loss, Marie would eventually find strength, hope, and a renewed faith.

To learn more about Marie's story and find hope on your own journey, please read her book, *Beyond Broken*, and sign up for free resources when you visit her website: beyondbroken.net

Julia, age 21.

Julia's tombstone.

Childhood photo (left to right), JoJo, Stephan, Andrew, Julia.

Last photo together - Chritmas, 2009.

NATALIE M. MILLER

"Give love no matter what."
- Natalie M. Miller

Nudged by the Universe

I envisioned working for the best, high profile, downtown law firm, so I was determined to make it happen. After tenaciously progressing through a grueling interview process, I FINALLY landed an offer for a litigation paralegal position with the company I had been trying to get into for several months. However, I soon realized I should have listened when my gut filled me with negative vibes because what I pictured wasn't reality at all.

My days felt like weeks in a toxic work environment with yelling, screaming, and phones slamming down. There was extreme cattiness, nepotism, and enough daily drama to star in our own reality television show. People quit or got fired as quickly as they were hired, and multiple attorneys made inappropriate comments or passes at many of us as if it was normal, daily conversation. Unfortunately, due to the high turnover rate, I lost my dear friend and colleague, Samantha, who was like an angel to me during those taxing days.

I was determined, so I gave my job everything I had. Later that year, the director selected me to be his paralegal. I felt honored, but I could tell by the dirty looks and passive aggressive remarks that the others in the department were disgruntled. I had by far the least amount of litigation experience, and this drove three of the women in the department to collaborate and try to get me fired. When the director advised me of their conspiracy, I yelled, "This is BS, unacceptable, and what kind of repercussions are in place to ensure this doesn't happen again?" I was furious because this now created a hostile work environment for me. After I voiced my concerns about everything and was told nothing would be done, being a woman of principle; I could no longer represent this company. On December 3, 2015, I resigned effective immediately.

I had lost my best friend, Katie, in May of 2015, which was very painful. Now, I was at a crossroads in my career and I wanted to make a change. I began to imagine feeling free, starting over, and living the beach life in paradise, like I had always dreamed of. In April 2016, I relocated to Tampa, Florida.

When I arrived in Tampa on that dreary, rainy day, I'll never forget my feelings of triumph. It was an adrenaline rush to know that I single-handedly planned and executed a move across the country in less than three months. Tears rolled down my face with overwhelming feelings of fear, excitement, and courage as I embarked on this new chapter in my life.

After discovering a probate paralegal position, I felt an immediate connection, so I applied for it. I began my career working in probate law, and I loved it. From the moment I walked into the office and throughout the interview process, I felt nothing but positive energy. I was offered the position a few days later, and I graciously accepted.

On my one-year anniversary at the probate firm, I scheduled my annual review. I went through my outline and spreadsheet that contained a list of cases I helped settle, the amount of money I brought into the firm, as well as positive words from my boss. One quote stated, "Wow, Natalie you have transformed the office, I should just put you in charge." With my heart racing, and hands trembling, I asked for a substantial raise.

My boss looked surprised and said he had to think about it. The following Monday, I was blindsided when I was introduced to a business strategist who was hired to continue my negotiations. My mind raced and then went blank. I pulled myself together and the strategist and I debated. I explained my expectation was to meet somewhere in the middle; however, he stated affirmatively that would not be the case. I continued to strategize, and fight for what I felt I deserved. In the end, my boss would not be able to pay me what I needed to consider staying there long-term, so I had to start looking. In the meantime, I missed home and consulted with friends and family. My mother's health continued to deteriorate. It became increasingly more difficult as I watched my niece, who is like the mini-me, grow up, and to not be there for my mom, family, and core friends.

I landed a unique position as a site inspection coordinator for a national construction defects law firm. This job was going to allow me to travel. I really liked the people as well as the ability to work outside of the office, plus I was in charge.

When I turned in my resignation to my boss at the probate firm, he told me that he wished he could give me everything I wanted because I was the best paralegal he had ever employed.

On August 21, 2017, (the day of the eclipse), I woke up in my hotel room, while on a business trip in Jacksonville, Florida, with a shock wave exploding through my body and one clear message: *It's time to go home.* It was core-shaking, because it felt like a nudge from the Universe. I finished my scheduled work that week, but I kept thinking about how much I wanted to go back to Wisconsin. I had built a great life in Florida which felt like one long vacation, but without my family and close friends, I didn't feel whole.

I had just renewed my lease, so I was contractually obligated until August 2018. If I broke the lease before then, I would be obligated to pay a $2,200 termination fee, plus one month's rent of $1,110. Since I didn't have that money readily available, I had to find another way.

While sitting at my kitchen table the next morning, overwhelmed with thoughts of how I was going to get home to Wisconsin, I noticed what appeared to be a black smudge on my wall. I tried to wipe it off, but the spot grew larger the more I tried to remove it. This was black mold and just the sign I was looking for. While working as a site inspection coordinator, I routinely examined black mold, so I knew it when I saw it. I researched everything I could about black mold and any incidents in my apartment complex.

The next morning, I finalized my plan and strategy. I was

supposed to travel for work, so I had to act quickly. I drove my company car, filled the trunk with my electronic devices and other firm belongings, and dropped the car off at the firm lot. I then called my office manager, and trainer, and left them voicemails, and I gave my immediate resignation, along with my sincerest apologizes.

The next morning, I went into the leasing office and informed my leasing manager of the black mold. As expected, she tried to deny it was black mold. So, I stated affirmatively, that I routinely examine and assess black mold for my job, so I know it when I see it. That afternoon, their engineer expert confirmed it was and stated my apartment would need to be quarantined as soon as possible. Considering the findings, I proposed they waive the $2,200 termination fee and next month's rent. She agreed to waive the termination fee, but said, "I really doubt my regional manager will waive the rent because it's against policy." I assertively replied, "I have been subjected to black mold, my health could be in jeopardy, and I now have to be uprooted from my home while it is quarantined; waiving the rent is the least that should be done." Thirty minutes later, she called me back and confirmed they were also waiving the rent. I couldn't believe it. I thanked her, and she said, "It's the right thing to do." I began to cry and almost fell to the ground in disbelief. I knew it was a long shot dealing with a huge company on my own, but it was confirmation this was all meant to be.

For the next two days, I packed only my belongings I couldn't live without and left the rest behind. My intuition was telling me to get home as quickly as possible. On Wednesday, August 31, 2017, I packed up my car and began my journey back home.

Hurricane Irma hit Florida as I left, and the entire four days of travel were filled with extreme stress; the skies produced strong winds, fog, and torrential downpours. On my last night of travel, I planned to stay in Nashville. The rain blasted my windshield, traffic was awful, and I could barely see the car in front of me. I white-knuckled the steering wheel, with hands at 10 and 2, driving far below the speed limit as my heart raced—terrified for my safety. I prayed with conviction begging to make it to my hotel safely, and when I turned into the hotel, my car almost flooded. It was the scariest drive of my life, so I was beyond grateful when I finally arrived safely.

It felt amazing when I drove into Milwaukee on September 2, 2017. It had been such an onerous journey that I felt victorious with a rediscovered, stronger, and more confident *me*; I was *home*. I always had this unsettled feeling while living in Florida, but I felt whole in Milwaukee.

Within weeks of my arrival, my mother suffered a severe fall that placed her in the hospital; and my sweet cousin, Shelly, suddenly and unexpectedly passed away. A few weeks later, my *estranged* father died. Part of me knew that intense and constant feeling of anxiety was telling me to get home for a reason, now it suddenly all made sense. The months that followed proved difficult, and I couldn't imagine not being near my family and close friends to get through it all. I am thankful I trusted my intuition, and it assured me I would get home, no matter what.

I began applying for jobs the following week, and then I interviewed the next few months. By October, I had undergone many promising interviews, but no offers. The money I had to live off was dwindling, and I really needed to acquire some income and start paying off multiple credit cards. Thankfully, I landed a temporary position doing contract administration work at a national healthcare law firm. Then my best friend, Patricia, encouraged me to apply for a bartending position working with her at the Milwaukee Bucks stadium which I secured.

After analyzing contracts, I walked to my evening job. Without any training, I started on the biggest night of the Bucks season. It was the home opener against Lebron and the Cavaliers. I had to learn the bar, the cash register, and everything I could in just five minutes before we began serving customers. Right then, I took a deep breath in and felt this incredible rush—knowing I was part of such an awesome franchise. From start to finish, we were nonstop busy the entire night. Everything that could go wrong did: one of our tappers stopped working, one of our receipt printers stopped printing, and then one of the credit card machines stopped working, but the endless line of customers didn't stop. I remember looking up during the chaos and seeing the mile long line of customers, and thought, *OMG, this is the most intense shift I've ever worked!*

Over the next five months, I worked both positions, often

multiple double shifts per week, without taking breaks in between, and working up to 17 hours in a day. Simultaneously, I continued to apply, interview, and follow-up for a paralegal/legal role. Some weeks, with everything going on, I put in 70 to100-hour work weeks, with at best five to six hours of sleep per night. Despite working harder and more hours than I ever had in my life, getting financially caught up still seemed daunting. To cut down on costs, I didn't drive my car for the first few months. However, during the winter months, that 45-minute walk home in the 16 degree weather, after working over 15 hours was enervating. Most days I felt like a walking zombie, and a few times, I almost collapsed from sleep deprivation and exhaustion. I kept telling myself *this is going to pay off soon*. I looked at my vision board every day that included pictures and words of how I wanted my future to look like, including a "Fortune 500 Company."

Throughout those grueling six months, I made many sacrifices. Since I wasn't driving my car, I walked as much as possible even when it was less than 20 degrees outside, sometimes for nearly an hour, after working 17 hours without a break. Since I stopped using my credit cards, I lived off my small payroll, so I ate a strict, cheap diet, and kept my personal expenses and entertainment to a minimum. Oftentimes I had to decline on events, trips, and fun because I simply didn't have the money, time, or energy. Due to the credit card debt I had accumulated after two relocations, I was making substantially less than what I was accustomed to; I was afraid I may have to declare bankruptcy. However, I was determined to avoid it and land something big! That something would get me caught up on my bills, pay off my credit cards, and allow me to live my life the way I was used to. It was hands down, the hardest six months of my life. I was making barely over what I needed to pay my bills, but that left next to nothing for food, personal items and needs, and entertainment. I held it together, but inside I didn't know how much more I could take, so I needed my big break, and I needed it soon.

A paralegal position opened in the firm I was contracting at, so I applied. I interviewed very well; however, since I did not have the compliance experience they wanted, they said they'd be seeking other applicants. Instead of allowing this to disappoint me, I used it as motivation to continue with my search and find something even better.

After extensive interviewing, I received an offer for a paralegal position, as well a sales/marketing professional position. I finally began to feel the positive energy and was excited for the opportunities coming my way. It was then, that I received a telephone call from a recruiter, for a contract legal administrative role, at Harley-Davidson. I thought, this is the kind of opportunity I was holding out for, hoping for, and thought could be my big break. From the recruiter's call, to the moment I entered the building, to the interview itself, I only felt positive energy and great vibes. I had always been a mover and a shaker, but there was something about the "feel" of Harley-Davidson, that made me think this is where I want to be for the long-term. The interview couldn't have gone better. It almost brought me to tears because I just knew this was it.

The following Monday, the recruiter called and told me the interviewers liked me so much, they cancelled the other interviews because they wanted to extend me an offer. The offer was even more than I envisioned on my vision board and would more than adequately get me financially caught up. This new role would also allow me to pay off my credit cards, and allow me to live my life even better than what I was accustomed to. Of course, I accepted. She said, "Natalie, I don't know what you said or did, but this has never happened to me in all the years I've been recruiting for Harley-Davidson." I was beyond excited and couldn't believe it; I wanted it so badly, and it just fell into place. I was overcome with emotion because my journey had been so arduous.

Meanwhile, the office manager for the law firm I had been contracting with approached me to extend a job offer. I told her I had three other offers on the table, and that I was making my decision by the end of the week. I wasn't even going to consider their offer, but I wanted to appease them, finish up my project, and leave on good terms. I strategically planned to be off that Friday, and then declined their offer via email that afternoon. For the first time in a long time, I felt my dreams were really coming true. I had moments when I thought, *is this really happening? Did I really manifest this?*

My first day at Harley-Davidson was such a rush. I felt unbelievably honored to work at such an iconic, innovative, and progressive company. Harley-Davidson was just the kind of company

I had dreamed of working for. Fortunately, I was trained quickly, and my wonderful manager, Lisa, and I bonded from day one.

After all the stress, and ups and downs I went through, and then with the anticipation and celebration of my new role, it took a toll on my body. An old back injury I suffered during my gymnastic days flared up and started to really bother me. It progressively got worse with each passing day. By the time spring rolled around, I was unable to run, workout, or do other simple daily activities, and it became increasingly difficult and painful to walk. I started to get really scared, so when I had to cancel meeting a *friend* because the pain was so bad, she insisted I see her chiropractor for relief.

Fortunately, the chiropractor helped me, but through this process, the *friend* who referred me to him, sabotaged me. After I told her the doctor had asked me out, *she* began to aggressively attempt to drive a wedge between us. The turning point was when *she* insisted on scheduling me for an appointment on Monday, May 28 (Memorial Day). Given this was a holiday, and her demeanor was aggressive, the situation seemed *off*. I confirmed the date and time of the appointment with her on two separate occasions and since *she* seemed annoyed, I wasn't entirely surprised when I showed up at the clinic that day, and it was closed. When I informed *her*, she lied and continued to lie thereafter and change her story. I later confirmed with the doctor that he did not schedule any appointments on Memorial Day, despite her telling me he had two others scheduled before mine. She scheduled a fake appointment for me and then lied about it. I believe she did this hoping after what she played off as a "mix-up," that I would not return to the clinic. I believe she wanted to keep me away from her boss because she has romantic feelings for him.

For the next several weeks, *she* continued to lie and change her story, so I stopped communicating with her. Five months later, *she* finally admitted to what she did. This sabotage caused me exacerbated physical pain and distress, that ultimately led to my cutting *her* off as a friend. However, I am grateful for this experience because it taught me the importance of slowing down, paying attention, and always remaining present. Had this setback not forced me to do so, I may not have caught on to *her* deception. What I didn't know at the time was, this experience was teaching and preparing me for another act of sabotage. Despite what *she* has done, I will always be kind to her, be there if she ever needs anything, and wish her nothing but the best. When the time is right, I expect to have a conversation with her in hopes this situation will teach and inspire her like it has me.

My *friend* R. is beautiful, intelligent, and successful. After I connected with a male friend of hers, she exhibited a heightened competitiveness towards me and a peculiar interest in my personal life. Despite her telling me NOT to get involved with *him*, the two of us continued to get close. After this, R. would only engage with me to ask probing questions about *him* and me, and other untimely questions. Multiple times she asked if I talked to an ex of mine. I wondered, *why does she keep asking me that and seem discontented when I say, "No. I'm not interested in him anymore."* I believe she hoped I would say yes, so that she could tell *him*, in hopes that would steer *him* away from me. It soon became clear she had romantic feelings for *him* and would stop at nothing to try to pull us apart.

R. said things about *his* past relationships including *he* will, "cold cut," a girl as she witnessed him do this to someone, he was previously involved with. She also said, "Well, you know he is a Leo and they are BSers." I thought, *if she was saying negative and conflicting things about him to me, it's possible she was also saying negative and conflicting things about me to him. She is his friend, so why does it feel like she is intentionally saying negative things that she believes will steer me away from him, and is she doing the same to him?*

One night when R., he, another friend, and I, were all going to meet up, R. lied to all of us. She told *him* that we were going to come meet the two of them, but told us, they were going to come to where we were at. However, R. never told us where they were, despite us both asking her multiple times. I have no doubt she lied to us because she didn't want *him* and me hanging out. I thought, *if R. could lie about this, what else was she lying about to him and me?* It was clear she was doing everything in her conniving power to try to tear us apart. Once I caught on to her lies and deceit, the closer I looked, and the more I discovered about the depths of her deception. This cut me deep considering she pretended to be my friend the entire time.

When I walked onto the volleyball court one night, R.'s eyes gave me the evilest daggers I've ever felt. It stopped me dead in my tracks and brought negative chills through my entire body. Later, the team was standing around and talking. Out of nowhere, R. whipped a ball so hard, I could feel the wind graze my face as the ball zipped by my head. I looked at her and said, "Woah!" She threw her hands up in the air, and with this insincere look on her face, replied in a very scheming voice, "Oops." I could see the hostility on her face and feel it in her voice, as it brought negative chills through my entire body. This felt intentional. I stopped going to volleyball after this because I did not want to subject myself to her threatening, aggressive behavior. Her deceitful actions caused me distress, so I considered talking to her. However, since she was lying, I felt she wouldn't be honest or admit to it. Further, I felt that letting her know I was on to her, might motivate her to retaliate and further sabotage and hurt *him* and me. It really hurts that she didn't even try to talk to me about her feelings and work through this with me in the beginning. Instead, she stooped to dishonest and conniving acts to intentionally sabotage *him* and me, while seeing the consequential conflict, drama, and pain inflicted on us. I will never comprehend how a person can do this to anyone, especially while pretending to be their friend. Now I understand what R. meant when she said she, "likes to mess with people's minds."

Unfortunately, R.'s lies and conniving behavior proved she could not be trusted and was no friend to *him* or me, so I cut her off. What is more discouraging is R. and *he* have been friends for years and someone *he* has trusted to confide in when he has girl problems. I can't help but think, she has been intentionally trying to sabotage all his relationships over the years.

I have prayed for R. to find peace and happiness, so that she doesn't feel the need to intentionally sabotage the happiness of others, especially true friends. Despite what she has done, I'm grateful for the experience. It strengthened and challenged me, while teaching me how to be two steps ahead of someone who is trying to sabotage me. It forced me to be more aware of dishonesty, deceit, and conniving behavior. It reminded me to always trust my gut about people, and to pay close attention whenever I'm feeling negative vibes. I will always be kind to R., be there if she ever needs anything, and wish her nothing but the best. While I hope one day, she will own up to what she has done, I don't expect she will. If she does, I would welcome a conversation with her, in hopes that I could inspire her to communicate her feelings before she sabotages anyone else, because after all, love conquers evil.

Both acts of sabotage caused me mental and emotional distress. While these situations were difficult and painful for me to go through, I am grateful for how I persevered, for what I learned, and the strength and grit I gained. I am further thankful for these negative situations because it led me to a newly discovered way of handling sabotage, adversity, challenges, and negative people. I now use sabotage, adversity, challenges, and negative people as motivation to do something positive and amazing!

While going through these situations, I was asked to coauthor a book about manifesting a dream. Since I had always planned to write a book— "published author," is on my vision board—I knew this was all part of my journey. I felt unbelievably honored and blessed to be a part of such an amazing opportunity. I thought, what an incredible opportunity for me to channel these negative situations into something positive and inspirational.

Since starting at Harley-Davidson, I have been acknowledged for my talent, hard work, and positive attitude. I love the vibe, culture, challenging and progressive opportunities for continued learning and growth, and cut-throat competition at Harley-Davidson. I am confident my career goals and dreams will be met there, or it will be the stepping stone to an even bigger opportunity.

No matter where I go, there will always be challenges, adversity, and people who may try to take me down. I must go through adversity to gain the grit and understanding needed to be prepared for and thrive with the most challenging people and circumstances. Each hurdle and challenging person I overcome, strengthens me, teaches me something valuable, and prepares and propels me closer to my destiny. Hurdles, heartbreak, disappointments, and grief finally propelled me to follow my dream and relocate to Tampa, Florida. However, it took me following that dream and moving away from everyone and everything I knew to truly put life into perspective, and I know now without a doubt Milwaukee is home and where I belong. It's where my heart is, where my people are, and where my career goals and personal dreams are meant to flourish.

"It is better to risk starving to death than surrender.
If you give up on your dreams, what's left?" - Jim Carrey

About Natalie

Natalie grew up in Eau Claire, Wisconsin, with her mother Linda and her twin brother, Matt. She competed as a gymnast at the club level, and for Memorial High School, where she earned an athletic award for Most Improved. Natalie also played tennis for Memorial High School, where she never lost a competitive match.

Natalie obtained her Associate's Degree in Paralegal Studies from the Chippewa Valley Technical College in 2001. From there, she relocated to Milwaukee, Wisconsin in 2001, and began her career as a Paralegal. In 2014, she obtained her Bachelor of Arts Degree in Business Administration and has spent her career in various legal roles. She also instructed gymnastics from 2015-2016, before relocating to Tampa, Florida, in 2016.

She relocated back to Milwaukee, Wisconsin, in 2017, and has been working as a contract administrator.

Natalie has passion for gymnastics, dancing, playing tennis, running, the Milwaukee Brewers, the Milwaukee Bucks, and the Wisconsin Badgers. She enjoys spending time with family and friends, traveling, running, and working out, cooking, baking, reading, writing, psychology, and the law.

"In the middle of difficulty, lies opportunity." - Albert Einstein

"We are only limited to the extent our minds dictate."
- Natalie M. Miller

"Dream without fear.
Love without limits."
- Dilip Bathija

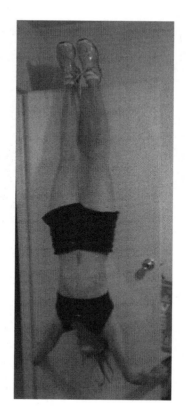

"You always gain by giving love."
- Reese Witherspoon

CHERYL THOMA

"Pay it forward, and leave a lasting footprint for others."

- Cheryl Thoma

Perseverance – Bullied Into Better

Confidence? Self-esteem? How do these characteristics develop in a person who wants to reach his or her goals...to create aspirations that are achievable?

As a young child I knew I was different; I was hesitant to make choices or decisions for fear of rejection. Today, I want to help others feel good about themselves, empowering them to achieve their goals and fulfill their dreams.

As I reflect back on my life, my first memories were of beautiful things. I remember wearing lace, ruffles, and tights...shiny shoes and pretty dresses. When I was three years old, I received one of the best gifts ever, my first dog. He was a poodle, and my mom named him PomPom because Mom did a lot of knitting. She made my sister and me matching ponchos we proudly wore with our plaid pants.

Christmas was an overwhelming yet exciting time, as we were spoiled with a surplus of toys. Dolls, board games, Slinkys, and Shrinky Dinks, just to name a few. Then, things changed. I knew my physical appearance was different from the others at my First Communion. My dress was so much shorter. I could tell I was a bit wider than most of the girls, but my veil made me feel so pretty. I loved my rosaries and Bibles I received as gifts. I already wanted to be like the nuns at school and maybe a teacher when I grew up.

Shortly after this time, other kids started asking if I lived with my grandparents, as my parents were older than the norm. They also made fun of my last name, laughing, snickering behind my back, and calling me fat. Instantly I withdrew and thought, *Why am I bigger?*

Then there was more change. It was in fourth grade when another student informed me that my parents were not my parents. *WHAT?* I felt sick to my stomach on the school bus heading home that day and I asked my mom as soon as I got inside. She explained I was adopted, as well as my sister, having different birth parents. At that time I thought, *What did that mean? Why wasn't I wanted by my real parents?* I withdrew even more as I continued to get bullied at school. My coats and boots were thrown into the trash by students who were laughing and whispering. I knew they were making fun of me. It was humiliating when I found Weight Watchers coupons in my desk, and this made me feel ugly. Physical Education class didn't help either, as I was almost always the last one chosen for any team, and the first one to get hit with that damn dodge ball. The smell of rubber to this day makes me sick.

More fear entered my world at home as Dad's drinking altered his behavior, and he became aggressive and mean. I found myself spending a lot of time outside, locked out of the house with my sister, wondering what he planned on doing to my mom…as I knew he had butcher knives and guns in there. I always tried to keep my sister busy so she wouldn't know what was going on. Scared to death to go to the neighbor's, and feeling secure under the swing set, I prayed for him to stop drinking and for Mom to be okay. Sundays were better as we went to church and sometimes stopped to feed the ducks at the convent. I often wondered, *Why couldn't we have more days like this? What could I do to feel more accepted by my dad? Why did he drink so much?*

Summers were spent in the yard alone with my sister. We couldn't have neighbor kids over because my mom feared they'd corrupt us or start trouble. I enjoyed being outside and played hopscotch and tag with my sister. I was able to ride my bike a few houses each way as long as I stayed on the sidewalk. My mom planted flowers, and we caught monarchs together. I found relief and peace in the breezy winds and the stable ground beneath my feet.

Mondays were great in the summer. I had butterflies in my stomach looking forward to that day. The simplest things brought me joy. We rode the bus downtown with Mom, and she would pay bills. On the weeks when she had a few extra dollars, we stopped at Kresge's and looked around, and sometimes I got a new toy or ice cream. That old familiar counter and stools felt as heartwarming to me as the hot fudge on my ice cream sundae with the cherry on top. I loved Mondays!

During the school year, my mom helped us with our homework making sure all was correct. In the winter, we played many board games. I still love the idea of getting together to play one.

I took guitar lessons and was asked to play at a recital in our church. I played in front of the entire school and was scared to death wondering what they thought. "My nerves are on end," Mom used to say when she took her Valium. I knew how she felt; I was so nervous and unsettled.

I wouldn't look up or make eye contact with anyone. The nuns scared me a bit, but I respected their authority. Sister said I did well, but this good feeling didn't last long.

After we got into the car, Dad started acting strange, making comments that we were going to get hurt. "They are after us," he said. We were instructed to get down on the floorboards of the back seat as he drove around winding up at the police station. Scared to death, and once again uncertain of what would happen, my father ended up giving me a knife to protect my mom and sister before he left. I don't recall much more of that evening.

Overcome with stress, we were told a few days later that Dad was in the hospital, and he was seeing snakes slithering on the walls. I didn't know it then, but he was going through detox. The arrests of DUIs (driving under the influence), possession of firearms, getting pulled over by police, had all become too much for my mom to handle. She had once again given Dad an ultimatum to quit drinking, and we safely retreated to my uncle's house…as we had done so many times before. My dad's drinking had caused psychosis, which I didn't know much about then. *Would he come back? Were we disappointing him? Did he see what he was doing? Did he care?* All of these thoughts scrambled through my mind.

When he returned home, we kept quiet as we didn't want to wake him. He got very upset and agitated when we did. I felt so inadequate and knew my mom wanted better for us all. I tried my best to achieve good grades hoping that would help. *What could I do to help my mom learn how to drive or get a job?* She said she had a job after she married Dad and worked in a factory as a secretary; however, once she adopted us she quit and gave up her life. "Putting you girls first," she would say. We were to be grateful she adopted us. In later years, she reminded me of this often. The more I grew away from her, as I connected more with friends and my first job, the more she said it.

As I continued through middle school and my early high school years, I felt so fat, and eagerly wanted to "fit in" with peers and just have friends. *What could I do to be accepted? Why didn't they like me?*

I'm not sure where I got the idea, but it started with diet pills, saran wrap, and a foil sweatsuit. I put that on and ran around the basement for hours. I felt the pounds melting off. This became a routine my first year in high school. Guess what? It actually worked too! I lost 30 to 40 pounds, and it really boosted my self-esteem. I felt more attractive and started feeling better as I received compliments. My confidence would always remain a little shaky.

Then something unexpectedly happened as I caught the attention of someone, an older man, who I thought at the time, would make me feel more valuable. All of a sudden it didn't matter what happened at home or my fear of what might happen. Now I felt whole because someone outside our household cared about me. I felt on top of the world because I saw my worth increase. Although I didn't know it at the time, this was not a healthy relationship. It was also one I could not share with others. It was a secret. It almost felt like a game. My idea of him, what I thought was reality, was actually a fairytale. I believed he was my prince, and he had come to save me. Those dreams were shattered by betrayal. *Why wasn't I good enough?* I had believed everything he said. Looking back now, this was so grandiose, but it did keep me looking ahead to the future.

Why wasn't I good enough? The question continued to arise as I continued to attract those who would bring me down.

Did I not know any differently? I wrote my feelings in this poem:

"Where Do I Fit In?"

Sweet, sweet girl
with bounces of curl,
why do you feel so alone?

They call me fat.
I feel it's a trap.
Where is this place called home?

I was given away.
Because I was a stray?
My thoughts would always roam.

For the beauty is within
which started very dim,
and grew until my spirit found its own.

I showed some interest in new activities and attempted to focus on more positive relationships. My uncle was a huge support system for me. He took me to basketball games, bowling, and the zoo. I looked forward to spending time with him and thought he was a pretty smart and cool guy. He cared and made sure I had transportation to Junior Achievement. This was my first outside involvement in a social group. The purpose was to learn how a business operates. We made cheese cutters and ice scrapers and sold our products. I found myself thriving on the challenge and opportunity to sell. I would be out in the rain knocking on doors striving to reach the sales goals I had set for myself. This was my first experience in the outside world I felt good about. It helped me feel better about myself too. Boy, was I surprised that next year when I received recognition for sales and was asked to be vice president of the group. I felt of value, and others thought so too. Wow!

I even met a boy my age. He started to visit me, and we would sit on the front porch and talk. I couldn't allow him to continue to visit though for fear he may find out how we lived.

School inspired me too, but at the time it didn't seem like much of an achievement because my mom expected me to excel. She expected me to get good grades. The nuns were very strict, and defiant behavior was swiftly corrected. I am grateful for the discipline they instilled in me to be successful in this life and for the faith I still have—*that all will happen as it is meant to be.*

I quickly learned in high school that what happened in my house didn't go on in the homes of others. My friends' moms didn't get Kool-Aid poured over their heads at mealtime because their dad said the food was cold. Other moms let their kids leave the house and have friends visit.

My mom was not happy with me the day I told her I got a job. I had to cash out a savings bond I received for my communion so I could pay for my shoes and uniform. I wasn't sure if I was doing the right thing, but my intuition told me, *Get to work and make some money for yourself.*

I was scared to death, but I was driven to buy a car and have a plan for college. Waitressing in a coffee shop, I sure learned a lot and had fun too. That scared, fat girl started to emerge from her cocoon. This however, caused much stress and turmoil at home. Verbal insults grew physical as my mother punctured her fingernails into my arms to get me to stay with her. My feelings for the older man grew as I imagined he was my prince waiting to rescue me. I was so vulnerable.

Now I know I rescued myself. *No one can love you unless you love yourself first.* This was a lifelong lesson.

As I started to make a few new friends at work, I found myself having to lie to my parents when I wanted to go out to a movie or dinner. I figured if I said I was working, I could still meet up with some friends once in a while. I was only to be gone a few nights a week and only for work or the library. Often I would say I was working when I wasn't, just to be accepted and have a friend. When the busses were done running for the day, I'd have to walk home. My dad had lost his license so many times that he quit driving and the car rusted out. We would take cabs or busses to school, work, the grocery store, and church.

I was elated when I could purchase my first car. It was a 1976 Ford Elite. My uncle helped me secure a small loan. In a month's time, one check would go towards my car payment, one for gas, one to insurance, and one for repairs…but that was okay. It was mine!

Little did I know at the time how much that car would benefit me toward my immediate future.

It was my first taste of freedom. I had to get out of that house, learn job skills, and make a life. I've been asked, "Why did you leave?" Well…for many reasons, but the final straw was when we had no working furnace and Dad couldn't afford to fix it. We had space heaters and a ton of clutter in the home. Mom had quit cleaning years ago after her parents died. Bills were piled up on TVs, stereos, tables, etc.

One of the few things I enjoyed at this time was playing records in the bedroom I shared with my sister. I started listening to Donny and Marie Osmond, and then REO Speedwagon, and Rick Springfield. Their music and lyrics inspired me to keep going. Asking myself, *What do I want to do with my life? Who do I want to become?*

Soon the pipes broke, and the water had to be turned off. Dad would fill buckets and flush the toilet every couple of days. Then the roof started leaking and caving in when it rained. Buckets collected rainwater. That wet insulation and wet carpet smell, mixed with cigarette smoke and stale beer, made me sick. *Yuck!* All personal belongings became damaged and ruined. I later was able to collect my stereo and a few records. All those games and toys I loved to play with for years were gone…ruined.

Once I moved out, that car was my best friend. I named her Betsy. I left the house with only the clothes on my back after my mom exploded one day. I snuck into friends' houses when their parents were gone just to take a shower. *What if they would have come back when I was there? How embarrassing would that be?* The hot water beating down on me felt so good but I was rushed to get out before I got caught. The mornings I could afford an egg sandwich with the extra change I had were the best sunny days for me at that time.

That car was the best investment. It not only provided transportation, but the bench seats were a comfortable place to rest my head. I lived in my car that entire summer, taking occasional relief from friends who offered an extra bed or couch from time to time. I frequented food pantries and found there were people out there wanting to help me without judgment.

One day I ran across an ad in the paper and moved into a

boarding house. *How do I pay the rent?* One job, two jobs, three jobs! As I worked to provide for myself, my confidence increased. I felt stronger and more driven. I became good friends with my roommates. My emotional side still struggled as I was continuously drawn to that man who needed to be helped or rescued, rather than surrounding myself with healthy fulfilling relationships. *How did I even know what a healthy relationship was?* I knew what I wanted, but since this was all I knew, I found myself drawn to more chaos. Anxiety was my norm. Chaos kept me motivated and driven.

My father informed me I didn't need to go to college. He said, "You'll just end up pregnant and have kids like all the other girls." I was adamant at this time that I was not going to have any children. I was not going to let that happen to me! I enrolled in college, and once again poured myself into learning. It was the one thing I felt good about and received recognition for. Fear of being rejected again kept me in punitive friendships, and even more so, relationships with men. I only knew men who had addictive personalities—gambling, drinking, and workaholics.

College years were filled with hard work and challenges with 16 credits per semester, and two part-time jobs just to get by. Living in a boarding house with other women was truly a gift. These beneficial years shaped my independence. Since I received help from so many during this time, it inspired me to pay it forward. I chose a major in which I could help others.

Once I graduated, I answered a job ad for a community social worker in mental health. I couldn't believe it. They offered me the job! I was extremely torn. I was ambivalent about moving, but in the end I decided to take the chance, accepted the job, and was on my way to helping others and living my life's purpose. Little did I know at the time, but all of my life experiences and the obstacles I struggled through made it more comfortable for me to help others.

For over eight years, I worked as a social worker, as well as working two additional part-time jobs. My school loans and credit cards bills had really piled up, and I wasn't sure what I was going to do. I was working 60 hours a week between all jobs and still not getting ahead.

A delinquent account call sent me into a debt repayment program and changed my behaviors with money. They set me up on a two-year plan and talked to creditors about agreeing to accept lower payments and eliminating interest. I had to agree to abstain from all credit cards and loans. This phone call saved me financially. I paid off my immediate debt, and it took me 13 more years to pay off my school loans. Mission accomplished, and I have never looked back.

I have great mentors to thank who I met along the way. I know I was destined to find them to show me there was more to life than working nonstop and spinning my wheels.

I depended on others so often to make me happy. I didn't give myself time to experience happiness myself. This became evident from my two failed marriages, and each time the feelings of loss created insecurity and fear again. *Why get attached? They will just leave anyway? Did I sabotage myself for failure with human relationships?* I felt overwhelming feelings of abandonment over and over again. *Did this all go back to being an adoptee?*

I worked as a social worker for 10 years, and then I made a career change into retail management and sales. I earned recognition for high volume sales and successful store audits. These achievements reminded me of ones I had during my days in Junior Achievement.

Later in life, an opportunity arose, and I was introduced to a fun home party experience with jewelry. I saw women happy with friends and getting good deals they could afford. *Could I make a business out of this? Discounts* **and** *income! Let's give it a shot!*

I was scared to do demos in front of people, but they seemed to enjoy it. It started out slow, and I questioned myself often. I was inspired by a Rick Springfield television interview; he talked about how many years it had taken him to hit number one on the charts. He had kept going and didn't give up. He had referenced the book, *Rich Dad, Poor Dad* which had inspired him. I went on to read that and many more uplifting and positive titles. These books and *The Secret* have changed my way of thinking and assisted in providing me with the positive attitude I hold dear to this day.

That part-time job grew into a full-time business empowering women to feel better, physically, emotionally, and financially. I came across women who were like-minded, inspiring, and motivating. Like attracts like and before I knew it, I was doing the same for others. This team of women I acquired was looking up to me as their leader. *What? How did this happen?* That scared, fat girl had really blossomed into teaching and sharing her passion to empower. That debt disappeared, and I was able to pay for extras. In the past, I'd have to make sure I had enough cans to return to pay for laundry. I now knew how to budget and save, and I wanted to pay it forward. I am so grateful for all I have achieved and want to share this mindset with others.

That scared, fat girl who was adopted by a family she never felt secure in, was on board for some great achievements, outstanding recognition, and certain success. *When opportunity knocks, open the door. What do you have to lose?*

This success did take a setback. After 10 years with the business I loved, the five-star trips I had earned, positive and healthy relationships I had developed, and the recognition I had received, the company chose to close. *Why? How could this happen?* This was another hit, but I was used to starting over. Anger and sadness were present, but self-growth has healed me.

I was once told life is a gift, live in the *presence* of it. The past creates depression, and the future creates anxiety. I was looking to others to make me happy all of those years. Since I now had more time on my hands, I learned to slow down and find happiness in the moment. I took time to reflect and found comfort in and with myself. I have found what it takes to form healthy relationships. The time I was gifted with has provided me clarity to know it's okay to be calm. It has given me the opportunity to be open to new ideas…I started to journal and meditate.

I have experienced how good it feels to learn about the right foods to put in my body. I take time for myself without feeling guilty. I am no longer afraid to find out who I am.

I have once again lost 40 pounds and want to help others become healthy. I now find gratitude in being grounded, meditating, the beauty of the sunrise and sunset, walking on wooded trails with my dog, and learning new and healthy ways to live and inspire others.

Healing my inner child and nourishing those insecurities has transformed me into who I am today, and I have no regrets. I have a new and fresh appreciation for life and the friendships I've had and learned from. I have an ability to recognize, *it's okay to say no, and distance myself from unhealthy toxicity.*

In years past, I would have felt bored. Now I know that feeling is peace. I had never experienced that before, and now I have learned and grown into the person I am today. My insides were so unsettled in childhood and early adulthood; I just couldn't relax. I had to keep busy so I wouldn't have time to think about things. Now, watching nature and just being at peace is who I am. That scared, fat girl who began life as an orphan, and after 25 plus years, had became one again.

My purpose now is to help others who may be in similar situations. I want to leave my mark on the world. You are the author of your own story; go out and live it! Smile, be kind, encourage, and empower others. If I can inspire one person to overcome challenges, and create a good life, I have served my purpose!

About Cheryl

Cheryl Thoma grew up in Northeast Iowa and graduated from Loras College in Dubuque with a Bachelor's Degree in Social Work. She has held many positions in the social service arena, management, and network marketing, most significantly as a division leader with Lia Sophia Jewelry.

She continues to pursue entrepreneur opportunities, coach and mentor, and has recently worked as an independent social worker. The process of writing this chapter has inspired her to do DNA testing which has led her to find closure with her adoption, and in addition, more family members.

Cheryl resides in Southeast Iowa with her companion, Steve, and golden retriever, Woodrow. Outside of helping others, she enjoys the outdoors, camping, hiking, kayaking, reading, self-growth workshops, yoga, working with dog rescues, and traveling.

You can reach Cheryl at: cheryl1anne@yahoo.com

Kayaking at sunrise...so peaceful.

Sunset on the Lake...one of my favorite places.

DEBBIE TRUNCALE

"Sometimes you have to let go of the picture of what you thought life would be like and learn to find joy in the story you are living."

\- Rachel Marie Martin

Surrendering Conditional Dreams

From as far back as I can remember, I've had immense love for two things—babies and dogs. I could not wait to be married and one day become a mom. I was blessed with our first child, a beautiful daughter. Our second child, my handsome son, and then our third child was another beautiful daughter. My children were all spaced about five years apart. I loved having each of them relatively independent before the next baby arrived. Babies, I quickly learned, are a lot of work! They are much more work than the puppies we've welcomed into our family. You never know what each baby will be like. You only have hope that what you dream about is what will be. You don't dream that your child may not be perfectly healthy or normal. That's never part of the dream. *But what if it happened?* Are you willing to surrender the conditional dream and accept the unconditional dream? There isn't a lot of discussion out there about how to handle it if your baby is born with unexpected complications. The doctors don't prepare you for this. The baby books don't prepare you for this. They only prepare you for the perfect baby and the perfect dream.

It was May 22, 1997 when our third child, a daughter, was born. I remember the beautiful full moon that night. I always think of that because she was several days early, and although it's not a scientific fact, it is believed that a full moon can cause a woman to go into labor. A full moon is always noticed as it lights up a dark night. Full moons are special, just like all babies are special; and my baby was no different.

For about the last four months of my pregnancy, I kept telling my family that something seemed "off" with this baby. She didn't move around much. I even reported this to my doctor. His response was that I was doing just fine; the baby sounded fine and was growing on schedule—all was normal. All the tests were fine. "You are just going to have a mild-mannered baby," the doctor explained. He must be right; he's the doctor. *Wow*, I thought, *how lucky will I be to have a mild-mannered baby?* In truth, I really wasn't so sure. I remember thinking as we drove to the hospital, (but not allowing myself to say it out loud), *if something is wrong with the baby, our lives will be changed forever.* What an odd thought; not about our baby, that's a usual thought but about our lives changing forever. I never thought that with my first two children. I quickly brushed fear aside, just as I had for the last few months, and prayed for a safe delivery and a healthy baby. My thoughts then changed to, *of course my baby will be healthy, and of course our family will change. I'm young and healthy, and all families change when a new baby is born...*but you know what they say about a mother's intuition? Some believe it's intuition, but I believe it was the Lord. I believe He was whispering in my ear. Not just during that moment in the car, but for the last few months—a gentle preparation of what was to come.

It was just six hours later, and our baby girl was born. Her name would be Alyssa Lee. Our family was indeed changed forever. She was born safely without complications, weighing in at a robust 8½ pounds. They whisked her right over to the warming bed to be evaluated and weighed. She wasn't in distress, but we heard the doctor tell one of the nurses that a pediatrician should perform an evaluation. The room was not filled with the usual happiness and excitement, but everyone seemed to be full of concern. My husband and I just waited and watched. I kept thinking, *How is this even possible? This can't be real.* It was such a surreal moment. My heart literally dropped to the floor. After a few minutes, they brought our new daughter to us, our beautiful baby girl. The doctor explained what he suspected…she would likely need surgery in the coming year. We needed to consult with specialists for a full evaluation as soon as possible. That fear I suspected and felt earlier in the car was suddenly staring right back at me; this was now my new reality. Our sweet baby girl was perfect, yet imperfect. We really didn't even see what they saw. We just saw our little girl. As I looked down at her, all I could do was smile. Just six hours ago in the car, I felt only fear. Now, I felt fear and unconditional love. Fear and love together are powerful. Fear is a feeling. Love is something you do. Fear alone will push you away from something. If you love something you fear, it pushes you toward it. Just a few moments after her birth, my love for her grew greater than my fear. I wouldn't let this fear of an unknown future stop me. I just knew I would love and protect her fiercely. Some refer to this as fight or flight. I call this faith. Faith is believing in the unknown and trusting the outcome.

As the months went on, it was evident that Alyssa had a complicated and complex combination of issues. She was thriving in the area of physical growth, but she was not meeting any milestones that a typical baby would make. This had no bearing on how much we loved her. She was my sunshine, my angel on Earth. I knew she had disabilities, but I didn't see them. I only saw her. Alyssa was blessed with a brother and sister who adored her and still do. They are constantly doting over her and helping take care of her. Daddy also loves her fiercely. He has told her she would always be his baby girl, and he'd take care of her forever.

Alyssa didn't talk much, but she had the biggest smile and the sweetest disposition. When she laughed, she carried the deepest belly laugh, and it made us laugh too. During the hardest time of our lives, our family thrived. The things that should have pulled us apart actually made us grow stronger as a family. We loved her, and we loved each other. We pulled together as one. I'm not saying it was always easy because that would not be true, but it takes a strength we never knew we had. We just knew that pulling apart, or taking things out on each other, would not cure or change our daughter.

More importantly we wanted to set good examples for our older kids. There was a huge lesson for them to learn, for all of us to learn, because sometimes in life—things don't go as planned. Sometimes our dreams don't turn out like we thought we wanted them to. We wanted all of our children to feel secure even on the hard days, to know we all would be fine.

I was a stay-at-home mom so at three months our daughter began to receive physical therapy services in our home. Over the next few years, we spent an enormous amount of time on in-home therapies and traveling to hospitals and specialists while trying to figure out her diagnosis and better understand her special needs. At that time and in the state we lived in, a child with special needs would transition into the public school for all therapies and other programs. It also meant that she would need to ride a school bus. To say that we were fearful is an understatement, but we knew it's what she needed, so that's what was going to happen.

It was at this time, that she needed to transition from a baby stroller into a wheelchair—*a wheelchair for my toddler? How and where do you even begin that process?* But, as with everything else in this new life, we started researching, asking, pushing, and figuring it all out. The more we learned and adjusted to this new idea, the fear disappeared, and we actually became excited. *Yes, excited about a wheelchair.* This chair was going to be her legs and her daily companion. A friend to us all—her new set of "big girl" wheels. The baby stroller or training wheels were now gone, and in its place was a hot pink and teal colored wheelchair. It was super cute and completely customized for Alyssa. When the day arrived for pickup, we pushed her into the building in a baby stroller for the last time. We headed to the fifth floor. We weaved in between people, rode the elevator, and sat patiently in the waiting room. No one paid much attention to us. Why would they, she was just a little girl in a stroller. When it was our turn, we anxiously went to the back, and there it was—our new family member. My husband picked up Alyssa from her stroller, and then he placed her into her new set of wheels. Adjustments were made, and off we went. My husband proudly pushed our daughter ahead of me as I followed behind them pushing the empty stroller. We repeated the same route. Back out to the waiting room, down the halls to the elevator, into the lobby, and finally to the parking garage. Our daughter was so happy enjoying her new ride, the same happy girl that she was a few hours ago. When we arrived back to our van and my husband lifted our daughter out of the wheelchair, I had the same thought I had the day she was born…our lives had just changed forever. Just two short hours ago we had rolled our toddler in a baby stroller through that building without anyone paying attention. We put our exact same toddler into a wheelchair, and suddenly people noticed. The looks, the quick head turns, the trying not to look, and the half looks. Though that chair was super cute, and of course so is my daughter, I knew then and there it was the wheelchair. It was the wheelchair that made them look. I assumed people would be looking at me, pushing an empty stroller. It was then that I knew, from here on out, we would be noticed. I reflected on that over the next week. I had so many different emotions to work through. The one thing that persisted was my smile every time I looked at my daughter. I loved her. I didn't care what she was sitting in. I didn't care what other people saw. She was just a little girl using a set of wheels. Once again, my love for her was greater than the fear and stigma associated with a wheelchair.

Shortly after this experience, we encountered another one. While shopping, a little girl about three years old saw us. She and her mom stopped near us and without hesitation she said, "Wow, that's a big stroller." I laughed and said, "It sure is." The curious little girl looked at it for a few seconds and then asked me why she needed a big stroller. I explained that her legs were sleeping—that even when she is awake, her legs still sleep. She thought about that, and then she simply replied, "Oh," and our conversation was over. That was all she needed to know. It made perfect sense to her. I loved that she was not afraid to ask. I also loved that she thought the wheelchair was a stroller.

Over the next week both of these stories were fresh on my mind. They both made me happy and sad at the same time. I had always enjoyed making up rhymes, songs, and little stories. I had created several for my daughter. We all enjoyed saying or singing them to her. Something about those two experiences made me once again compose a rhyme in my head. It was a kind of therapy for me in a way. It started as a little rhyme then kept growing and expanding. Before I knew it, my rhyming poem led to a rhyming story, which led to a story I scrapbooked complete with pictures. It became "her story." It became my way of letting her know that Mommy always sees her. I don't see her disabilities or her wheelchair. It's just a set of wheels, and we all use wheels to get to different places. I decided this little book would be a daily reminder that no matter where we are or what she uses to get there, she is a person like everyone else, and she is so very loved. Our family all began reading this to her over and over for years—17 years to be exact.

Over those 17 years, family kept telling me I needed to get "Alyssa's story"—my book—published. I kept wondering, *How in the world would I go about doing that?* Does anyone really know how to get a book published? Back then, we didn't have the Internet like we do today. So, like many things in life, it went on the mental "someday list." Plus, I was busy raising three kids, which in and of itself is a full-time job...along with the added work and stress involved with raising a medically fragile child. Every time I read that book (which at this point was memorized), I believed the Lord was whispering in my ear...when the time was right, I would know it. He would help me get this book, my dream for my daughter, published. I believe things always have a way of falling into place. My faith and trust in the Lord has proven this to me time and time again. Our lives changed quite a lot through those years. Our older children grew and flourished into the best people and siblings one could have. They always loved, protected, and helped us care for their special little sister. They were never embarrassed or afraid to introduce her to their friends. None of us were—her extended family included. This was Alyssa, the only way we ever knew her—the way God intended her to be. Like with any child of our own, we only see the person, not the disabilities. It's quite a unique experience to celebrate her birthday every year. Chronologically she ages, her body grows, but mentally and physically she remains a very young toddler stuck in time—stuck at the sweetest age possible. The age you always forget about. The age in which you say (but know it's not possible), I wish they would stay this age forever. It's that same feeling we get with baby animals. SO...the next time you see a family out and about with a special needs child, don't feel sorry for them. Think about how lucky they are to have a love like that.

It wasn't until she was 13 years old and through extensive genetic testing, we finally learned her exact diagnosis. And we definitely learned the meaning of faith, patience, and believing that when something is meant to be, it will be. Finding out was important to her physicians and for her health (which had become fragile), but we really didn't find the name of her diagnosis important to us. Her name was what we named her...beautiful Alyssa.

The diagnosis is what she has, not who she is.

It was also during those years that we moved 900 miles away from all of our family, friends, and the secure life we had always known. We did this for a number of reasons but mostly for our daughter's needs. At that time, I wasn't a fan of joining social media, but because we were away from our family and friends, I decided I needed to. It really was a great way to keep in touch regularly with family and friends. It also opened the doors and possibilities to meet new friends. I discovered some great groups, especially the special needs support groups, dog lover groups, and a group for a particular 1980s rock star and a soap star who I had enjoyed watching since I was a teen. He had just visited our city and performed in concert shortly before I joined. Often in these groups, I would see the same names pop up. I started to feel a connection to these people, like real friendships. There was this one particular person in our group who had just announced she was about to have her very first children's book published. How exciting! I could totally relate to her story of how this book came to be. It too was written from a personal experience with her daughters—an experience very different from mine, but still she felt the passion to write it down and pursue this dream. For the next six years I watched as she then published her second and her third children's books. I wanted to reach out to her, but I was apprehensive, nervous, and frankly not sure I even had the energy. Anyone who is a caretaker knows how much it drains every aspect of your life. It's like having two full-time jobs. However, I also knew this was a permanent situation. I had waited this long, and life was not going to get easier. The more I saw her excitement with each book, the more I felt a nagging about my own book idea and the exciting possibilities. I began to think about this a lot, and I began to hear the Lord whispering in my ear that it was time. I was trying to get up the courage to message her and kept putting it off. Then one weekend as I sat on my back porch, I read one of her Facebook posts. She was offering to assist anyone who may have a story of their own to publish. I had to reread her post a few times to let it penetrate into my head. I literally felt like the Lord dropped this in my lap. Not just a whisper but a loud and clear voice shouting, *It's time!* All those years ago, pre-social media days, I had no idea how to or who to go to for help, and here it finally was, my answer, my invitation to transform my dream into reality. I knew I had to message her. So, without waiting and any further hesitation, I sent her a private message. She was thrilled! We set up a time to talk about my book, and she helped me navigate through the world of publishing. We talked about how my book idea began. I shared with her my experiences over these last 17 years. I sent her a copy of my scrapbook, and she instantly agreed that this was a little book that should be published. Much to my relief and excitement she agreed to speak with her publisher and arranged a meeting with him. Nervous was now an understatement. As I waited to hear from the publisher, I thought about our journey to get to this point. It was then that I began to really understand why the process of waiting so long was a benefit.

There were so many other layers to living this life with a special needs child. We still have many more to go, but we feel well equipped and experienced at this point in our journey. We all changed in so many ways…but all in good ways. I believe the Lord knew back then that my message was from a raw and emotional time, I'd only just begun to understand. It was now that I was able to expand on my book and its message through all of these years and so many more experiences. There was also a very important character that was added to this book. I can't even imagine this book without her. This was another sign that things are meant to be, when they are meant to be. Sometimes the Lord's whispers are soft and quiet and other times they are loud and clear. So, now with much anticipation, it's time for the characters in this book of mine to come to life—time to leave our home and our family and become a part of other families.

After the publisher was in place, the illustration process began.

I had a few choices. Once the illustrator was chosen, the contracts were in place, and we were ready to begin. Waiting for that first picture was so exciting. It felt like the first time you see your baby on a sonogram. You get that first glimpse and know that baby is a real living and breathing, beautiful life inside you. You also learn that it will be a slow growing process. It takes time to bring your words to life. In my case it was going much slower than normal. I kept telling myself to be patient. Finally, for various reasons, my publisher and I agreed it was unlikely my original illustrator would be able to complete my book. Part of me was relieved and I didn't know why because this meant finding a new illustrator, and I would be starting all over again. But I felt complete peace and was ready to begin again. Once again, and without any doubt, that was the Lord whispering in my ear. This turn of events was His plan and in His timing. He was so right.

It didn't take long to find a new illustrator. We instantly connected. He had an excitement from reading my book that brought all of these months of waiting full circle. He had so many wonderful and unique ideas to make my children's book the best that it could be. It became very clear the Lord placed roadblocks in our way over the last year for a reason. My book was to be drawn by a completely different artist. I waited 17 years to make this happen, so I knew that one more year was His plan all along.

We cannot wait to share our message through the words and illustrations in my children's book. It has had quite a journey from its little beginnings—just like the lives we live. We grow and change. We dream and hope. We love and fear, but through it all we ultimately rely on faith to walk through life. We each have our own story and journey, one that makes us all special. So now it's time to give our daughter a voice and show you who we see when we look at her.

My book is titled, *Who Do You See...When You See...Me?* My little scrapbook story grew up, and it's ready to leave my hands and be held in the hands of so many children and adults. It's a big dream come true for me. Dreams, whether big or small, can come true if you believe in yourself and in your dream. Take that very first step past fear. Let the love of your dream be bigger than your fear.

About Debbie

Debbie Truncale is an author, wife, and the mother of three children. She is also a full-time caregiver to her youngest child with complex special needs. This life requires so much on-the-job training, while continuously switching hats throughout the 24-hour day.

Debbie was privileged to have been a stay-at-home mother to her three kids Amanda, Nathan, and Alyssa. Debbie's youngest daughter Alyssa, now an adult, was born with multiple special needs. She requires 100 percent care on a daily basis. Debbie has devoted her life to caring for Alyssa in their home. Alyssa's sweet and docile disposition brings the entire family so much joy. She has taught them the real meaning of unconditional love.

Debbie has written a new children's book that is currently in illustration. This book was written for Alyssa many years ago. As time went on Debbie knew it had a very important message for not only kids, but for adults as well. She hopes it will instill in its readers a different way to look at wheelchairs and the people sitting in them. She also hopes it will help kids and parents feel more comfortable knowing what to do or say when they encounter a disabled person.

Included in Debbie's book is one of the family's dogs, Ember, an airedale terrier. She is funny, mischievous, and smart, but most importantly she loves Alyssa unconditionally. Debbie believes animals can be very therapeutic to so many. This is a beautifully illustrated book with an unforgettable message.

For more information on Debbie's children's book, please contact her at debbietruncale@gmail.com or follow her Facebook page: *Who Do You see...When You See...ME?*

A seat is a seat to our Ember.

Alyssa's contagious smile started young.

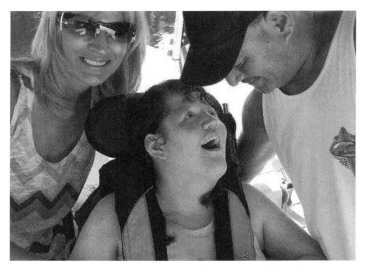

Our angel on Earth with Mom and Dad.

My scrapbook turned into a real book.

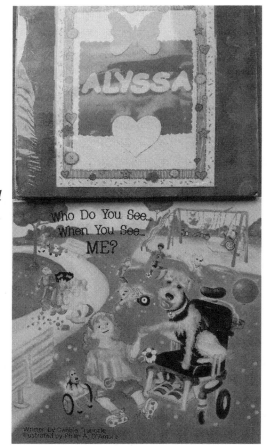

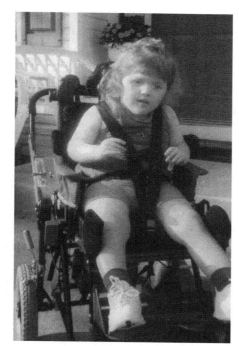

Alyssa's first wheelchair.

Sibling love!
Nathaniel, Alyssa, and Amanda.

SHARON MANIACI

"Scars remind us where we've been. They don't have to dictate where we're going."

– David Rossi
(Criminal Minds)

Surviving Life's Challenges

Everyone has a way of coping and adjusting to the day-to-day challenges life throws at us. When I was younger and wasn't getting my way about something, I would often say to my mom or dad, "That's not fair!" to which their reply was always the standard "Life isn't fair." How right they were.

I guess I can say I have been a survivor literally since birth. I was born February 13, 1970 (a Friday no less), and my due date was not until April 28. I weighed a mere four pounds and was hooked up to tubes, wires, and needles for quite some time. I was so premature, that my body still had the lanugo (soft thin hair found on a fetus or newborn baby) on it. When I was finally ready to go home, my older sister told my mother that she wanted a baby pig, not a baby monkey.

My first Easter dress was a yellow doll's dress, and growing up I was always very thin and as you may have guessed…short. I ended up back in the hospital with pneumonia and my weight dropped to only two pounds. As a premie in 1970, I probably should not have survived, especially given the fact that medical technology was not as advanced as it is today. But, I did survive—because even then I was a fighter and determined to prove everyone wrong.

I never let my small size and low weight deter me from achieving anything. If I wanted to try it, I did. I am sure I gave my parents their fair share of gray hairs, but they never discouraged me from doing something I wanted. I have never been the type of person who would listen to someone tell me, "You can't do that." I would just reply, "Watch me!" That's not to say I haven't suffered a few bumps, bruises, and even a couple of broken bones along the way, but I kept going. I played softball for a very long time and much to the dismay of my parents, who only encouraged me and never let me see their fears, I became a catcher on the team. The equipment weighed more than me, but I still did it, and I was good at it. I caught for my youth softball team for 10 years, so naturally I tried out for my high school softball team; I wanted to play catcher. That isn't the position I was given. I was now an outfielder and while I had a great arm to throw the ball back to the infield, I dropped balls. It wasn't my natural place or the position I was used to. I was a catcher.

One day during practice, while I was retrieving a pop fly from deep centerfield, the ball had rolled into the football field where the team was practicing. They stopped practice when I approached their field. I wanted to quickly get out of the way, so I picked up the ball and threw it to the pitcher. The ball never hit the ground; I purposely missed the cut off person and trotted my way back to my outfield position. As I headed back, I heard some of my friends on the football team talking about the "gun of an arm she has." Later, after both practices were over, Coach Hoekel, the freshman football coach, told me they still needed a quarterback and asked me if I would like to try out for the team. I said, "Yes!" I immediately told my parents when I got home that day. Mom was none too thrilled, as her now 95 pound, 4-foot-11 premie wanted to play football. Neither of my parents said no, but they made their concerns to me known. Over the next few days, news made it around school (and the town too since it was such a small community). There was both support and some pushback.

The next week, Mom stopped at school for something, and a group of guys on the team told her how excited they were for me to try out. They reassured her, "Don't worry Mrs. Maniaci, we will protect her." She didn't know why I would need protecting, since all I had to do was stand there and throw the ball (she didn't really know much about football). One of my teachers, who was also a coach on the team was not very happy about the prospect of a girl playing a "boy's" sport. He started asking my mom if she was really going to let me play, if I knew how much negative attention this would get from the school, the town, other parents, etc. Like I said, she wasn't thrilled with my decision, but became more supportive when this teacher told her that girls didn't belong in sports that boys play. She informed him that now she would make sure she did everything possible to support me. He then asked her if she knew what the position of a quarterback did? She replied...she knew all I had to do was throw the ball and the other players would protect me. He then explained that the reason I had to be protected was because 11 players from the other side would be trying to take that ball from me and tackle me to keep me from throwing or handing it to my own players. That was the end of my budding football career. I did however become a team manager and kept stats for the games.

I didn't play softball after my freshman year, but I did become a member of our student council. It wasn't very exciting, but I was still involved in activities. I was not a very big fan of school, and I struggled with my grades, especially math but I muddled through the teasing and name calling that was hurled my way. Bullying isn't anything new today; it's just more noticeable and more relentless due to social media. When I went to school, students didn't have the capability of tweeting or posting on Facebook; we passed notes or slipped things in the lockers. Some people were extremely blatant about their actions and words. During my sophomore year, I had gained quite a bit of weight but managed to lose it the summer between then and my junior year. I went to dances with groups of friends and didn't date any of the guys I went to school with. Most of them were like brothers to me, and we had great friendships. I don't think I was "girlfriend material." I had three very good friends I had known for years, and to this day I still count them as great friends. These are the kinds of friends you can go long periods of time without having contact with, but the moment you do it's as though time has not passed.

I started looking at colleges my junior year and had made

251

an appointment with my guidance counselor to help me with applications. I researched information from some schools in the area, and the only out-of-state school I looked at was West Point Military Academy. When I met with the counselor, and she saw the schools I was looking at, she did absolutely nothing to help me. She looked through the brochures and said to me, "I'm sorry, but I cannot help you. I think you should just go apply for a job at McDonald's or stick with your job at the grocery store, because you are just not smart enough to attend college, especially West Point. You just aren't college material. There is a new community college, maybe you could get a general degree from there."

My heart sank. It was the day I stopped trying as far as academics were concerned. I had also been told by an AP (advanced placement) history teacher that he would not let me in his class because I wasn't smart enough. Two art teachers told me they would not help me put a portfolio together for schools because my art and photography was just not good enough. These were adults, teachers, and guidance counselors who were supposed to be helping and encouraging me to grow. I thought all of that had ended when I was in sixth grade. I had a handful of good teachers the last two years, and my senior year was my favorite. My English class was the best. I was in class with an amazing group of people, and the teacher was just as wonderful. I keep a journal and a planner to this day because of him. When we had to do a writing assignment, his advice was always the same, "Write your papers the way women should wear their skirts…long enough to cover the subject, but short enough to make it interesting." When I was older, I ran into him and he offered another piece of advice, which came from Hemmingway, "Write Drunk. Edit Sober." (*I am completely sober at this moment*).

My senior year was not perfect. A new student, a good-looking guy from Texas, walked into my English class. I struck up conversations with him, and he soon came over to my house for dinner and to hang out. One night, as he left, I walked him to his car, and we sat inside the car since it was a cool night. We started kissing, and it suddenly took a turn for the worse. He became very aggressive, and in moments he had me in a headlock. Out of the corner of my eye, I could see the front porch light flashing on and off, which meant it was time for me to go inside. Through the tears and not being able to breathe, I said to him if I didn't go inside soon, my dad would come out. That was the only thing that saved me from being raped by him that night. I didn't tell my parents what happened until many years later. He came into the grocery store where I worked one time, and before I could leave the cash register and have someone else take my lane, he made it up to me and told me if I ever said anything about what happened that night, he would hurt my younger sister. So of course I never said a word. To this day, if I smell that same cologne, I stop in my tracks and look around to make sure he isn't there. A few years ago, I searched public records and discovered he had more than one conviction in Missouri and in Illinois for sex offenses and, of course, is a registered sex offender.

After graduation, I did attend that community college, and I have on several occasions advised high school students to consider attending a two-year college before transferring to a four-year school. I don't encourage this because they aren't smart enough or are not college material; I encourage this choice because it's the best way to get the general courses out of the way and gain those credits, and then transfer to a school that offers their major. Plus it's also more affordable, and if they are undecided, it gives them a chance to figure out what calls to them. I didn't have that type of advice from my guidance counselor, and once again, I plugged along. I achieved my associate degree and met a guy in one of my classes who I dated for four years. He had wanted to join the Army at one point, but was turned down due to an open-heart surgery he had when he was a child. His next plan was to join the St. Louis Metropolitan Police Department. As I helped him study for the written portion of the test, I began thinking of joining the department as well. I changed my major in college from education to criminal justice, and aside from certain classes, my grades jumped up a little, but not enough. When I entered the four-year college, I was told I needed a 2.0 to graduate and, in my mind, I still wasn't college material, so I did the bare minimum to get by. During this time, I told my boyfriend I wanted to study for the police academy exam to which he replied, "If you do, and you join the department, I will break up with you." Given my history of proving people wrong, you would have thought I would have acquired better grades, and I would have told him to, "Stick it!" But I didn't. I stopped the process, and my grades diminished to barely passing.

Months later, he broke up with me, I was fired from my job at the grocery store, and my life seemed to just go down the drain. I was devastated. I lost 25 pounds in a matter of two weeks, and those were 25 pounds I couldn't afford to lose, especially since I only weighed 120 pounds. I cried all the time, and there was nothing my friends and family could do to console me. One day, I became eerily calm, and started to walk out the door and do something I would have never been able to take back. My mom was sitting at the kitchen table and asked me where I was going and what I was doing. I told her, and she said to me, "Sharon Christine, you have been a fighter and survivor since birth. You have never let anyone, including your father and I, tell you what you could or couldn't do. Are you really going to let these circumstances break you? If you walk out that door and do what you are planning on doing, you will never get on the police department."

The very next day, I got up, showered, got dressed, and my mom and I went down to the police department headquarters to pick up an application. I worked at a department store with one of my best friends while waiting to hear about my application. In December of 1993, I received a letter stating everything I needed to prepare for my January 1994 academy start date. I only had one semester left, one class, before I graduated with my (first) bachelor's degree; however, the academy was a full-time job, and they wanted it to be our only focus. My college degree was on hold. In my mind that was okay because I had already been put on academic probation once. My grade point average was just under the 2.0 minimum needed for graduation.

I was so excited to start the academy, until I realized it was like high school, only the students were adults. The worst part I realized was that these people were going to be protecting other citizens in the city. In a class of 47, there were only seven women, and we lost one to an injury just a week before graduation. It saddened me because she was the only other woman in our class I had a connection with. Once again, I had made friends with the men more quickly than I did with the women. One woman set her sights on me and harassed me daily; she made it her mission to make me cry. I put my head down one more time and made it through.

I have never been a runner, so the running aspect of the academy proved to be the hardest for me. I received decent grades in the courses but by no means excelled to the top of the class. The day we took our final physical fitness test, which included 1½ mile run in 13 minutes or less, I heard the voices of all of those teachers, all of the adults who told me—*I couldn't because I wasn't smart enough or good enough*—all of the classmates and academy mates who picked on me in one way or another; these voices fueled me. They fueled my desire and determination to prove that yes, I absolutely can! I was the last one to complete the run, just under the time demanded of us. There I saw the one woman who had consistently harassed and picked on me as she waited for me to cross the finish line.

After graduation, I was assigned to the district that had the highest homicide rate in the City of St. Louis. I heard fellow coworkers call it "The Bloody 5th" and "Little Beirut." Despite leadership by a training officer, who was not exactly ethical and expected me to be the same way, I absolutely loved my job. It was the first time in a very long time that I felt as though I was good at something. But because I would not "fall in line" with the activities of my training officer, I was almost fired, and when that didn't happen, he told everyone I could not be trusted, and I didn't back other officers. In the police world, that is almost a fate worse than death. It elevated to the point where some of the criminals and gangbangers looked out for me more than some officers. I still loved my job. I would not have changed it for the world. I had some amazing partners after training and will never forget the lessons they taught me.

I was then transferred to a different district and began working the downtown portion of St. Louis. Eventually I was assigned to the downtown footbeat and had two more wonderful partners. After a while I was transferred back to the 4th District (downtown) and rode solo. My sargeant was not a pleasant woman, and she continuously preached to me...I was a woman in a man's job...I needed to act a certain way. She had to prove herself, and I would have to do the same. I became very discouraged with my job and life in general. I had been dating a police officer from a different district and unbeknownst to me, he was dating another woman who he eventually married. One day after roll call, I went to retrieve my radio and an officer on desk duty told me I needed to switch to night tours. I asked him if he thought it was so great, why was he on days? He had just had surgery, and it was the swing shift that needed the help.

During the time he was on desk duty, we became friends, and eventually, we started hanging out after work as well. Our friendship turned into a physical relationship, despite the fact he was married. It was also during this time he started talking to me about moving to the night shift. I have never been a night owl. I can fall asleep on my couch the minute I lay my head down to watch a movie. But swing shift events finally swayed my decision to request the night shift. What an AMAZING difference it was. I worked for one of the best sergeants and lieutenants, and our squad was bar none. I loved working the night shift with everyone in the 4th District.

We would frequently go out after work to a bar called Area IV (it was a play on the way our districts were divided up; I worked in Area II Command). They were open early in the morning, so the night shift people could unwind as well. One day after work, the man I was involved with and I, along with another group of people, met at Area IV. I was tired, only had one drink, and something to eat. I was nursing my second drink when I excused myself to the ladies' room. When I came back, my car keys were missing and there was a fresh drink in front of me. I remember my *friend* told me to finish my drink, and we'd go back to his house after a stop at the grocery store. That is all I remembered…until almost 20 years later.

In 2013, I started having haunting nightmares, very vivid, as though I was cast as a character but playing the part in my own life. It was at this time I remembered what had happened that early morning. I had started to recover memories of a rape that was perpetrated by my *friend* and another police officer. Between being drugged that day and the trauma that occurred, my mind completely hid that part of my life in a box and sealed it into my subconscious until I was ready to grip its reality.

I don't know that I ever was ready to handle that kind of information, but I had. I've spent multiple occasions going back and forth to St. Louis, the first time to file criminal charges, do the photo lineup, and interview with the Sex Crimes Unit. It was a very daunting experience and had it not been for my family, especially my younger sister and my best friend traveling with me to the police department, I would not have made it through. I was in therapy at the time, which was helpful to a point, but I have always found myself leaning on the people who have been there from the beginning of my life as I remember. As I went through this process, I learned a lot not only about myself, but about those who I thought I could trust and believe in. The police department sadly, was no help. Part of this was their own doing and some was out of their control. Criminal charges could not be filed due to the statute of limitations on rape at the time of the incident. In 1996, the statute of limitations from 1995-1997 was three years. This means I would have had to have remembered by 1999, and I didn't.

When the detective called and told me this news, I was in my car and ready to meet my mom and dad for lunch. I sat at the wheel and sobbed. I sobbed until I had no more tears. Yet again, I pulled myself together and I got out of the car and enjoyed the day with my parents. When I returned home to Virginia, I discussed it with my then husband, and I attempted to file civil charges against both perpetrators. The second law firm I visited was fantastic and explained all the ins and outs of what would happen. They were very thorough in their explanation, and then the one partner in the firm explained to me that even if I won and was awarded a monetary settlement, both men could counter sue me for defamation of character. I had until July of that year to decide, and they would be more than happy to represent me. He asked if I didn't go through with it, what was I hoping would come out of it all? I told him I would want an apology from both men, in front of their wives in that office. He asked if I would be willing to sign a non-disclosure agreement, meaning I could never speak of it again and could not mention their names. I turned that down. My older sister was with me that day, and when I walked out of the conference room she saw the disgusted look on my face and the tears pouring out of my eyes. This time they were not tears of sadness but anger. I was angry I went through that trauma brought on by people I had trusted, angry at the justice system for failing me, and angry that after everything those two men had put me through, they would have been given the opportunity to traumatize me all over again.

As we left the city, my fictional book, in which I changed their names to protect the not-so -innocent, and of course, me, was already forming in my head. THIS was my survival; it was my justice.

When I went back to Virginia yet again, I went to my therapist and cried until I couldn't cry anymore and then made plans to start a support group for anyone who wanted to attend. Not just for people who had been through some sort of trauma like I had, but for anyone who was struggling with life events. "Life isn't fair." I could hear my mom's words ringing in my head, but I was going to do whatever I could to find peace and justice for myself and others.

Since that year, I have been surviving those memories, and have put them down on paper. Remember that woman from the police academy who picked on me so badly? Her name is Elizabeth Powell, and almost 20 years to the day of our academy graduation, I had lunch with her on one of my visits to St. Louis. We have reconnected and have been best friends ever since. She too was instrumental in my ongoing healing process. In 2015, I met an amazing group of people at a Rick Springfield fan event in Florida, including a woman who is more than my best friend. Tamie Price has become an invaluable part of my life, and I am convinced that somewhere, in a past life, we were sisters. I believe we just happened to meet again in this lifetime…call it good karma.

To those teachers and the guidance counselor who told me I was too stupid to go to college, wasn't college material, and I should just work at McDonald's for the rest of my life (which I am not discounting in any way—ironically, I did work at McDonald's for a week, and it was not easy work): I currently hold an associate degree, two bachelor's degrees, one of which is with honors in anthropology, and I'm completing my master's degree thesis for which I graduated with honors in forensic science.

At this very moment I am going through a separation and divorce, and like many times before, I would not make it through without the support of my friends and family. There are events that have taken place in the last year that made me question again whether I wanted to even be part of the living. I was thinking of all the ways I could part from this world and then all the reasons why I wouldn't do them (mainly I was too lazy…haha). As I was going through this list in my head, I heard the logic from the two people I told I was feeling this way, and I thought of how it would affect others in my life. I stopped for a moment and realized some very important, selfish reasons to stay here. I would have proven all those naysayers right, and I am just too stubborn for that, and most importantly—I have been a fighter and survivor since birth and the degree of the fight has varied and still varies depending on the situation. It is not without the love and support of so many around me that I have made it through all of my fights, battles and wars…I have learned that not only is it okay to ask for help, it is imperative. Lean on the people in your life. They cannot fix things for you, but everyone gives snippets of tools to use to build that support system.

About Sharon

Sharon C. Maniaci was born and raised in St. Louis, Missouri. She was raised in a small town west of the city and moved back to St. Louis when she joined the St. Louis Metropolitan Police Department. Sharon served on the police department for four years, and in 1998, she moved to San Diego with her husband. In October of 2000, they were relocated to Hampton, Virginia. In addition to obtaining a second Bachelor's Degree in Anthropology and a Master's Degree in Forensic Science, Sharon fosters kittens for a private not-for-profit organization and the local animal shelter. Most recently, Sharon accepted a position with St. Louis County Health where she will be working for the Office of the Chief Medical Examiner as a Forensic Death Investigator.

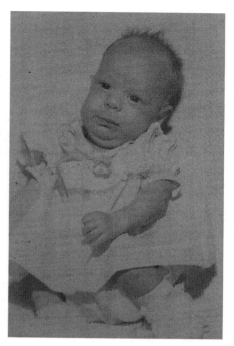

*May, 1970, my 3 month photo
(wearing a doll dress because
it was all that would fit me).*

*1996 St. Louis Police
Department studio photo.*

Me with my Georgie Girl.

Taking Jefferson Kitty home to Virginia. He rode like this most of the way from St. Louis to Virginia.

Jasper "Jazz" doing his favorite thing.

KRISTI ALLEN

The meaning of life is to find your gift. The purpose of life is to give it away.

\- Pablo Picasso

Rock Star Wishes and Crochet Dreams

When I was 10 years old, I had two gigantic dreams. The first was to meet Rick Springfield. The second was to learn to crochet. What I had not realized at that young age was how both of these dreams would intertwine throughout my life.

My Great-Aunt Margaret initially piqued my interest in crocheting. I had been an admirer of Aunt Margaret's beautiful afghan work while growing up. She would create very elaborate afghans in no time at all. Her crochet hook would easily pull at the yarn thread, and then go through many loops and turns before one shell stitch would be completed. She had quite the skill set, and what was even more fascinating was her creative process. She would watch *Days of our Lives* and carry on conversations with family at the same time while quickly crocheting those same shell stitches, without even looking at her work and without any evident mistakes. I was in such awe.

When I finally felt comfortable enough with the knowledge my aunt and my mom (who was also a bit of a crocheter) had gifted me with, I began to experiment with some scrap yarn myself. My mom taught me a basic chain stitch with one of her hooks. I then learned "how to" start a second row. It was at that time I also learned something "magical"—how to pull every single stitch out and start over from scratch. *(Insert sarcasm here.)* I was not crocheting like Aunt Margaret; I was not even close.

In those early years, I would put Rick Springfield's latest album on my record player, grab a skein of whatever yarn I had, as well as my gold crochet hook, and just crochet away. I was simultaneously frustrated and thrilled at the discoveries I made as I learned. It was never easy trying to determine my strengths, yet at the same time I found more weaknesses than I cared to admit. Yet, I pushed myself and continued to muddle through this creative process each and every time a crochet hook was in my hands.

One day, not far into my teenage years, while my record player blasted Rick Springfield's huge hit, "Don't Talk to Strangers," I had an epiphany. I could not explain it, but it was like my mind somehow conformed to my crocheting knowledge. I tried it again, really taking the time to concentrate and focus on what I needed to do, and it finally clicked. I crocheted something that looked decent. It was only two or three rows, but it was uniform, and I felt so proud of myself. Finally, I was making progress.

I completed a zigzag-patterned afghan not too long after my epiphany, and after I finished it, I realized just how hard my Aunt Margaret had worked on all of her projects. I could not believe how much effort went into crafting something that elaborate until I did it myself. As much as I thought my great-aunt's work was beautiful and detailed, I knew that wasn't the right choice for me. I wanted something that was uniquely my own.

Despite being a novice at this hobby, I started having visions of crocheted stuffed animals. I could actually describe in exact detail what they looked like, their size, and approximate dimensions. The visions were so vivid. I never understood why this happened to me, but it did. I'd like to believe there was some heavenly intervention steering me toward my crocheting goals. What I failed to realize, at this young age, was that these visions were going to be the blueprints of what would become my life's work.

I wanted to see if I could replicate what was in my mind. I felt so inspired to try. I was able to put my unique skills to use, and I crocheted a teddy bear. I was so happy to finish it, but I was NOT as impressed as I thought I'd be. The bear was crocheted with a bright, yet burnt orange yarn, sewn-on black and gray large button eyes, and a tiny white button nose, with an extremely crooked crocheted lilac mouth, and white stuffing sticking out all over due to my very loose crochet stitches. It was the saddest, strangest, homeliest yarn creature you could imagine! It still haunts me in my dreams. You definitely could tell it was a bear, but it seemed so square and full of harder edges. I wanted something more rounded, softer, for the completed animal.

I tried so many times after that, unsuccessfully, to sync my mind's eye with what my hands composed. Imagine having an elaborate symphony in your head, only to realize you can't write sheet music or don't even know where to start. Even though I had the tools at my disposal, I was at a loss. My mind was always three steps ahead of what my hands could do. Despite the numerous obstacles, I challenged myself, and never once gave up.

Several months after "the teddy bear incident," I had yet another vision. I couldn't explain why, but I saw a crocheted dalmatian dog in my mind. It was bigger, rounded, and so full of stuffing. Once again though, I was at the mercy of having an incredibly detailed vision with a very limited skill set. I thought if I had already come this far, it was worth a shot to try it again, only this time, I would approach it much differently.

I had first learned how to crochet in straight lines, back and forth, but I felt this was not the right approach for a stuffed animal. I picked up my crochet hook and yarn yet again, and basically taught myself how to crochet in a circle. After seeing the completed circle in my hands, I thought to myself: *Why didn't I try this years ago?!* Once I conquered crocheting the circle, I could expand from it, crochet it further, and form it into a piece for the middle part of the body. Then I started the next piece, the animal's head. I attached the head to the body. Next came the legs, the tail, and the ears. I channeled all of my effort and energy from my vision and actually completed the dog. I was sixteen years old, and I did it. Finally!

For the first time ever, the vision closely resembled what my hands had produced. I had, many frustrating years later, finally crocheted one right. In those moments, holding the completed crocheted dog in my hands, I knew that not only had I found my formula, I had also found my calling.

I never anticipated these stuffed creatures (which my mom sweetly dubbed "Kritters") would be seen by anyone outside of my own family. The dalmatian Kritter, prominently displayed on my grandmother's sofa for a long time, became a conversation piece for all who entered her apartment. This dog Kritter I had crocheted for her had brought smiles and joy to everyone who saw it, and it also put my work, and my calling, in demand. My grandmother took orders from people who also wanted me to make them one too! This was something I never expected in my wildest dreams.

As I approached adulthood, I carried my Rick Springfield fandom with me. Around the late 1990s, I located a chat room on his website and met some great people. I had fun talking to my newfound friends and decided to disclose to them my interest in crocheting. I had decided to crochet my new friends, black and white dogs made to resemble Rick's black and white bull terrier, Ron, the canine star of Rick's album, *Working Class Dog*. In giving my new friends these special Kritters, I found a novel way to bring two things I love together. Although the happiness for me came in doing something nice for others, it was wonderful to hear how happy one of my Kritters made a fellow fan. One of Rick Springfield's lyrics states simply, "Every little bit of love I give to another, you know what I believe? It comes back to me." I do believe that.

After much encouragement from my new chat room friends, I decided to crochet Rick Springfield a Kritter and somehow get it to him during one of his concerts I would attend. I crocheted him a dog to resemble another one of his dogs, Scooby, from his 1998 CD, *Karma*. I took this Kritter with me to a 2001 concert in Columbus, Ohio. Luckily, midway through his concert, I got close enough to the stage to throw the "Scooby Kritter" up to him, and it landed within inches of his feet. I couldn't throw to save my life before those moments! (Again, another moment in my life I chalk up to heavenly intervention!)

Rick had stopped playing his guitar when he saw the Kritter, picked it up, and asked the crowd who had made it. I think he could tell by my craziness, jumping up and down, and yelling, "ME!!!" It was indeed yours truly who crafted his cute canine. Rick smiled, held it up for the crowd to see and announced to everyone, "This is my dog, Scooby!" And he looked right at me, smiled again, and said, "Thank you!" That was the first moment I ever *talked* to my hero, and it touched me so deeply. It was brief, yes, but that moment in time stood still for me. I still remember it to this very day.

But it didn't stop there. When Rick performed in Branson, Missouri, in 2003, I crocheted Kritters that looked like Rick's dog Ron, and I dressed them to resemble each musician in his band at that time. Try to picture how funny that looked, me carrying all these stuffed, crocheted Kritters in my arms at the venue. At one point during the Branson show, Rick saw them, and he motioned me over to him. I presented the armload of Kritters to him while he was out in the audience during the concert. He then spoke to me, and asked why I had so many of the crocheted animals with me. When I told him why, he said, telling the crowd through his microphone headset, "She said she crocheted a dog for me, and one for each of the guys in the band!" He then proceeded to introduce each band member to the audience, one by one, and then threw their dog Kritter up on stage. The Kritters were a big hit at that show and generated plenty of laughs and smiles which had been my ultimate goal. And…I had an actual conversation with Rick this time! *WOW!*

On another occasion, I crafted "Scooby Kritters" that resembled Rick and the band (much like the ones in Branson but using Rick's dog Scooby as the template that time). I took the Kritters with me to a concert in Cleveland, Ohio, in 2004. Heavenly intervention occurred yet again, in bucket loads that night, as not only did I get the "Scooby Kritters" to Rick and the band during that show, but I got the thrill of a lifetime when Rick came to my seat, handed me the microphone, and asked me to sing part of his hit song, "Don't Talk to Strangers." I didn't know how loud I would be, once I had the microphone in hand. I summoned all of my courage, strength, and energy, and I belted it out. I probably should mention that not only do I think I overdid it because he jumped back about 10 feet when it happened, but I am completely tone deaf. Rick Springfield, the comedian, told the crowd of many that night after my singing debut, "It's a good thing you crochet better than you sing!" He couldn't have said it any better.

Another instance where I am convinced I had divine heavenly intervention in my life is when I met "Lynnie" (name changed) at a Rick Springfield concert in Columbus, Ohio, in 2003. She lives in another state, but that didn't stop us from becoming fast friends.

One day, months after the Columbus concert, we discussed meeting up at another concert. Lynnie asked me if I was ready to meet Rick? As she had already known from our many discussions, I had never met Rick before, but I said I was always ready for that. But then she said, "No, I mean, *when* you meet him in *a few months*. I'm giving you a backstage pass!"

Truth be told, I am pretty sure, right in that moment, I screamed for a good, solid five minutes. You should have seen the looks I got from my coworkers when I read that email!

So when Lynnie told me all of this in her email, that she was going to donate that coveted backstage pass to me to meet the one and only Rick Springfield, a pass that she won in an online contest, I really thought she was crazy! *How in the world would she be able to part with that "Golden Ticket," and why was she willing to give it to me, of all people?* She insisted I take it, her reason being that I never met with Rick one-on-one, and it was "my time." I couldn't believe her generosity. And even to this day, I thank God for what she did for me. Without Lynnie, and her selfless act, I can guarantee that I'd still be dreaming about meeting Rick Springfield at that time in my life.

Prior to meeting Rick that summer night, I kept thinking about everything I wanted to say to him, how his music was always there for me, motivating and inspiring me, taking me to creative heights I never fathomed. Plus, with any luck, I would be able to divulge to him that he kept a young girl on track with her crocheting destiny just by simply being the music in her life.

I was tongue-tied when I finally came face-to-face with my idol. Fortunately, Lynnie was with me backstage. She introduced me to Rick Springfield and said, "Rick, this is Kristi. She is the person who has been crocheting you all of the dogs over the years."

I smiled humbly at the rock-god before me, wondering what he would say and how he would react to this tidbit of information. After all, this poor man had been inundated with crocheted dogs over several years, no thanks to me, and likely was sick of seeing my creations. I was a little scared of what words would emerge from his mouth in that moment, and the fear alone caused every muscle in my being to freeze. With this thought process brewing inside of me, I never expected what occurred next.

The rock-god said to me with his killer smile, "I love the dogs! You have captured my dogs so perfectly!"

The Kritter Lady was rendered speechless.

I hugged the man I had waited a lifetime to meet, willing myself to say what had been on my mind since I was 10 years old, with my gold crochet hook in my hand and "Don't Talk to Strangers" playing on my record player. I had hoped everything I wanted to say would finally come out of my mouth and be succinctly summed up when I could find my voice.

I said three words that contained far more meaning than Rick Springfield will likely ever know.

I said, "Thank you, Rick." And I absolutely meant every single word.

I remember that ten-year-old girl, dreaming two dreams that she thought were so big, so enormous, that she thought neither could happen, not even in a million years.

But both dreams came true. Spectacularly true. Bigger and more epically true than she could have ever dreamed possible.

But...my story does not end there.

My lovely Aunt Margaret has been gone now for over 13 years, but I still remember her creativity, and how she challenged herself on each and every project. She was always determined to complete an afghan, and she would never give up. It is something I try to remember when I have my own difficulties on any projects I try to tackle. If she could do it, then so can I.

My wonderful Rick chat room friends from the late 90s, as well as Lynnie, are all still friends of mine. They are my heroes. Their kindness, warmth, and generosity of spirit remain intact. Anytime I need to be reminded of the good in the world, I look no further than their beautiful hearts.

I have continued to crochet many Kritters for Rick Springfield over the years. At last count, I have made him over 20 (although in my heart, I have a sneaking suspicion that total is actually higher). The most recent Kritter was gifted to Rick in Columbus, Ohio, in 2018. I made him yet another black and white Ron, dressed in the white dress shirt and black tie resembling the outfit from the *Working Class Dog* album. After presenting it to him, it was placed on the drum set, where it remained for the entire Columbus concert that night. *How awesome is that?*

I feel incredibly lucky to say that I have met Rick Springfield quite a few times, each time even better than the last. I have gifted him with a Kritter at every concert I have attended, whether it be backstage or during the actual show. The times when I have been able to talk to him, he has been so very kind, gracious, and sincere. I think he is, without a doubt, one of the most generous people in the world, especially to his fans.

In late 2017, I was able to present him with (again) a black and white Ron, only this time I dressed him as a king with "diamonds" and a "crown" and a crocheted red cape, which was sort of a play on Rick's then new CD, *The Snake King*. Rick seemed to look over this one rather attentively, admiring every detail on the Kritter as he held it in his hands. It brought so much happiness to my heart to witness his genuine reaction.

I never expected what came next.

Rick then said to me, so very sweetly, almost as if he was trying to find the right words, "You made me a Ron before like this. My mom loved it, and she had kept it all these years."

Tears surfaced in my eyes in that very moment. Not only was that one of the most amazing stories, knowing I brought joy to his mom oceans away (in Australia) without even knowing it, but he had just lost his mom not quite a year prior. I told him it truly warmed my heart, and it meant so much to me. What an incredible story he shared with me, a story I will never forget.

I would like to think at this point that Rick does know me through my work, and I admit I fully intend to continue to crochet him even more Kritters as time goes on!

Probably the single biggest highlight for me is knowing I have become the "Kritter Lady" in Rick's fan community. I take such pride in my work—and to be known for it by so many people, some I don't even know, is phenomenal. It astonishes me that some people will call out for the "Kritter Lady" before or after the concerts, trying to locate me. Because of this, the shows I attend are like a family reunion for me. The fan community has embraced me with open arms, Kritters and all, and I couldn't be more thankful.

Which of course brings me to...the Kritters.

I am floored I am still crocheting them some 30 plus years later.

I am still getting visions of the Kritters. That has never stopped in all these years. I have at least five to 10 Kritter ideas floating around in my head on any given day and the only obstacle I seem to be faced with now is the lack of time to devote to these project ideas. I am sure if I get a chance to retire, I will be crocheting Kritters in my free time—but free time...*what is that?*

I have never set foot outside the United States, but my Kritters have "travelled" worldwide. I have sent them all across the United States, and to Mexico, Canada, England, China, France, Trinidad, and Tobago, and as mentioned earlier, Australia. To know something I've handcrafted is present in all of these locations is mind-blowing, as well as heartwarming.

I have a Facebook Kritter Lady page that showcases my latest creations, whether that is a Kritter gifted to a famous rock star, or a Kritter made to resemble a favorite pet, animal, or sports team. I am so proud of the work I do, and I am proud I can share it with so many.

That first ever Kritter I spoke of earlier, that one I labeled the "homely" bear—I actually still have it. It serves as a reminder to me that through determination and perseverance, you can accomplish anything. I did not become an expert at this overnight, and I didn't expect to with that first creation. But reflecting back now, it's a huge reminder to me—that's exactly where my dream truly began.

Along my life's crocheting journey, one thing has remained the same. Each time I am fortunate enough to gift a Kritter I have created, I bring happiness and joy to someone's life. Perhaps they feel they have received the greatest gift in receiving my Kritters. But

I have realized I am the one who actually has been given the greatest gift of all—my dream goes on and gets even bigger each and every time a crochet hook is in my hands.

Hmm...I wonder what vision I'll have next that will transform into one of my Kritters?!

About Kristi

Kristi is known in many online fan communities as the "Kritter Lady." She is an avid crocheter, and has spent over three decades perfecting her craft. Using her own visions as her inspiration instead of relying on patterns, she designs and creates her own unique stuffed animals, called Kritters. She can be found on Facebook, via her Kritter Lady page.

Rick Springfield hugging one of my Kritters that I gave to him.

Rick Springfield, me, and a Kritter.

My first-ever Kritter, the "homely" square bear.

More Kritters!

JENNIFER LONGHOFER

"In the end she became more than what she expected. She became the journey, and like all journeys she did not end. She simply changed directions and kept on going."

— RM Drake

The Power of El Camino de Santiago

In April of 2015, I made the decision that the following April I would walk the El Camino de Santiago or The Way of St. James. The Camino or "The Way," as it is often referred to, is an 800 km pilgrimage to the shrine of the Apostle St. James in Santiago De Compostela, Spain, where it is believed the remains of the Saint are buried. The first record of pilgrims visiting the shrine of the Saint date back to the 9th century.

I learned of the Camino when I was about 18 years old; I'm not exactly sure where. I'm assuming it was in a book I had read. Over the next 25 years it would periodically reappear in my life either through something I'd read or had seen on television, even a movie. I always thought it sounded like an amazing journey, but the idea of pilgrimage was something very foreign to me. I couldn't grasp how someone was able to walk/hike over 500 miles with a backpack, and that's all they had. I wondered, *Where did they sleep? Eat? Go to the bathroom? What if it rained?* I admired the courage and commitment made by the countless people who had decided to do something like this; however, I never imagined it would someday be me. I wondered, *What drives someone to do this? What do they get out of it?* It would be almost 30 years before I got the answer to my questions.

When I decided to do the Camino, I wasn't in a very good place in my life. There were so many things that had transpired over the previous seven or eight years, so many things I had never dealt with. My mom had passed away. I made the decision to leave the man I had been with for 13 years. I moved back to Chicago. I then got involved with someone from my past who I deeply loved, and I let myself believe that we had finally gotten it right this time only to have him completely deceive me once again. This was the proverbial straw that broke the camel's back, and I wasn't just broken, I was shattered. I knew I needed to gather all the pieces and start to reassemble myself, and my heart. I didn't know where to start. I knew I was the only one who could figure this out. I also knew I had to face some early childhood trauma that I had also never dealt with. It was frightening facing what felt like my private emotional tsunami.

The first thing I decided I needed to do was take a *timeout* from toxic relationships, both friendships, and romantic. I really needed to learn to be my own best friend. I needed to do some soul searching. I slowly started to withdraw, never really expressing to anyone what was really going on with me. I've never been someone who battled depression, but during this time, I was probably the closest to it I had ever been. I look back at pictures, and I can see the vacancy in my eyes; I can see how sad I was. The smile was there, but it never reached my eyes. It was during this time that I really started to examine my life and saw how little I shared about myself with others despite the close friendships and bonds I had. I really felt like no one truly knew me or saw me for who I was—including my family. I had to realize a lot of that was my own fault. Vulnerability is something I've never been good at expressing, and I don't share my feelings easily. This stems from my past.

Between the ages of eight and 11, I lost three very important people in my life. One of them was a result of a violent crime. These losses had a major impact on me and who I've become. I was sad and confused for a long time when I was a child, and I never expressed it. I think that's when I began to keep my feelings tucked away and shut off from the world. I really believe its when I stopped being a dreamer and became a goal setter. I think in some subconscious way I didn't allow myself to dream for the fear of it not coming true, and if you don't have dreams then you don't have disappointment. It was about this time in my life, I started to view the world as a very unstable place. Life and death became a reality for me; and no matter what, it changed my behavior in relationships for the rest of my life.

During this time in 2015, I had become very close to someone I had known for years. He was someone I had grown to love, trust, and rely on. So when he suggested doing the Camino de Santiago together, I was immediately on board. I knew this was right, more importantly it seemed right that we should do it together, although I didn't know why? I felt he may have had his own healing to do. Maybe this was the purpose of our deepened friendship.

I started researching the best times of year and picked the date of April 21, 2016. It gave us about a year to mentally prepare for this journey. Through my research, I quickly understood a few very important things. First, decide if we're going on pilgrimage or if we're going on a "pilgrim vacation," and then commit to it. Second, this is a deeply, personal, spiritual journey, and although I may be traveling with others my experiences would be completely different. Lastly, an honest pilgrimage was something I was being called to or driven to do. It's not a decision based on a movie or just a walk through Spain; there is a purpose, and although I may not have known exactly what that purpose was, I had faith that in time I would. I needed to open my heart to the Camino, and it would provide what I needed.

I began to have my doubts whether it was a good idea for Jack and me to take this adventure together. We had very different views on things, which I had always known, but there was part of me that didn't really believe a lot of the nonsense he spouted. He claimed to be an atheist which went completely against his actual character. He is one of the kindest, most generous human beings I've ever met. A man so connected to nature and animals that it just didn't seem possible he didn't believe in something bigger. He kept saying, "I'm just taking a long walk through Spain." I ignored it, but it honestly bothered me. I knew it wasn't a long walk through Spain, and I took the Camino very seriously. I told myself, no matter what, my heart was open, and I was going to experience the journey I was meant to. We had committed to experiencing the Camino together, and it's a commitment we kept. The year seemed to fly by, and before I knew it, we were headed to Paris. I left Chicago with what I thought at the time was an open heart, a backpack weighing about 15 pounds, and a mantra for the times I needed encouragement. That mantra was the Spanish/Latin word *Ulteria* meaning "Carry on" or "this takes courage." I hold it in my heart as my mantra today.

Although I had researched the Camino, I don't think I really grasped what I was in for; to this day I will say it was the hardest and easiest thing I had ever done. Find the irony in that! It was hard physically and emotionally, the easy part was I just had to put my boots on and go. It became clear from the beginning; it probably wasn't the best idea that Jack and I were doing this together. At first I felt anger toward him as if he was ruining my journey, and the more I grumbled in my head, the worse it got. Suddenly I realized that I controlled my journey and what I would experience—*me and only me*. Once I settled into that mindset, I cleared the wide open path for the gifts I was about to receive. Every day was another beautiful adventure I felt very fortunate to be able to experience, however; I wondered, *when I would have my great epiphany? When would my healing begin?* I would walk for hours lost in my thoughts. I thought a lot about my mom and how much I missed her. She loved butterflies, and so many times when I was struggling on the Camino, I would see a white butterfly in front or along side of me, and I imagined it was her telling me to keep going. When she died a little bit of me died too. It was a sobering reality that I no longer had biological parents; it was a very lonely feeling. I thought about my biological father and how unfortunate it was that we never got the chance to know one another. I was seven when he was killed. I don't have many memories of him. I know I look just like him, and I have a lot of his mannerisms. I had spent a lot of time telling myself that I can't miss something I never had, but I was wrong...I did miss him. I wish I would have known him. I finally gave myself permission to grieve that loss, something I'd never done before. I thought about my beautiful Aunt Becky and how much life I'd been able to live—when her life was cut so short. I imagined the Camino was something she would have embraced. I thought about my Grandpa Joe, and how I would give anything for one more day to meet him at Marie's for a jelly doughnut. But time is something we can't get back, and I didn't want to waste anymore of my precious time letting life live me. I wanted to live my life. It was at this point on my Camino that I was entering the Mesetta. It's a part of the Camino many people avoid for a myriad of reasons—most commonly because its flat and ugly, but I think "fear" may be the main reason.

It's said about the Camino—the first part is the physical, conditioning your body to carry your pack for what often feels like endless hours of hiking/walking.

The second part is the emotional side of the Camino; this is the Mesetta, it's where all the emotional baggage confronts you.

The third is the spiritual side, and these are the insights and lessons you've learned along the way, and hopefully what you bring back to your "real life" once you return.

I neither feared nor looked forward to the Mesetta. I honestly didn't know what to expect.

The first day of the Mesetta, I was met with threatening, gray skies, blustery wind, and torrential rain. The Mesetta is extremely flat and vast, and with the rain the trail transformed into a thick, red, clay type of mud. Each step I took felt like I was pulling my boots out of quicksand which made the journey even more challenging; and my tears fell just as hard as the rain. I cried out to God, "Do you think this is going to break me?" I'd endured harder struggles than this, and I wasn't about to allow myself to be defeated now. It was on this day...stomping through the muddy flatlands of Spain that God answered my question. I heard His voice speaking to me deep in my soul—a reminder just how strong I really was. I realized I had become someone I didn't even recognize anymore. I had given into my brokenness. And I had given that brokenness so much power by closing my heart that I was building calluses, and with those calluses in place, I would never heal. That realization triggered my anger. I had become someone I didn't even recognize, and I committed to myself that it had to end and now! I didn't exactly have a plan, but I knew at the time I was here for serious life changes. It was on that day, I asked myself the tough questions.

What was it that I really wanted to do?

What are my gifts in this lifetime that could propel my dreams forward into what I want my future to become?

With each step all the clutter in my mind slowly started to clear. All the things that I had, all the material things that I had accumulated, meant nothing to me. I had always said I could give it all up, and I'd head down to a little island somewhere, get a job working in a bar… shorts and flip flops; that's all I would need. *What was stopping me?* I had a job that allowed me to travel anywhere in the world. I used airplanes like most people use their cars. *Why wasn't I living in the world?* I had always dreamt of living in a foreign country. Why was I paying for an apartment in Chicago that I only spent a few days of the week at? I don't have children. I wasn't in a relationship. I had no one to take care of other than myself; nothing was holding me back but me! Over the next 300 km, I decided that when my lease was up, I would become a global citizen of the world. Each day my plan became a bit clearer…with each step on the Camino, I started to regain my confidence again. I saw glimmers of the real me. I was excited about this new adventure. I knew there would be people in my life who would question my decision, all wondering what I was running from? I had all those conversations in my head, and when and if they happened I would have my answers ready. I was confident that I wasn't running from anything; I was finally running toward something, and that was my life, my very best life.

I returned home from Spain ready for my new adventure to begin. It was a tough transition returning to my "real" life. The transformation wasn't external, it was internal, and I longed for my days on the Camino. I craved the simplicity. My lease was up in a year, and it seemed as if this was the longest year of my life…never ending. I knew I wasn't changing my mind and a few months prior to the end of my lease, I started planning for my first big adventure—a month in Greece. I started researching different islands and followed my instincts on where I should go, places that seemed to call out to me. I also started booking and paying for apartments and *pensiones*, and that's when it all became a reality. I couldn't afford to keep my apartment and go to Greece. I needed to figure out what I was going to do with all my belongings.

I made the decision I would basically give everything away for free. I didn't want to haggle with people over prices. I just wanted it all gone; none of it meant anything to me. It was all replaceable. I posted a notice on an online site, and a month later I had committed all my belongings to different people. I scheduled their pickup dates for the end of April with the promise to reconfirm one week prior. It felt like a fire sale! Everything must go! I did secure a small storage unit because in life we do have some personal effects we can't give away. It was both freeing and frightening. The time flew by so quickly that before I knew it, I was standing in my apartment watching strangers claim their new belongings as each piece of furniture, dish, fork... whatever it was, left my possession; my emotional load seemed to get lighter. I never really realized how cumbersome "stuff" can be.

I spent the next few months working a month and then traveling a month. I saw and experienced sights I only read about in books. I knew I had taken a huge leap of faith with my decisions, and this new journey was only meant for me. During some of my travel, other people joined me, and instead of it being my journey, it became their vacation; it was something more than that for me. It was a journey of my soul. It was nice to have friends with me for a week or so, but I was happiest on my own. I didn't go out at night.

I often didn't even talk to many people. I really spent time getting to know myself in a way that I never had before. I was clearing the path to plant new seeds.

I needed to start thinking about my next Camino. In April, I planned on experiencing both Camino Frances as well as Portuguese Camino—about 1,200 miles total. I knew I needed to start the mental and spiritual preparations. That is when Assisi happened. This is the trip that changed everything, the trip that was most important to me.

The decision to go to Assisi came about very quickly and unexpectedly. I started researching convents in Rome, and Google was interceded by divine intervention and sent my search to Assisi, which didn't surprise me in the least. This brought back memories from almost 20 years ago when I met Father Stan and a group of Franciscan friars who made a huge impression upon me. I met them on a flight, and then like now, I was once again at a personal and spiritual crossroads. It was through my encounter with this band of brothers that my deep love and admiration for St. Francis began. I've always felt St. Francis is the one who always brings me back to God.

January 3, 2018, is the day I landed in Rome and took the bus to Termini Station in central Rome. It was about 10:30 a.m., and my train didn't leave until 2:30 p.m. On previous trips I tended to want to hurry up and get there, but this time I was much more relaxed. I knew I was exactly where I was meant to be, and instead of changing my train ticket, I wandered about the terminal, sat, and just stared off into space. I just really enjoyed being there. I enjoyed traveling, and found serenity in my alone time. I was much more present and in the moment. It's interesting and at times a bit uncomfortable listening to a language you don't understand. I suppose it could even be isolating at times; however, I wasn't lonely. I had this calm and peaceful feeling, something I hadn't had in an extremely long time. Maybe I was just tired, but I felt my whole body unwind; perhaps I would get some much needed rest.

I felt like I was there because I needed to make some changes both within myself and some relationships I had in my life. Maybe they weren't good for me and blocked me from the happiness I was longing for.

When I arrived at the train station in Assisi, I was overwhelmed by the majestic sight of the basilica, a golden glow atop the hill. I had this rush of gratitude overwhelm me as I witnessed its beauty. Again I was overcome with a calming, peace, and contentment. I knew I was exactly where I was supposed to be. Assisi is a commune in the Province of Perugia in the Umbrian region on the western flank of Mt. Subasio. It sits high above the valley with beautiful stone walls and winding cobbled streets in which both cars and pedestrians share the road. I was in awe of its majesty as the village twinkled with fairy lights artfully strung in intervals. I knew the convent overlooked the basilica, and as we drove up winding hills and sped down narrow streets I couldn't imagine where it was. Then we turned the corner, and there it was, the basilica, with a beautiful life-size nativity scene and the convent Beata de Angelina only steps away. Sister Claudia met me, and we did our best to understand one another. As she took my passport and saw my middle name, Rae, she said, "Ahhh Raffaella, like the angel, I will call you Raffaella."

So just like when a sister joins the order and their name is changed, my name too was changed. Later I would learn Raffaella also meant "Child healed by God," which was fitting since I felt like I was on a journey of healing. Sister Claudia took me to my room, and it was perfect—a simple twin bed, a desk, wardrobe closet, and my breathless view out the window was priceless. I couldn't believe this is where I could pray for the next 14 days.

I showered and went to bed early as I was exhausted. I woke the next morning before the sun rose and just marveled at my good fortune. I went downstairs, enjoyed my breakfast provided by the sisters, and set out to explore my new surroundings. Assisi reminded me a lot of Santiago, and later I learned they are sister cities. Both are considered to be two of the most spiritual places in Christendom. That day I explored all the tourist destinations, and it was wonderful; however, I knew this was about much more. It was the second or third day of my stay, and I awoke to my breakfast, just like every other morning and headed to the basilica. I walked to the lower portion where the Tomb of St. Francis was. It's a small simple chapel used for prayers and meditation. I began my prayer, and the next thing I knew I was weeping uncontrollably. It wasn't heaving sobs; it was silent weeping, and I just couldn't stop. I sat there for more than an hour, and I wept. It was like I turned on a faucet and all the hurt, pain, guilt, and shame that was so unnecessary was finally released like heavy flowing water. It was one of the most uncomfortable moments in my life. As I was on my knees praying, I opened my eyes and saw this pool of water on the pew. I couldn't imagine that it all came from me, and it was still flowing. I left the tomb of St. Francis that day emotionally and physically exhausted. I read most of the day, but I think I cried even more. From that day forward my days were quiet. I experienced the same routine everyday—the tomb of St. Francis and the Basilica of St. Clare. Then I would wander to the small park and read or write in my journal, but mostly I sat and looked over the Umbrian Valley. At first I thought I was perfecting the art of doing nothing, but I soon realized I was in constant communion with God, and He had been waiting for me. It was here in Assisi my healing began, and what started as just a crack on my first Camino became a crevasse that allowed the magic and love I encountered on my second Camino which truly healed me.

I'm happy to say I did all 1,200 plus miles on this Camino. It was a journey of healing, love, and magic, and I feel like in this moment I am living a dream. I have been given an opportunity to share my story, and not only does that heal me—I hope to inspire others to believe in themselves too. Life is hard, and it chips away at all of us, but we are all so much stronger than we realize. I took an extreme route to get down to the basics of who I am and who I was meant to be. For me it was essential to unload the trappings of material things and to put my faith not in myself—but in something much bigger.

About Jennifer

This is the beginning of Jennifer's beautiful and courageous journey that embarked in April of 2016 on the El Camino de Santiago —The Way of St. James, a 900 kilometer spiritual pilgrimage through Spain to Santiago de Compestella where the remains of the Saint are believed to be buried. The life changing pilgrimage led Jennifer to make the decision to live her very best life. She divided her time working a month in the airline industry, as she has for the last 24 years, and taking a month off to travel as a "global citizen of the world."

It was never a series of great vacations for her; it was a journey into her heart and soul to find out who she really was apart from family, friends, and occupation. It led her back to the Camino de Santiago in April of 2018, this time to complete both Camino Frances as well as Portugues Camino, approximately 1800 kilometers. It was 57 days. She laughed, cried, struggled, and connected with new friends.

Through many unplanned and unexpected turns, she reflected on her life, and she let the best path for her future unfold before her very eyes. Ultimately she found peace, happiness, and direction.

Jennifer is currently dividing her time between work in Chicago and Assisi Italy where she is writing her first book chronicling the story of her quest to get to the core of who she really was and is.

108 Santiago. Only 108k to Santiago! This photo was taken by my good friend and fellow pilgrim KC. This is my favorite photo of me ever, it's the only photo of me from that first Camino that I see the hope in my eyes. It is a peace that I hadn't known before. I can see I was looking forward to the future with a new spirit.

Cruce De Farro
The Iron Cross marks the highest point of the mountain
pass and is a very special place for pilgrims. Tradition is to
bring a stone from your hometown and leave it at the cross,
symbolically leaving your burdens behind.

The special stone my nephew gave to
me to leave at Cruce De Farro. There
is a saying on the Camino that your
pack is only as heavy as your burdens.
I consciously laid my burdens down
that day and started to believe in the
dream that had started to take shape,
excited about this new adventure
in my life.

LUCAS J. ROBAK

"What the mind can conceive and believe, the mind can achieve."

\- Napoleon Hill

My Dreams Always Come True

Throughout my teenage years I entertained the various ways I'd kill myself. Thankfully, I noticed my wicked thoughts leaning toward action and checked myself into a mental health clinic.

At every clinic and hospital I checked myself into, or was forced into, there was someone there who treated me differently than the other patients. These weren't isolated incidences either; for decades I attracted people into my life who saw greatness inside me and took the time to point me in a better direction.

The final straw occurred in my late teenage years when I chose to actually attempt suicide. While locked up in the hospital's mental ward for those 36 hours, I realized the life I was living wasn't meant for me; I wasn't being my true authentic self. Instead, I was living the life society expects of us.

I'd be ashes if it weren't for the world's leading expert on success, Bob Proctor, and his YouTube videos. He provided me with all the tools needed to control my thoughts, and therefore, my results. Go to YouTube and subscribe to the Proctor Gallagher Institute channel, he'll change your life too.

My Silver Platter

For weeks, the left side of my body was numb and tingly to the point of feeling extremely painful. Everything around me became a makeshift walker and cane. Walking along the walls, using chairs, holding on to strangers' shoulders, I used anything to keep my balance.

One evening I delivered a speech while sitting on a desk in front of a room full of people. Afterwards I drove myself to the emergency room thinking the doctors would tell me to stop working so hard and eat healthier. In not so many words, that's exactly what they said.

To date, Memorial Day weekend 2014 has been the most positive moment of my life. If I wasn't diagnosed with multiple sclerosis (MS), I wouldn't be on the path I am today.

What is MS?

Who cares?

What it is, and what it might do is useless information; all that matters is what's in my control and implementing what I learned with how to successfully live with a chronic illness.

Practicing daily gratitude and appreciation since attempting suicide rewired my brain to know that only good can come from every situation. This view on the world is more empowering than choosing to become a victim. No one is a victim until they consciously choose to think themselves into one.

When the doctors wheeled a flat screen television into my room to talk about my MRI and CAT scans, my thoughts began racing toward a positive direction. The neurologists didn't know they were handing me my life's purpose on a silver platter.

After years of learning from failing, I chose the right thoughts to be mentally prepared to instantly see all the great things that can come from MS. Aside from handicap parking, student loan forgiveness, and being a federally protected citizen, this diagnosis inspired me to lead people towards natural health and wellness.

Community of Natural Health & Wellness

One of the biggest dreams I have is to use my MS to inspire people. If I can achieve anything worth mentioning in a conversation, then there's zero reason why you shouldn't be able to create a life worth talking about too!

The Internet is flooded with memes illustrating the real world path leading to success. One meme in particular shows a straight line from point A to point B depicting what most people believe a successful journey looks like. On the other side of the image has a cloud of scribbles to show the path of what it really takes to be successful.

While sitting in the hospital bed for those 72 hours after my diagnosis, I researched "how to successfully live with a chronic illness" leading me to many facts that are suppressed from society.

Within a couple weeks after leaving the hospital, I was asked to contribute to the first book in *The Change: Insights Into Self-Empowerment* book series. The next month I was asked to be a leader of a positive MS support group. Then, 10 months later I became the leader of a wellness community simply because I started surrounding myself with that world.

I'm now leading a community of qualified wellness professionals who are just as passionate about healing the whole mind, body, and spirit to those seeking a natural and healthy lifestyle.

Nothing's Easy Breezy

When I first started *The Wellness Fair*, I incorporated Dr. Stephen Covey's Habit #2, "Begin with the End in Mind." All of my actions revolved around creating a 10-year goal within just one year, sprinting instead of taking baby steps.

After the first year, I was not remotely close to achieving those results I daydreamed about. But they were far superior if I played it safe by thinking small.

In 2015, I vividly visualized driving up to an expo center which displayed our signs and flags outside letting the 100,000 attendees know this is *The Wellness Fair*, checking in, walking around, and meeting the 100 qualified vendors.

Remember the concept of the path to success is made with scribbly lines and not a direct path? Today, that fantasy is finally starting to manifest itself, but not in its entirety. I'm now visualizing going international even though that original goal hasn't been fully accomplished. I've learned to celebrate achieving my goals well before I actually achieve them so I can set bigger ones and not lose momentum.

Even though this happens every now and then, my fantasy still includes people coming up to me asking if I'm Lucas Robak, re-verifying I'm the organizer of *The Wellness Fair*, and thanking me for doing what I do while detailing the results they've achieved.

Then there are those whiners, complainers, excuse makers, and dream stealers every accomplished person will warn you about.

I was dreadfully wrong to think the idea of qualified professionals educating people on health and wellness would be widely accepted by everyone. Negative people have this inept need to crawl out of their dark holes to force their opinions, and then hate you if you don't fall in line and conform to their demands. Some people would rather put their health in the hands of an uncertified hobbyist instead of a qualified professional.

One of the greatest learnings I've realized over the years is to question those who tell me what to do. *Are they competent? Do they have noteworthy results in the area they're talking about?* Many don't attain any notable achievements which is why they're not worth listening to.

Since 2015, we continue to grow, we're being talked about, and I've been interviewed many times on podcasts, syndicated radio shows, and TV stations. In time, *The Wellness Fair* will continue to positively impact a limitless amount of lives around the world every year.

Come Live Your Vision

Jack Canfield is the cocreator of the *Chicken Soup for the Soul* series and is the author of *The Success Principles*. In this incredible book, Principle #12 is "Act As If." When I read this chapter I instantly adopted its theory and even started hosting the event he mentioned.

Mr. Canfield calls the event "Come As You Will Be," and I renamed it to "Come Live Your Vision." This is a party where you act as if all your goals are your present reality. By attending this event, you come living your vision board. It's a fantasy party that drives your goals deep into the subconscious mind making it more likely you will achieve your enormous dreams.

In January 2015, I hosted the first "Come Live Your 2020 Vision" party. Out of all the dreams I bragged about "achieving," one of them came true within a year.

I found a picture of Jack Canfield with Lady Gaga at the Grammys and replaced Lady Gaga with me using Photoshop. During the event I bragged how Jack called me out of the blue and invited me to one of his events so he could meet me, shake my hand, and take a picture. Within a year, I answered my phone and Jack Canfield invited me to an event in Chicago so he could meet me, shake my hand, and take a picture with me. Granted, this was a voice recording but I got exactly what I talked about.

In spring 2017, I received an email with a short video from Bob Proctor holding my first children's book saying he can't wait to meet me. *Seriously? See you soon!*

The first week of January 2019 I won a free ticket to Bob's *Art of Goal Achievement* seminar and shook his hand in Los Angeles, CA, on January 14, 2019…just in time to get back and host the next "Come Live Your 2020 Vision" event.

Want to manifest your dreams? Expect it to happen while doing everything you can to make it reality with no excuses!

Because I achieved my own results due to this event, it was easy to continue doing it so more people could start *Manifesting Their Dreams*.

I write, rewrite, and study my goals almost on a daily basis because I know that's what it takes to create a life worth talking about. Taking time out every day to visualize each goal as reality while getting emotionally involved in the fantasy is what jumpstarts every cell in my body and ignites the "Law of Attraction."

Every event I organize, I fantasize about hundreds of thousands of people showing up because thinking big is far better than playing it safe. A teacher told me once not to think so big because I'll just be disappointed when I don't achieve it. One thing failures know how to do is remain stagnant and drag everyone else down to their level of mediocrity.

I've failed at every event I've organized because 100,000 people haven't shown up…yet. I'd rather fail at achieving massive results than being successful at something average and ordinary. The only way to succeed is to fail many times along the way. Failure is only feedback; learn to love it because outrageous success leaves a long trail of failures.

For me personally, what keeps me going and staying positive is "Acting As If" in my mind because I'm working towards something bigger than myself. I'm always working towards something that is forcing me to become someone better than I am today. If my big dreams don't positively change me and force me to grow, then it's not worth my energy. Nothing great will be easy and nothing easy will ever be considered great.

Published 75 Authors in One Year

In 2012, I was reading a book to my friend's two-year old son. Laughing at how basic it was, I looked this cute child in the eyes and told him anyone can write a children's book. At that moment, the decision was made...I'm a published author!

Contacting numerous publishers and book agents, no one wanted to publish my idea nor did anyone point me in the right direction. So I chose to figure it out and published the book on my own because if one person can do it, everyone can do it!

Soon enough I was selling my children's book from the trunk of my car. I still carry copies of *I AM: Children's Book for Positive Thinkers* with me everywhere I go.

USA Today did a study and found 84 percent of people want to write a book but .02 percent of people will actually do what it takes to get the job done! Think of that. If you're in a room with 5,000 people who talk about writing a book, odds are only one person will prove themselves to be a doer.

Being so proud of myself for achieving something the major majority of people in the world will never do, I had the crazy idea to see my book on the shelf in a store. I took action and was thankfully told by two different owners that I was an arrogant narcissist to think my book could go on their shelves.

I was an arrogant narcissist because it was staple bound (saddle stitch) versus a perfect binding like this book here. For customers to see my book, it would require a lot of real estate to have the front cover facing out rather than just the spine. *Challenge accepted!*

Within a year, my book could be purchased in many different hobby shops and stores. This book also helped me achieve my dream of becoming a paid speaker too!

To achieve my challenge of publishing a quality book, I also published a workbook series entitled, *Master Your Life Using Transformational Quotes*. Because I was dumb enough to put more value on money rather than quality, I lost a great deal of money hiring amateurs and chose to figure it out on my own. This "poor person" mentality was a blessing in disguise because if I didn't hire affordable amateurs, I wouldn't be an Entrepreneur Publisher today.

Around my sixth book release, people started asking me how to do it themselves because I overcame a ridiculous amount of screwups, failures, and permanent mistakes which would've stopped most people. Just for fun, in 2016 I helped all those who asked.

When December 2016 rolled around, I looked back at the year and counted all the people who became authors because I read a book to a child years before. That year I helped exactly 75 people in a couple countries become published authors.

When I began this publishing journey, my initial dream was to learn how to successfully publish a book; mission accomplished. I now continue to experiment by publishing my own books so I purposefully can have real world experience when training clients on how to use a book as their greatest marketing asset.

It's the Worst Book Ever Written

Once you become an author, what's next on the list? Becoming a #1 Best-seller!

By now you're realizing I have a peculiar way of thinking with outside-the-box tactics. Why would this be any different?

In 2017, I hosted a weekend training for authorpreneurs to become best-sellers and brought in the #1 International Best-sellers of *Bankroll Your Mind*, Rich Perry and Larunce Pipkin, to do a panel Q&A on what it takes to become best-sellers. The only issue I faced was knowing the theory behind it but didn't have my own real world results to back it up.

Earlier that year while putting together an author's book, I had an idea to publish a joke. Literally, my goal was to publish a full-blown piece of trash. All within 45-minutes of conceiving the idea, I wrote the book, did the layout, created a cover, and uploaded it on Amazon as a paperback and Kindle. Because people love wasting their money on stupid stuff, I named the book, *It's the Worst Book Ever Written: Don't Waste Your Money Buying This, You're Not Getting a Refund.*

While facing this predicament, I went through all the books I published and chose this one to make a best-seller within a week.

With nine 1-Star reviews already on Amazon, I went to Facebook and started insulting everyone who bought it for being dumb and wasting their money. When it came time during the training to show everyone how to monitor all the best-seller lists, my book was at #1. It actually stayed there for 10 days, a best-seller for almost a month, and racked up over 20 hilarious 1-Star reviews.

When you have an idea, do it. Simply make the decision to achieve something you desire, just like you make the decision to go home at the end of the day. Have that same level of expectancy with what you desire most, and you will begin *Manifesting Your Dreams*.

All Within Six Months

After publishing those 75 authors in a year, my first official client for *Authorpreneur Academy* was Dr. Anthony Piparo because he's a doer, not a talker!

A couple months after his son committed suicide he asked me to meet him for coffee to find out how to get the media's attention and promote suicide prevention. With my past experience and deep respect for Dr. Piparo, I shared with him the only way I knew how to achieve any dream in record time, publish a book and leverage it as a tool to open any door of opportunity.

Even though he already accomplished his Ph.D. and published other books, the best way to become a credible authority figure on the topic is to simply become the first six letters in the word **author**ity.

When you have a passionate fire lit up inside you, along with a group of people who believe in you, incredible things will happen.

Six months after we met at Starbucks, Dr. Anthony Piparo's book, *Freedom From Depression*, became an International Best-seller and Amazon #1 New Release the day before we even prepared to launch it.

Today, Dr. Piparo is a positive force in the mental health world by actively participating on various boards and steering committees. He's also being interviewed by the media and asked to speak at events.

Manifesting Your Dreams

In the video I received from Bob Proctor holding my first children's book, *I AM: Children's Book for Positive Thinkers*, he gave me a piece of advice, "The mind is the most powerful force in all of creation, hold the image of what you want, surprise the whole world."

If you can hold the idea of what you want in your mind, there's nothing stopping you from holding that idea in your hands except for you and your thoughts.

When I first went to college for Flight Operations, I wanted to graduate being able to fly multi-engine airplanes; done deal! When I want to attend various trainings and seminars, I consistently find thousands of dollars in a matter of hours to attend those events I truly desire.

Seriously, make the decision to achieve your desires, expect it's going to happen, and get to work on *Manifesting Your Dreams*. It's literally that simple, just three steps!

If you believe you deserve it, go out and earn it. If you don't have it, that means you didn't earn it and don't deserve it. Make it happen with no excuses!

Just Do It

In 1987, the founder of Primerica Insurance, Art Williams, gave a speech called "Just Do It." It's a video on YouTube which I encourage you to take 20 minutes every day and watch.

At the end of this speech, Art said something which I'll leave you with in hopes it'll inspire you to actually capture your idea, formulate a plan, and take persistent action until it becomes reality:

"I hear too much talk in these United States, everybody can talk a good game. We need people in America, who can do it. I go all over this country and I have people say, "Art, you can count on me." Wonderful. Just do it..."Art, what's the primary difference between winners and losers?" The winners do it. They do it, and do it, and do it, and do it, until the job gets done. And then they talk about how great it is to have finally achieved something you need. And how glad they are that they didn't quit like everybody else. And how wonderful it is to finally be somebody they're proud of. And make a difference with their life."

About Lucas

After flying multi-engine airplanes in college, today Lucas is a #1 best-selling author and a contributor to numerous publications like *Addicted 2 Success*, *Good Men Project*, and *Thrive Global*. Lucas also has been interviewed on many podcasts, radio stations, and TV shows.

In 2014, a diagnosis of multiple sclerosis (MS) empowered and motivated him to bring more value to the world. Within 10 months Lucas became the organizer for *The Wellness Fair* and is also the president of *The Health & Wellness Network of Commerce Southeast Wisconsin Chapter* (HWNCC-SEWI).

While reading a book to a friend's son, Lucas decided anyone can write a book. To prove this, a year later parents began reading his first book to their kids, *I AM—Children's Book for Positive Thinkers*. This fun experiment found its way into Bob Proctor's personal library and is being read to Jack Canfield's grandson. Any and everything is possible as long as you believe it is.

Be Different! Be You!

LucasRobak.com
TheWellnessFair.org
Authorpreneur-Academy.com

The Change: Insights Into Self-Empowerment
(Book 1 - 2014).

Wisdom-sharing community of natural well-being.

Bob Proctor endorsing
my first book.

My photoshop image signed by Jack Canfield.

Me actually meeting Jack Canfield.

Dr. Anthony Piparo is a successful Authorpreneur.

*#1 International Best-selling Authors:
Rich Perry and Larunce Pipkin*

*Proof that people
waste their money.*

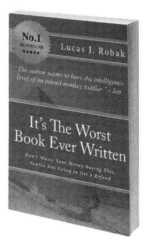

Entrepreneur publishing company.

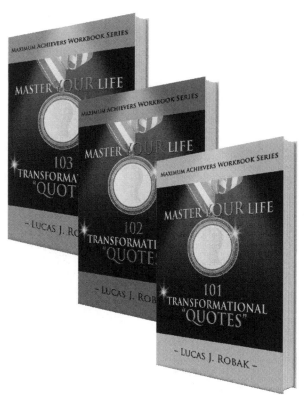

Quote Workbook Series.

Milwaukee's **The Morning Blend,** *2018.*

NASTASSIA PUTZ

"My life then—a wild spark, my life now—a roaring bonfire. I just needed stronger sticks."

- Nastassia Putz

Manifesting Ms. Wrong Into *Mrs. Right*

I've had a bad attitude ever since I can remember. I took every ounce of positivity around me and turned it into this congealed bowl of negative soup with a dash of self-sabotage. Some called it my gift for easily attracting negative energy. My dad tried for many years to break me of this cycle, but that thorn grew over time as I lived with a negative and emotionally fragmented mother (sorry Mom). I went trudging through life with bags of dirty laundry sewn to each hip. I collected a pool of negative people around me and left a trail of codependent exes in the dust. I knew one thing was for certain; I didn't want to be married, and I didn't want to be like my mother. I had a better plan.

That plan began with binge drinking, partying, dropping out of college, and then working in the service industry for little to no pay… *great plan, huh?* Well, it took me years to really settle down and start to care about my future. At age 26, I was still lost. I met a man at a bar in Brown Deer, Wisconsin; he was a bartender to be exact. He was quiet, dark, and so good-looking. And in a drunken slur, I proposed my undying attraction to him over a sticky bar top. He, of course, was in a relationship with another woman and was disgusted by my poor taste and inebriated body language. So I took my grotesque self *(that's what I thought of myself)* and left that night never to return again. I continued to pursue other like-minded individuals when it came to intimacy and failed to see why I was so utterly alone. *Ever lie next to somebody and just feel more alone than if you were lying there by yourself?* It's probably one of the worst feelings a woman can have because it does absolutely nothing for her self-confidence. However, the drinking was not my actual problem, it was just a symptom. My view of myself was my problem. I had such a distorted perception of how I wanted to live my life. I suffered from what some may refer to as the "unique syndrome." I felt uniquely different in all of my daily enterprises, and I didn't need to answer to anyone else. My problems were unique. I didn't want to be my mother, trapped in a cycle of ongoing failed relationships and a nine-to-five job she hated. I wanted to be a writer and move to glamorous New York. Therefore, I continued on my college path I had so reluctantly failed to finish in my earlier twenties. One thing was for certain, college was really good for me. It kept me sober (during the day) and busy most nights.

A year after I met that bartender, you'll never guess what happened…he broke up with his girlfriend and found me on Facebook. Score! I finally felt like things were turning around for me. We met at a poetry reading on the eastside of Milwaukee… HIS! There is nothing like a good-looking artist…if you ask me. Charisma just radiates off of them and shouts, "I want you!" After seeing him in action, I was hooked! I wanted to be this man's muse. So, we started dating. The physical attraction and magnetic pull to this other tortured soul-type was so intense I felt intoxicated in his presence. We spent many nights going to bars and partying with friends, waking up hung over, and going to work late. It was the start of a downward spiral for us. Neither of us was a highly motivated, independent individual, nor were we spiritually stable enough to foresee the poison we were injecting into each other's lives. We were now both stuck in this "unique syndrome" together, and it caused a lot of fighting; but it was the kind of passionate fighting you see in movies like *The Notebook* or *Blue Valentine*. It was not a healthy kind of fighting a couple should do at all.

After two years of this on-again, off-again toxic relationship, I got pregnant. My dreams of New York died as my belly grew bigger each day. We tried to make it work over and over again but the stressors were building a mountain between us. He was finally working on his sobriety while I was fuming at home alone. I didn't want the same things as he did. We both felt alienated by the other. As he dove further into his self-improvement program, I fought against my own uniqueness. I was huge, uncomfortable, oozing hormonal negativity, and just not fun to be around. My path of self-sabotage and victimization was underway. Night after night, he would go to meetings and not come home until late. I was livid. Then at 7 a.m. on September 2, 2013, I awoke to my water breaking followed by 36 hours of labor until our son Ezra came into this world. He was gorgeous, and I was scared to death. As new parents, we were drowning in quicksand. After the birth, I developed post-partum depression, and my partner worked all the time to pay our bills. I felt envious and stuck raising our son alone. Eventually, we separated yet again only to discover I was pregnant with our second child.

Was this going to be the missing piece to complete our puzzle and make it work for us? We plunged right back into a living nightmare; I was so stressed and hormonal. And he really just tried to stay sober and find some serenity in the storm we had once again created. I was completely absorbed in self-pity. *How was I going to take care of two kids every day? How was I going to love two kids equally? How was I going to find the time I needed to work on myself?* Worry and anxiety masked any clarity I may have had regarding who I was. That was it. My life, as I knew it, was completely over. Unfortunately, our beautiful daughter's birth caused the ultimate storm. She unknowingly swooped in and tore off the blindfolds. We were done! I took our son and our newborn baby girl and moved out of the unhappy home we had built. My aunt was nice enough to allow us temporary refuge in her home. Each day the anger and self-victimization grew inside of me. *How dare he leave us? Who is he with? What did I do in a past life to deserve this?* It was complete self-annihilation. My self-esteem was gone. I wanted someone who no longer wanted me, and a big part of why he no longer wanted me was rooted from my unwavering negativity. I had put an unrealistic version of this man above my kids, my God, and myself. I had successfully become my mother. Tears filled my bloodshot eyes continuously, while thoughts of suicide floated in and out of my brain. Something had to give. I could not go on like this forever.

Along Came Al-Anon

At this time, I had not admitted to myself I had a problem or was at all responsible for the breakup. What I did know for sure was that I was in love with an addict. I had become addicted to the addict in my life. Eventually, meetings ignited the only flickering light in the dark cave of isolation I resided in. I was ready to seek help, but it had to be on my terms. I went to as many meetings as I could each week and met some very wonderful and supportive people. One woman, in particular, gave me the idea of the "God Boxes," as she called them. You gather three boxes, one specifically for letting go of the past, one for gratitude, and one for future desires. I took heavily to this notion, as I needed something to help me manifest some good in my life. I also spent the next year trying to find my own spiritual footing. I attended church, I prayed A LOT, I went to meetings, I talked with mediums, I went to spiritual expos, etc. I was on a mission to find answers and feel better. This was the early start of my footwork for manifesting a better *me*.

Hitting a Wall (literally)

Even though I actively searched for meaning in my life, I still tried to drown out the pain of my past with booze. During the nights my kids would stay with their dad, I would go out. I could not stand being alone. One night in particular, at a benefit to support rescue dogs, I had way too much to drink, and against the advice of those around me, I drove. I started texting my ex while I was driving and before I knew it, I crashed into the wall of a church. *If that isn't a sign, I don't know what is.*

> *That was it; I was certainly going to jail.*
> *I spent the night in a holding cell.*
> *My car was totaled.*
> *My pride, all but gone.*
> *My moment of awakening was upon me.*

The next day I got sober. I checked myself into an intensive outpatient program and faithfully attended meetings. My kids and I deserved much better than what I was manifesting. With the support of family, I was able to complete a two-week program and travel along a new path. I had finally admitted to myself and to another human being that I was messed up. I had lost control of my emotions. My world was filled with so much hate and sadness…the only way out was to now climb up.

Resurfacing Out Into Humanity Again

As the new year approached, so did my desire to transform into a better person. My "God Boxes" worked beautifully, but I needed another manifestation project. I started my vision board…a board comprised of photos or whatever you wish to use to demonstrate your real desires. *If used correctly, this vision board can become a very powerful manifestation tool.* After I created this board, I visualized these desires happening to me, and I felt the compatible emotions as well. I hung my vision board directly in my daily sight and meditated near it, strengthening my connection to the Universe. The one I created this time was quite different than the one I previously had done. In 2016, I had manifested a better version of *me* on a board with pictures of myself surrounded by quotes and past writings. This awakened me to face many trials and changes within myself. In 2017, I wanted to manifest myself as a better mother, and so I focused on family values and displayed pictures of my kids. This board helped me manifest my first apartment with my son and daughter; it helped me establish a new life for us. We moved to Dundee, Wisconsin, and I acquired a day care job to help pay the bills. It was so hard living on my own, but the kids and I had a blast. We spent a lot of time walking the trails of the northern Kettle Moraine area and going to the lake. My ex and I also began working things out, and we spent a lot of time together as a family again. But it was different; I was different. As a result of the manifestation tools I had been using, I became a healthier, more independent person. I knew what I wanted and how to get it now. My perception changed, and I was more easily able to accept the ups and downs of life better. It's progress, not perfection.

My Life's Resurrection…

In 2018, we got engaged! We just started to discuss combining our households when life happened…I lost my father to small cell lung cancer. This was a setback for me and for everyone who loved him. He was my rock, and my life did not make sense without him. I wanted to pause everything at this point, but the manifestation process had already taken off. I was evolving into my third year as a dog magazine owner, working part-time, planning a wedding, and looking for a house. Knowing my father, he would have been disappointed in me if I had given up everything I had worked so hard for. I moved forward with my life during the grieving process, and we bought a house and got married. Our house and our wedding were byproducts of manifestation. It was everything I had written down and placed in my "God Boxes," plus much more.

As I work on my newest vision board, I plan to ramp it up a notch with more meditation and the use of crystals. *It's a forever process. You must continually climb up mountains and fall down in order to reach a point in your life where you are ready to start manifesting the good.* Each day I must work on creating a better version of *me* by attracting the positive in life and letting go of the negative. Life is very subjective, and how you choose to view it will either help or hinder the goals you want to manifest. I spent so many years collecting negativity and regurgitating it unto others. I had to hit my bottom so that I could have only one direction to go…and that was up. *So are you ready to go up?*

Here is my brief step-by-step guide I comprised as a starter tool for helping you begin *manifesting* a better you.

My 6-Step Manifesting Guide:

1. Want It!
There must be something in your life you really need or desire. So begin visualizing it.

2. Find A Spiritual Connection
For me, this was my understanding of God and His presence in my life. Going to AA and Al-Anon meetings for things I wanted to change in myself really helped!

3. Work On Letting The Past Go
For me this was praying and writing the past down and putting it in one "God Box." You can also visualize it disappearing or breaking down in your life through meditation.

4. Kick It Into High Gear

For me, this meant going to more meetings, reading inspirational quotes and books, praying to God, going to workshops, etc. Basically, do some preliminary work.

5. Find A Manifesting Hobby

I have a lot of these. I make vision boards of what I want for the year ahead in my life and hang it somewhere I can revisit it daily. I write on my mirror with dry erase markers: "You are beautiful..." or "You're a great mom." I hang things on my refrigerator door or put notes in my "God Boxes."

6. Never Forget To Be Grateful

Remind yourself often how far you've come and where you still want to go. And have gratitude for everyone and everything that has helped you get there.

God Boxes: (one for letting go, one for future desires, and one for gratitude)

Future Box: In three years all of this has manifested: A marriage, a house, a family, and a strong sense of self.

Gratitude Box: Mine is filled with sobriety coins and lists of things I am thankful for like my kids, my magazine, my creativity, my strength, etc.

Letting Go Box: Mine is filled with anger and resentments I held toward my husband during our split and prior to our marriage.

Based on my experiences, I encourage you to try these steps, and use the God boxes. You have manifesting to do, so what are you waiting for? Get to work!

About Nastassia

Nastassia Putz was born in Milwaukee, Wisconsin, and now resides in Cedar Grove with her husband James and their two kids, Ezra and Scarlett. She currently owns a free dog publication called *FETCH Magazine* with a strong emphasis on finding rescue dogs homes. She has interned with various publications such as *Shepherd Express* and *Milwaukee Magazine,* and she graduated with her Bachelor of Arts in Professional Writing from Mount Mary University.

Her immediate goals consist of raising her kids and writing a few children's books that focus on establishing self-help skills and individuality. She also dreams of having her own dog rescue one day, because it is good to dream!

With Sophy.

With my husband, James, and our children Scarlett and Ezra.